D1251156

occor Sep-01-1993 09:20

DATE DUE			

OAKLAND COMMUNITY COLLEGE
ORCHARD RIDGE LIBRARY
27055 ORCHARD LAKE ROAD
FARMINGTON HILLS MI 48334

DEMCO

The Economics of Cost, Use, and Value

The Economics of Cost, Use, and Value

The Evaluation of Performance, Structure, and Prices across Time, Space, and Economic Systems

Revised and expanded edition of *Cost, Use, and Value*
(Clarendon Press, Oxford 1985)

FRANCIS SETON

With a Foreword by Professor Jan Tinbergen
and a Special Annex and Appendix
contributed by Professor A. E. Steenge

CLARENDON PRESS · OXFORD

1992

HF
1456.5
.D44
K78
1993

Oxford University Press, Walton Street, Oxford OX2 6DP
Oxford New York Toronto
Delhi Bombay Calcutta Madras Karachi
Petaling Jaya Singapore Hong Kong Tokyo
Nairobi Dar es Salaam Cape Town
Melbourne Auckland
and associated companies in
Berlin Ibadan

Oxford is a trade mark of Oxford University Press

Published in the United States
by Oxford University Press, New York

© *Francis Seton 1992*

All rights reserved. No part of this publication may be reproduced,
stored in a retrieval system, or transmitted, in any form or by any means,
electronic, mechanical, photocopying, recording, or otherwise, without
the prior permission of Oxford University Press

British Library Cataloguing in Publication Data
data available

Library of Congress Cataloging in Publication Data
Seton, Francis.
The economics of cost, use, and value: the evaluation of
performance, structure, and prices across time, space and economic
system / Francis Seton; with a foreword by Jan Tinbergen and a
special annex and appendix contributed by A. E. Steenge. —Rev. and
expanded ed.
Rev. ed. of: Cost, use, and value, 1985
Includes index.
1. Prices. 2. Value. 3. Comparative economics. I. Seton,
Francis. Cost, use, and value. II. Title.
HB221. S418   1992   338.5'2—dc20   91–14793
ISBN 0–19–828383–0

Typeset by Pure Tech Corporation, Pondicherry, India
Printed in Great Britain by
Biddles Ltd
Guildford and King's Lynn

To My Wife

Foreword

by Professor J. Tinbergen

It is well known that comparisons across different economic systems are beset with great difficulties. To a large extent these are due to the fact that the prices on which the results are dependent are based on sharply different principles. Actual prices are generated by different mechanisms, e.g. on free markets or in central planning commissions, and do not in either case necessarily reflect scarcity, costs, or utility. A large amount of research has gone into methods of overcoming these difficulties. In his earlier work Bergson, a pioneer in this field, tried to make USSR data on national income comparable with those of the US by purging Soviet prices of non-market elements and reducing them to pure labour-costs. This approach, however, is not entirely satisfactory as these costs are not necessarily generated by a free market either. Marxian labour-values neglect non-labour-costs and utilities in their entirety. In Seton's characterization they suffer from both 'monomania' and 'cost-fetishism'. The United Nations International Comparison Project tries to ensure greater comparability by using so-called standard prices, i.e. by revaluing the physical flows of one country in the prices of the other, or the physical flows of both in some common price system held to be appropriate to a number of different countries. This method, however, has the disadvantage that the results are heavily dependent on the set of prices chosen, and cannot therefore be considered very satisfactory either.

In my opinion it is Seton's merit to have formulated a solution to the problem that is free from arbitrary assumptions and, moreover, takes account of as many factors of production as can be measured, and of the utility created by the final goods produced.

The usual procedure starts out from a given set of prices and asks for the final output-mix which would optimize a pre-set social utility function involving these prices. Seton's eigenprice paradigm starts from the opposite end, i.e. from an observed final output-mix, and asks for the prices (values) which the economy implicitly puts on its factors and commodities on the assumption that it has chosen the optimal output-mix available to it.

The starting-point for the computation of eigenprices is a description of the economy in terms of an ordinary Leontief input–output matrix (in terms of the country's own price system) and its fixed input-coefficients. From this table Seton derives two sets of results:

In the first instance he shows how the 'full' labour-costs of each commodity can be derived by aggregating its direct labour-cost and the indirect labour absorbed in the shape of raw materials, fuel, etc. The same method can be applied to derive the full costs of commodities in terms of the other factors specified in the table (full capital-costs, land-costs, import costs, etc.). These can only be synthesized into a *single* cost for each commodity by giving the factors weights reflecting their relative importance to the economy and constructing the average of the various 'monomaniac' full costs so weighted.

In the second instance he contraposes to the monomaniac costs a new set of valuations based on the monomaniac contribution to *final use* or *norms* of commodities and factors, i.e. when only *one* of the final commodities is held to be of benefit to the economy while all others are deemed useful only to the extent that they contribute to the selected one. Examples of such an approach can be found in the history of economic thought and policy. On a physiocratic view, for instance, one would compute the full contribution to *grain* production of each factor both as a direct input into grain farming and as an indirect input via the production of other inputs into grain; on a mercantilist view its full contribution to *cloth*-making for export; on a Stalinist view its full contribution to *steel*-making, etc., thus yielding as many sets of full contributions or 'norms' as there are final commodities in the system. Again, a *single* set of full contributions made by the factors or 'factor-norms' could be obtained only by averaging these monomaniac norms with every final commodity weighted according to its presumed importance to the economy.

With a set of commodity-costings based on factor-weights and a set of factor-norms based on commodity-weights it is possible to find the factor-weights producing commodity-costings which, when accepted as commodity-weights, would imply the same factor-weights from which one started. This set is unique (but for a multiplicative factor) to the economy and yields the only structure of factor- and commodity-prices that is self-consistent in the sense of pricing each commodity according to its factor-cost while each factor is weighted according to its contribution to the final commodities so priced. Mathematically, this set of prices emerges as the eigenvector of certain matrices derived from the input–output table and has therefore been named the 'eigenprice' set of the system. It is presented as the only rational price structure since any deviation from it would betoken that some commodity-producers were paid more (or less) than the complement of factors they had employed (including the normal mark-up) and some factor-owners were rewarded more (or less) than according to the contributions they had made to final output. It follows from this that eigenprices would coincide with actual prices in perfectly competitive economies producing the observed bill of final goods in which government taxation was strictly even-handed between industries, i.e. levied exclusively as value added tax at a uniform rate.

The first edition of Seton's book appeared in 1985 under the title *Cost, Use, and Value*. It is a pity, however, that in spite of its originality it has not so far received the attention of the scientific world to which it is undoubtedly entitled. Nevertheless it has already been hailed as a breakthrough by the well-known Hungarian economist Professor Andrew Bródy and a number of other reviewers have also given it a very favourable reception. Professor De Wolff, formerly Director of the Central Planning Bureau in The Netherlands has given valuable comments in a chapter of a Festschrift in honour of Professor Venekamp. I myself am particularly pleased by the fact that Seton's work has not only received a good deal of attention in my own country, but that the method has also been applied in empirical investigations of a number of countries by a group of economists at the Technical University of Enschede under the leadership of Professor Steenge. The results for The Netherlands and for Hungary were already published in the first edition, and further co-operative research is now in progress both in the theoretical field (especially by Dr Eric Dietzenbacher of Groningen University) and in its practical application. The present second edition contains extensions of the theoretical framework as well as extending and updating the empirical enquiries to which eigenprices are adapted.

It should be borne in mind that even if the method should be found wanting in various ways it represents a valid attempt to throw bridges between contending value-concepts by integrating them into a comprehensive system, and can therefore be qualified as an act of intellectual statesmanship which ought to be applauded and popularized. It is to be hoped that not only the economics profession, but wider circles of social scientists will join in the examination, revision, criticism, and practical application of this novel conceptual tool which is so rich in the promise of new insights.

Preface to the Second Edition

WHY a second edition? The 'eigenprices' treated here are still the same as those of the first edition. In spite of the occasional scepticism and severe strictures which a discerning public has infused into what was on the whole a kindly reception, not to say a chorus of guarded approbation, the author is still unrepentant and unregenerate. He does, however, need to clear up errors and misconceptions which have crept into the first edition, and he needs to widen the horizon by exploring concepts related to eigenprices and complementary to them which were left 'just around the corner' in the first edition. He needs to update and supplement the empirical findings, even though—alas— he cannot as yet claim to have improved their reliability and upgraded them from the status of illustrative material to that of genuinely usable diagnosis. Above all, he must try to address a wider public, including those who took flight on meeting the uncompromisingly algebraic treatment of the first edition.

In this edition he is attempting to do so in Part I by presenting three separate chapters, to be read not so much consecutively as alternatively: Chapter 1 is a purely verbal treatment for those who prefer to eschew both figures and algebraic symbols, but still wish to gain an insight into the nature of eigenprices in a quasi-impressionistic manner. If their interest is sufficiently aroused, they might wish to graduate to Chapter 2 which seeks to demonstrate the existence and characteristics of eigenprices for those prepared to put in more intensive concentration by following numerical examples verifiable with the aid of a simple desk-calculator. The hardiest souls who require rigour and are not afraid of algebra may then wish to plunge into Chapter 3, which expounds the theory of eigenprices in the fullest generality the author is capable of. Alternatively they might wish to start their reading with that chapter and ignore the preceding two though, I believe, they would be missing some of the rationale of the line of thought pursued here.

I have attempted to make each of these chapters into a self-contained exposition which can be read in isolation, as well as in supplementation, of the other two. This necessitated a certain repetitiveness for which the author must ask the indulgence of those who read the chapters consecutively. This is not to say that repetitiveness is absent from the three chapters in isolation, particularly from Chapter 1 which is, after all, an essay in persuasion as well as explanation. Those irritated by it will, I hope, skip the offending passages while suspending a stern judgement, and press on with the essential thread of the argument.

The original intention which gave rise to this line of thought was to conduct a relatively modest exercise in the much-maligned economics of comparative systems analysis, which only gradually revealed itself as a new conceptual analysis through which the notion of 'value' emerges from the two opposite poles of cost and utility. It is, indeed, little more than an illustration of this synthesis—one among several methods of achieving it; but even this may go some way towards justifying the main titles of the two editions which may strike the reader as unduly ambitious.

It would have been fascinating, and no doubt equally valuable, to trace the *Ideengeschichte* of this synthesis from the early toying with simple ratios through the selection of common *loci* uniting functional relationships, to saddle points, fixed-point theorems, and all the sophisticated tools of latter-day mathematicians who have not played their last card in this game (and probably never will). Such, however, goes well beyond my intention, and vastly beyond my capacity. Like an untutored child in a sequential question-and-answer game, I prefer to start out from simple perplexities as they arise in the attempt to grapple with concrete issues, e.g. the comparability of ratios internal to different economies, and to be lead step by step into the abstract realm by the manifest deficiencies of the naïve answers prompted by a series of questions of gradually increasing difficulty.

The first two chapters introduce the problem of intersystem and intercountry comparability in the simplest form and outline the desiderata of possible solutions in numerical terms, without the use of algebra. From Chapter 3 onwards a general solution is approached in abstract terms starting from the cost- and utility-sides in turn, and culminating in the proposed synthesis of these approaches in the concept of eigenprices. It may be appropriate at this point to emphasize that, as far as this book is concerned, I claim no originality for the use of dominant eigenvalues and eigenvectors as a way of finding fixed points in linear transformations and thereby forming the desired synthesis underlying the concept of 'value'. This device has by now a history covering a quarter century or more, in which the author may claim to have played a modest part (see Sect. 3.5, n. 14). The novelty, if novelty there be, lies rather in the particular choice of the matrices to serve as a base for these values, their definition, derivation, and interpretation.

Those acquainted with the first edition will notice that I have abandoned the somewhat idiosyncratic 'accent notation' for vectors and matrices in spite of its usefulness for the purpose in hand (and, I venture to assert, for other purposes as well), and have reverted to the established use of bold face type and primes, in the belief that a book designed to introduce novel concepts should not burden the reader with unfamiliar notation as well. The resulting changes and proliferation of letter symbols may make it necessary to refer more often to Appendix D which contains a full directory of symbols in alphabetical order— probably a small price to be paid for the avoidance of the deterrent effects of accents over letters on which they do not normally occur.

Part II is an attempt to elucidate the nature of eigenprices and eigenyield by establishing links with older established and more widely known economic concepts, some of which may be interpreted as the result of eigenprice calculations in highly simplified or 'degenerate' systems. Readers should find Chapters 4 to 6 of particular help here, while Chapter 7 is a new venture into related fields unexplored in the first edition which may remain unread without prejudice to the understanding of basic issues. They should, however, take special warning from Chapter 8.

The empirical exercises of Part III, as will be repeatedly stated in the text, are mere illustrations of where the method will lead when applied to the rough-hewn and ill-adapted data that official statistics have at present on offer. A proper application to data specially collected and tailored to the purpose in hand, which alone could yield reliable results, would require a research effort far beyond the scope of this book or our unaided resources. The tentative results of Part III are therefore no more than a 'game with figures' to ascertain whether meaningful and superficially plausible results emerge. This caveat applies with somewhat diminished force to the 1980 data for seven EC countries which were not available when the first edition was processed; for in these cases we have at least the assurance that the input–output tables offered were harmonized *inter se*, even though this must be taken with a grain of salt. The official source states explicitly that the flows of a given product are not valued uniformly; they may or may not include VAT, depending on whether or not the purchasers are entitled to a refund of VAT on the goods purchased, and tables for non-deductible VAT are not available for reasons of confidentiality.

The caveats apply with even less force to the Special Annex (Chapter 10) contributed by Professor Steenge who has made a special study of The Netherlands and Hungary. However that may be, the outcome of both exercises gives reason to hope that when increased resources are available a further, more intensive, research effort would be worth while, and that the new concepts introduced in this book could play a part in pushing back the frontiers of our knowledge of the world's economies.

My indebtedness to colleagues in the profession, both senior and junior, is profound and varied in scope. Professor A. E. Steenge, the contributor of the Special Annex and of Appendix A, paid me the compliment of choosing an earlier article I had written on the subject as the starting-point for his own independent researches on Holland and Hungary, and in this edition also the United States, and thus provided much of the encouragement without which this book might never have been written. In my Preface to the first edition I listed those colleagues who had made valuable comments on the work then in progress and had helped to bring it to fruition. In this edition, therefore, I need only record my gratitude to Dr Erik Dietzenbacher of the University of Groningen who undertook the complicated computations with a profound understanding borne of the valuable work on the theory of eigenprices whether published or as yet unpublished which he had undertaken in a different context.[1] I alone, however, remain responsible for errors and misconceptions and for the sheer presumption of launching two editions of a book on a subject in which so much unfinished business still remains to be done.

Oxford   F.S.
July 1990

---

[1] Among relevant publications we may cite: E. Dietzenbacher and A. E. Steenge, 'Seton's Eigenprices: Comparisons between post-War Holland and Hungary', in A. Smyshlyaev (ed.), *Input–Output Modelling*, Springer-Verlag, Berlin, 1985; 'Time— Series Analysis of Seton's Eigenprices for The Netherlands and Hungary', Paper presented at the Fifth World Congress of the Econometric Society, Cambridge, Mass., 17–24 Aug. 1985; E. Dietzenbacher, 'Seton's Eigenprices: Further Evidence, *Economic Systems Research*, 2 (1990), 103–23; 'Perturbations of Matrices: A Theorem on the Perron Vector and Its Applications to Input–Output models', *Journal of Economics*, 48 (1988), 389–412; 'Perturbations of the Perron Vector: Applications to Finite Markov Chains and Demographic Population Models', *Environment and Planning* A22, 747–61. These and other relevant works by the same author will be collected in his forthcoming thesis *Perturbations and Eigenvectors: Essays.*

Contents

II. Eigenprices: Historical Parallels, Special Cases, and Extensions

III. Eigenprices: A Foray into the Real World

List of Statistical Tables

PART I

Eigenprices: Meaning and Purport

1

Eigenprices: Verbal Exposition

1.1 Introduction

IT is well known to the point of notoriety that economics can never be an experimental science. The phenomena and relationships that the economist observes are not embedded in an environment that can be varied at will to isolate particular actions or reactions; he must forever find his way in a world where every effect remains assignable to diverse causes, and every cause is fraught with multifarious effects. Thus frustrated in his vying for honours with physicists, chemists, or biologists, he has to seek solace in a different aspiration—that of trying to achieve at least the status of an *exact* science, a body of systematic knowledge operating with concepts, aggregates, or variables defined to allow the largest possible number of logical relationships to be deduced between them, giving maximal scope for valid conclusions in a world of uncertainty, and spelling out the fullest possible implications of the choice between disposable means towards given ends or between competing ends within reach of available means. To the extent that this has been successful, it has been achieved by stripping economic reality down to bare essentials: a faceless assembly of factor-owners and 'economic men', the proverbial single factory, or even a single monster-machine with interlocking parts—a 'black box' into which are fed primary resources ('factors') at one end to be transformed into final commodities ('goods') at the other for the use of consumers, investors, or public policy-makers. The black-box vision is now so deeply ingrained in the minds of quantitative economists that even the traditional notions of cost, utility, and value—overlaid with atavistic impurities though they still are—have taken on formal meanings little different from mathematical functions, derivatives, mappings, or transforms on specially defined domains, with nothing left for thick lips to kiss or heavy boots to kick.

It should be stated from the outset that this book takes its stand on the black-box vision, not because its author believes that there is nothing to be explained outside it, but because he feels that the analysis to which it has given rise has been, and continues to be, one-sided in several important respects, and that some potential for generalization still remains to be explored. In particular, the backward linkage which relates final goods to primary factors, the process of costing, has seldom been matched in thoroughness and emphasis by the forward linkage relating factors to final goods through which the factors could be evaluated or 'normed' according to their ultimate productivity or *usefulness*; and the concept of *value* with which most people operate (outside the rarefied Paretian world of universal optimization) still fails to synthesize the twin ingredients of *cost* and *use* in an even-handed manner and remains tainted with an ingrained bias of 'cost-fetishism'.

With so much unfinished business still to be tackled in the conceptual sphere, we may be forgiven for sidestepping a number of well-known and probably unresolvable conundrums attaching to the black-box vision, such as the separate measurabilty of inputs and outputs (e.g. 'capital' and 'profit') or the criteria for the division between them (e.g. is 'work ethics' an *input* or *output* of the system, or merely part of the environment in which the system operates?). We beg leave to brush such stumbling-blocks aside in order to focus on the central question: How can flows and proportions of specified inputs and outputs be compared in rationally commensurable terms to produce internally consistent and valid criteria of economic structure and performance, consonant with established notions of cost, use, and value, and amenable to international and intersystem comparison without imparting biases inherent in country-specific, time-specific, or arbitrarily chosen price structures?

This comparability across time, space, and different economic systems is in the author's view the litmus test for the general validity of the value-concept or standard of value that has been applied. The value of, say, a ton of coal may need to be assigned vastly different numbers of units in countries with profoundly different cost conditions and economic needs such as Britain and China. We may not even be able to express it in commensurable units, and the same may be true of each and every commodity entering the national income. Yet if comparisons between the structures of gross national products (GNPs) are to be possible at all, there must be some methodologically uniform value-concept applicable to both countries whose adequacy to each environment and freedom from bias can be universally accepted. Conversely, a value-concept, however satisfying on philosophical, logical, or mathematical grounds, can never command universal credibility unless it permits direct international, intertemporal, and intersystemic comparisons of greater validity than country-specific or arbitrarily chosen price systems. Validity entails comparability, and comparability attests validity. It is for this reason that we put intersystemic comparison at the centre of this book, even though its basic objective is the wider one of exploring economic concepts and placing traditionally accepted value-systems in the context of the wider family to which we believe them all to belong.

1.2 Invitation au voyage

The journey on which we are embarked, then, is the quest for a concept of measurable value which can be applied in any economy to all the commodities and factors of production (labour, land, capital, etc.) in current use to serve as an unbiased standard of comparison between economies with widely different internal structures and price systems. Such a concept cannot accept the verdict of market price, since the economies to be compared may organize their markets very differently, and some of them may not be governed by markets at all. Our concept of value must therefore be distilled from features of the economy not necessarily measured, though inevitably co-determined, by market prices. It must, moreover, accord with general principles which, though applied to different countries and economic systems, remain essentially the same in each case.

The concept underlying such a measure, if it is to be universally acceptable, must reflect *both* the cost incurred in the creation of a product and the benefit derived from its use; for high cost by itself is not a guarantee of high value, nor is a high degree of usefulness. Ground foxmeat has no value because there is no use for it, even though it would cost much time, skill, and energy to procure; and highly useful, indeed indispensable, goods like air and water have no commercial value unless the cost of procuring them confers such value, as would be the case with *clean* air and water secured by pollution control.

Our value concept, to be embodied in the 'eigenprices' of goods and resources, if it is to serve the purposes of comparison, must also be computable from national or international statistics, and must yield the same numerical values when the laid-down procedure is followed, no matter who undertakes the computation or when it is undertaken.

The eigenprices introduced in this book are intended to fulfil these conditions. When explaining their nature and purport, it seems best to start with the signposts which have launched the author on his quest and have guided him on his way.

1.3 The Challenge of Comparability

Questions of the comparative size, growth, structure, or performance of different economies have for long dogged economic analysts as well as policy-makers and the common man. It is scarcely possible to decide on, or justify, crucial measures in the field of commercial, investment, or defence policy without giving credence to some such statements as 'The USA spends under 7 per cent of its GNP on defence[1] while the USSR spends over 14 per cent'[2], or 'For every unit absorbed in household consumption the Soviet Union spends twice as much on capital investment as the United States',[3] etc., etc.

It does not take much persuading to make the purveyors of such information choke on their own words. The ratios being compared are clearly dependent on the prices in which the underlying aggregates are valued. Those of the West are—in principle at least—derived from the interplay of market forces, transformed or distorted by random concentrations of monopoly power, fiscal policy, tariff protection, etc. Those of the Soviet Union derive from the edicts of central authority acting under historical, ideological, or administrative constraints, and unhampered by the need to use prices for market-clearing—a function that can safely be left to queuing, residual

---

[1] The figure for 1970–5 was estimated at 6.6%; see Joint Economic Committee, Congress of the United States, *East European Economist Post-Helsinki*, US Government Printing Office, Washington, DC, 1977: 274.

[2] The figure is implied by the CIA estimate of 40–5bn. roubles on Soviet defence spending (including R & D) for 1970 and official data for Soviet GNP (285.5bn. roubles in 1970); see Joint Economic Committee, Congress of the United States, *Soviet Economy in a New Perspective*, US Government Printing Office, Washington, DC, 1976 and Ts. S. U. *Narodnoe khozyaistvo SSSR v 1980 g.*, Finansy i Statistika, Moscow, 1981: 380.

[3] A. Bergson, *The Real National Income of Soviet Russia since 1928*, Harvard University Press, Cambridge, Mass., 1961: 277.

foreign trade, or direct administrative intervention. This being so, the defence share or investment ratio in GNP can be made to appear whatever the planners wish, and juxtaposition with the corresponding Western statistics makes about as much sense as comparing a bootlace with a piece of string. Yet the human mind lusts for comparisons of just that kind, and few statistics carry any meaning to economists unless they can be compared in their different manifestations in space and time. Can we devise a method, crystal, or prism through which they can be viewed in these different environments without losing the assurance that we are still looking at the same thing?

It is this hope that launches us on the quest for an unbiased price system in terms of which heterogeneous inputs and outputs can be made commensurable—a quest that has produced a number of holy grails in the past, and an even larger host of knights-errant. In this book we propose to add to their number, but instead of setting out from the famous Round Table of King Arthur, we shall take our starting-point from the equally famous Square Table of King Wassily (Leontief). Our indebtedness to illustrious 'Knights of the Square Table' like Sraffa, Morishima, and others, will become abundantly clear in what follows. But we hope to go beyond them and, in particular, to attempt to lay the twin ghosts of cost-fetishism and monomania which have frightened off so many who might otherwise have rallied to their banner.

Before the exorcism can begin, however, we need to pay our respects to the scholarship and ingenuity that have gone into previous attempts to circumnavigate the reefs thrown up by differently based price systems in the way of those who wished to make comparisons between different systems or to compile valid league tables of various sorts. To my mind these attempts can be brought under three main heads, and it might be as well to pass these in review, however cursorily.

Price-pruning

Professor A. Bergson, the pioneer and past master of the art of intersystem comparisons, originally put his faith in what might be called 'price-pruning', the careful pruning of conceptually empty or noncomparable prices of their extra-economic incubus in the hope of reducing them to a better reflection of each country's own factor-costs. His 'adjusted factor cost standard' forms the basis of the classical series of estimates of Soviet national income and product (SNIP),[4] which for three decades insistently and persuasively invited comparison with their US and generally Western counterparts.

The method has found distinguished followers, and an impressive literature of comparative assessment has sprung up.[5] Its sources, apart from the works of Professor Bergson himself, were earlier attempts to come to grips with the problem of differential or distorted prices, often in a slightly different and sometimes dynamic, rather than static, context.[6] Naturally there has been no lack of doubters and critics,[7] and the notion that, even with ostensibly free labour markets, a reduction to internal factor-costs would solve the comparability problem has been subjected to severe and to my mind quite damaging criticism.

Price-grafting

An even more popular method of seeking comparability takes its cue from the statistical methodology of index numbers, and revalues the economic aggregates of one country systematically in the prices of another in order to measure the results against the unadjusted data of the latter. The method could probably trace its ancestry as far back as the computation of standardized mortality rates or rates of incidence of disease, crime, etc., designed to eliminate the distorting effects of differential age or class structures on the crude figures, or the construction of output indices of the Laspeyre or Paasche type, which value commodity-flows of different time-periods in the constant prices of the initial or the final year. From this it is only a short step

[4] A. Bergson, 'Ruble Prices and the Valuation Problem', *Quarterly Journal of Economics*, Aug. 1950; *Soviet National Income and Product in 1937*, Columbia University Press, New York, 1953; *The Real National Income of Soviet Russia*, A. Bergson and H. Heyman Jr, *Soviet National Income and Product 1940–48*, Columbia University Press, New York, 1954.

[5] O. Hoeffding and N. Nimitz, *Soviet National Income and Product 1949–55*, RAND Corporation RM-2101, Apr. 1959; A. S. Becker, *Soviet National Income 1958–1964*, University of California Press, Berkeley, Calif., 1969 (for a discussion of the valuation problem see Pt. I, 43 ff.).

[6] N. Jasny, 'Intricacies of Russian National Income Indices', *Journal of Political Economy*, Aug. 1947; A. Gerschenkron, 'The Soviet Indices of Industrial Production', *Review of Economics and Statistics*, Nov. 1947; D. Hodgman, *Soviet Industrial Production 1928–1951*, Harvard University Press, Cambridge, Mass., 1954.

[7] P. Wiles, 'Are Adjusted Rubles Rational?', *Soviet Studies*, Oct. 1955; F. D. Holzman, 'The Adjusted Factor Cost Standard of Measuring National Income: Comment', *Soviet Studies*, July 1957.

to the use of 'neutral' price systems imported from third countries, intermediate years, or 'the world as a whole', a universal valuation system which has found its most complete expression in the United Nations' International Comparison Project (ICP).[8] Although this particular exercise was concerned primarily with the comparison of costs and purchasing power, the method has also been used to compile league tables of GNP, GNP per head, and the main components of final demand.

In all cases the method suffers from an inescapable ambiguity, as the results of comparing countries A and B normally give sharply different, and often conflicting, verdicts according to which of the two countries is chosen to furnish the uniform price basis. It may be concluded that such 'transplants' of organically alien valuations can at best eliminate the bias arising from *differential* pricing, but cannot escape the residual bias inherent in any one country- or time-specific price structure *per se*. When such hybridization between two countries is replaced by recourse to a common standard alien to both by drawing on the price structure of a third, supposedly 'neutral' country, the choice of that country introduces additional degrees of freedom into the result, which commands confidence only to the extent that arbitrariness is accepted as a substitute for neutrality. To cast the 'world as a whole' in the role of the third country appears to inject an element of objectivity by eliminating arbitrary choice, but hides other assumptions of doubtful validity, such as the notion that the appropriateness of a country's price system as a universal yardstick is proportional to its size, population, prosperity, or whatever furnishes the weight with which it figures as a constituent of 'the world' in international statistics.

On a more theoretical level, the use of Laspeyre-, Paasche-, or Geary-type ICP indexes can be justified as an approximation to a postulated single family of indifference curves representative of all countries involved, allowed to differ from one another only in the particular region of the indifference map they happen to offer for empirical observation. The Kravis–Gilbert method of taking geometric means would then be tantamount to fitting a homogeneous-quadratic family to the regional slopes detected in this manner[9] and

[8] Methods and procedures are fully set out in I. B. Kravis, Z. Kenessy, A. Heston, and R. Summers, *A System of International Comparisons of Gross Product and Purchasing Power*, Johns Hopkins University Press, Baltimore, 1975.

[9] I am indebted to Professor Samuelson for pointing this out to me.

accepting this construct as the 'substratum of common humanity' to which the idiosyncracies of every nation can trace their origin. Attractive though this notion might be, the eye of healthy scepticism will see in it no more than a sophisticated form of wishful thinking whereby unrevealed truth can be discovered by concocting suitably recondite averages from revealed falsehoods.

Price-implanting

With this fanciful expression we push our horticultural analogy to the technological limit of molecular biology which can cause natural organisms to display information on their functioning when tracer elements are implanted in their bodies or in certain of their cells. What we wish to 'implant' in the economies under review is a uniform *principle* of price formation rather than ready-formed prices in order to observe and compare the prices which these economies would generate if they all followed this principle or mechanism of price-formation.

To some extent this is also the approach implicit in Bergson's 'adjusted factor cost' standard. Historically, however, it has made its greatest impact with the emergence of what I have elsewhere called 'diagnostic' prices,[10] prices whose role is neither descriptive (of actual exchanges anywhere in time or space) nor functional (in the sense of pushing the economy towards an optimum, however conceived), but investigative, probing for hidden truths, unmasking or exposing. This purpose is certainly what motivated the use of the most influential representative of such prices, the Marxian labour-values, defined as the socially necessary labour-time spent in the making of a good. We shall return to this definition and its purport shortly. For the present we need only recall that Marxian labour-values have been used for international comparisons quite extensively,[11] presumably in the belief that their invariance to the prices implied in the input–output tables from which they are derived eliminated all elements of price bias from the comparison, and that they correctly reflected the values that should be put on commodities everywhere. This 'gut

[10] F. Seton, 'The Question of Ideological Obstacles to Rational Price Setting in Communist Countries', in A. Abouchar (ed.), *The Socialist Price Mechanism*, Duke University Press, Durham, NC, 1977.

[11] See e.g. A. A. Brown and J. A. Licari, in A. Abouchar (ed.), *The Socialist Price Mechanism*.

feeling' is widespread and stands in stark contrast to the teachings of mainstream economic theory according to which value cannot be derived from *costs* alone, and even less from costs in terms of a single factor only.

1.4 Value Theory and Intuition

For close on two centuries now 'value' has been identified with the price formed on a market where both demand and supply exert their influence, thus creating an unbiased synthesis of the *cost* incurred in the making of a thing and the benefit accruing from its *use*. Traditionally it has been held that such a synthesis would be generated by a free market where buyers and sellers bid against each other until the price settles down at a level where both sides are satisfied with the quantity exchanged. The resulting price will of course vary with the nature of the market, the relative number, knowledge, and strength of buyers and sellers (monopolists, competitors, etc.), and the dependence of price on these factors has been the bread and butter of textbook analysis for many generations. In the process the very word 'value' has all but disappeared from the vocabulary of mainstream economics except as a synonym for 'price' or 'perfectly competitive price' such as economists believe would lead to the optimal allocation of resources. The notion of a true or real value from which even the perfectly competitive market price might deviate is thereby banished. I wonder how much of the common man's distrust of economics as an amoral or dismal science is due to this excision and the resulting impression that economists, like business tycoons, 'know the price of everything and the value of nothing'.

Some notion of value independent of markets, however, appears to be ingrained in the human mind almost as a Kantian category like time, space, or causality. The untutored mind guided by nothing but common sense expects the value of a thing to be closely related to, if not determined by, the effort and sacrifice involved in its creation, as if the blood, sweat, and tears of the labourer were a fluid which had been made to flow from his body and mind to be permanently locked up in the object. When people are exchanging commodities on a market, therefore, they are bartering packets of human energy, and the ratios in which these are exchanged are reflections, whether true or distorted, of the fluid thus embodied; they are the *consequences* of their values, not their determinants.

This intuition no doubt stood at the cradle of the labour theory of value. It accounts for the immediacy of its appeal as a synthesis of costs and sacrifices obvious to all from introspection, demanding compensation as a matter of common justice and evident to the labourer without elaboration and beyond all art to make him feel in his bones: This is indeed the stuff that value is made of. It must have haunted toiling humanity ever since the emergence of agriculture, long before it was explicitly stated and codified by the great classical economists of the last two centuries and long before it made its impact as the cornerstone of the Marxian ideology.

1.5 Marxism as a Point of Departure

Misconceived and defective as the Marxian ideology may be, it is the child of intellectual movements which are rightly regarded as the flowering of Western culture: The age of enlightenment with its ethical impulses rooted in notions of human dignity and equality, and the scientific spirit with its relentless search for unbroken chains of cause and effect. Nevertheless it is a heretic's ideology, conceived and espoused by unrepentant scions of this illustrious ancestry in profound error—even though it is an error of genius which succeeded in revolutionizing the thinking and cherished beliefs of large sections of humanity and, for over half a century at least, shaping the world to its mould—an error, therefore, which must be approached with understanding and without passion or prejudice.

The betrayal of the search for truth of which Marx may be accused is enshrined in his own confession of his intentions: He does not seek to *explain* the world; he seeks to *change* it, and nowhere is this clearer than in his theory of value. This is inspired above all by the wish to expose and indict the presumed iniquities of capitalism, its injustices, and exploitative nature. That is why Marx starts by offering us, not an *explanation* of value, but a *definition* of it, a definition, moreover, which is an elaboration of the age-old common-sense intuition described above. It is no wonder, therefore, that he had no difficulty persuading his followers that this definition could be accepted like a Euclidean axiom which needed no justification, but could serve as the basis for all other proofs. Value is thus a deprivation, a pain suffered in the exhaustion of human energy, a cost in physical effort, a *disutility* which everyone knows from introspection. More than that, as we have seen, it establishes that in the exchange of things in proportion to their values each party gives to the other the same amount of effort as he receives and neither is constrained by force or deception to incur uncompensated labour; in fact it is not the two things of the same value that are equal, it is the *people* exchanging them. Value is thus the reflection of a power relationship between humans, and it is through unequal exchanges enforced by the class monopoly of the means of production that Marxists see the capitalists exert their exploitative power.

In spite of the widespread disillusionment with Marxism which has overtaken its former devotees, and indeed its high priests, the notion of value as a distillate of human effort and sacrifice is still ingrained in millions who find it too self-evident to admit any challenge from the supposed sophistries of more discerning analysts. On it was erected a structure of mutually supporting doctrines, development theories, historical materialism, epistemology, and dialectics which not only succeded in reinforcing the original intuition, but also claimed to reveal the motives and sources of error of those who refused to worship at that shrine. This edifice was offered to its devotees as the key to all understanding of the world, a blinding flash of insight eradicating error and confusion, besides placing the believer firmly and forever in the ranks of the great battalions of history. It is no wonder that such a doctrine produced intellectual rigidity, blinkers, fetishisms, taboos, and monomanias which consistently put it outside the mainstream of the search for truth, and that the tenets of the Marxian theory of value have earned it opprobrium, disparagement, and open contempt from the bulk of the economics profession, and at least a cold shoulder from those we recognize as our leaders in this field.

1.6 Input–Output Economics and Eigenprices

Yet there has been no lack of outstanding thinkers who have built on that tradition with greater understanding, sharper tools, and a deeper commitment to the search for truth than those whose main aim was to *change* rather than explain the world. Leontief, von Neumann, Kantorovich, Sraffa, Morishima, to name but a few, have greatly advanced our understanding of important aspects of economic concepts and processes which mainstream analysis had hardly touched upon, using Leontief's seminal invention of the square input–output table. These thinkers, the 'Knights of the Square Table', revived the ancient tradition of *tableaux économiques* and paid attention to the interaction of the various sectors within the economy, thus putting the role of produced commodities as inputs into the production process firmly on the order of the day, fully on a par with that of primary factors. In the process they forged the tools with which unresolved problems connected with labour-values and prices, the nature of the Marxian 'rate of exploitation', and the transformation of labour-value into 'production prices', purged of their metaphysical incubus, could be analysed with rigour and efficiency.

By now this mode of analysis has not merely dispensed with the original monomania of regarding homogeneous labour as the sole fount of all value but, through its linear programming extension, has also made serious inroads into optimization procedures, for long the preserve of mainstream marginalists. In this way the *utility* aspect of value, firmly rejected by Marxian economists as 'subjectivist' and therefore 'unscientific', has been readmitted into the ranks of value-forming principles. It is quite possible to be a practitioner of modern Leontief–Sraffa type of economics without deserving the odium of what we shall refer to as 'cost-fetishism'. This, however, is only achieved by admitting the existence of something like a collective utility or social welfare function, surely a notion which the original orthodoxy would denounce as the very queen of the subjectivist underworld. Ingenious attempts have been made to defend the social welfare function against this charge and establishing its 'objective' character by defining procedures for its derivation from statistically observable behaviour, e.g. by processing the market-demand functions for individual commodities into a single integral from which they could all be abstracted as partial derivatives. But quite apart from the practical difficulties of such a statistical *tour de force*, these attempts must come up against such conceptual reefs as interpersonal comparisons of utility, welfare effects of different income distributions, inconsistencies in social choice—all conundrums with which the acutest minds of the profession have grappled with only partial success for decades past.

Eigenprices have been devised as an attempt to integrate the utility aspect of value into the Leontief–Sraffa type of analysis without the need to specify a social welfare function—a marriage between the contending strands of value theory without the need to legitimize an illegitimate child. In a world of fixed input-coefficients, in which average variables are equal to their values at the margin, we can describe them as the set of valuations through which commodities are priced at their marginal costs in terms of the factors absorbed in their production, while the factors are priced at the marginal contribution they make to the total value of the commodities so priced—a mutual correspondence we shall refer to as the 'principle of reciprocal marginality'. The 'eigenprice-set' is therefore identical with the costs and prices which neoclassical theory posits as the outcome of perfect competition in all markets, the allocational optimum where factor-prices are equal to marginal revenue productivities in terms of goods prices and goods prices to marginal costs in terms of factor-prices. If we may take it, therefore, that in choosing the final outputs we observe, the economy had achieved the optimum allocation of resources open to it, the eigenprices simply reproduce the market prices which *would have had to prevail* for the economy to have arrived at the same final output pattern under perfect competition in all markets. In an important sense, therefore, the eigenprices are the values which the 'sovereigns' of the economy (whether consumers or planners) must implicitly have put on goods and resources for them to have acted as we observe them to have done in pursuit of an optimum. It follows that the economy's internal ratios (defence-ratio, investment-ratio, wage share, etc.) expressed in these prices will be proper measures of the relative efforts and sacrifice devoted to various objectives and of the relative benefits derived from them. Such internal eigenratios may therefore be used in international and intersystem comparisons with the reasonable assurance that we are measuring the apportionment each economy has chosen for itself *in its own implicit estimation*, i.e. without importing outside biases of any kind.

1.7 Labour Monomania and Multi-Factor Costing

Is labour really the fount of all value, even in the intuition of the common man? Can we say that two countries each devoting 10 per cent of their labour to, say, defence are making the same relative defence effort or sacrifice? Suppose half of this labour is embodied in metals, of which there is an abundance in one of the countries, while the other has so few metallic ore deposits that it can accomplish its defence programme only by depriving itself of tins for food and of heating equipment. Surely, then, the metal-poor country is making the greater sacrifice for defence; for in addition to toiling and sweating it also has to tighten its belt and freeze in the winter. In fact, labour is not the only sacrifice to be reckoned with; so also is scarce metal, the factor of production usually identified as land, and also machine-time, factory space, and all the things provided with past savings which could otherwise have been consumed or invested, in fact capital—not to speak of risk-taking or the entrepreneurship involved in making defence goods the demand for which is uncertain. There are in fact any number of factors of production other than labour in play, and what they all have in common is not disutility, but *scarcity*, the fact that in using them to make anything forces one to forgo their use for something else, a sacrifice which economists characterize as 'opportunity cost'. Even the pain or disutility cost of labour could be brought under this head by regarding it as the opportunity cost of ease or leisure. But the concept of opportunity cost plays little or no part in the Marxian scheme of things, and that is one more reason why it only recognizes the one factor of production which has direct and obvious disutility cost, i.e. *labour*.

In this respect the Marxian scheme is certainly flawed by a defect which, in a more general sense, I shall refer to as 'cost-monomania', the arbitrary exclusion from value formation of all but one factor of production. Since Marx regards himself as the tribune of the working classes this factor must be *labour*. But it is equally possible to imagine other forms of cost-monomania: A dyed-in-the-wool capitalist might argue that the only factor that genuinely contributed to value was *capital*; he would then define value as the total direct and indirect use of capital involved in the making of a thing; or a feudal landlord might define it as total *land*-content. In view of the popular intuition I have described, these claims would certainly appear less plausible than labour monomania; but they could be made *in principle*—as could others, even less plausible ones. If horses could write economics, they might define value as the total direct and indirect horse-power[12] involved in making a good. In fact, there can be as many cost-monomanias as there are distinguishable and separately measurable factors of production.

An unbiased observer would surely have to allow that each of these alternative monomaniac commodity-costings might have some claim

---

[12] I owe this quotation from Tugan-Baranovsky to Professor Alec Nove of Glasgow University.

to be included in a synthesis that could be identified as value. But in what proportions should they come into play? Simply adding a commodity's costs in terms of the alternative factors selected by the various monomaniac valuers (i.e. in terms of each 'mono-factor') would not do, as this would imply that each mono-factor was to be given equal weight in the cost of the commodity—a decision no less arbitrary than any other. If the weights are to be different and we do not accept preconceived ideologies or decisions, we must suspend judgement and adopt the time-honoured mathematical device of making do with functions rather than concrete numbers: We simply give the undecided weights algebraic symbols a, b, c, . . . and content ourselves with the formulae by means of which these would be translated into a single set of commodity-costings, leaving the numerical values to be inserted later, when we hope to be in a better position to a make a decision on this. This is as far as exclusive reliance on factor-costs will lead us. It delivers a set of functions transforming *any* adopted set of factor prices into the corresponding set of commodity costs or 'full costs' (when increased by a uniform mark-up for profit or tax charges). We shall refer to this set of functions as the 'downstream transformation', as it converts the weightings of original factors at the source of the economic flow into the full costs of the commodities at the end of the flow where it discharges into the sea. In this sense the full costs or prices are simply the *effects of the factor-weightings* and may be referred to shortly as the latter's 'price-effects'.

To get any further we must invoke value-forming principles other than costs; for factors are by definition non-produced items having no costs of production; any relative weighting system applied to them can therefore be justified (or rejected) only with reference to the *uses* they serve, directly or via the commodities they help to produce, and to the degree to which they serve them.

1.8 Use-Monomanias and Multi-Product Norming

Just as we have distinguished possible cost-monomanias in which the cost of a commodity was traced back to the use of one of several factors absorbed in its production, so also is it possible to distinguish a variety of 'use-monomanias' in which the contribution (productivity) of a factor is traced forward to one or other of the final commodities it helps to produce, i.e. we can measure its direct and indirect contribution to the final use of any commodity that may be regarded as the only one to confer benefit on the economy, its 'use-norm' or 'norm' for short. To emphasize the monomaniac character of this measure, we shall speak of 'mono-norms', e.g. mono-coal norms, mono-steel norms, etc., each of them computable from the same data as the mono-factor costs, though by a different procedure, in line with the switch from one end of the economic telescope to the other, i.e. from the cost-valuation to the use-valuation of economic flows. The history of economic thought and policy provides a number of examples. The physiocrats of eighteenth-century France held that the production of agricultural commodities (say grain) for human consumption was the be-all and end-all of economic activity. The value of all factors and commodities was therefore implicitly defined by them as the total direct and indirect contribution they make to the final output of grain, while their contribution to other final outputs (which were held to confer no benefit) was excluded from value-formation. To be consistently use-orientated, the calculation of these contributions has to assume that 'value' in this sense does not depend on production costs, i.e. not on the nature of commodities as they emerge from the production process, but on the *uses* into which they are channelled. Thus the unit ($-worth) of any input into a given sector (industry) must be valued at the norm attaching to that sector, regardless of the sector of origin (cost) of the input; e.g. if the norm of agriculture was 2, every unit of coal ($-worth) delivered to agriculture would be normed at 2, and so would every unit ($-worth) of electricity or oil serving agricultural production, even though the cost of coal, electricity, and oil per physical unit differed greatly from one another; for the *cost* of any economic flow per unit depends on its sector of *origin* (coalmining, power generation, oil extraction), while its *norm* depends on its *destination* (in this case agriculture). The mono-grain-norm of final uses would then be unity for agriculture and zero for all other sectors.

Each sector would have to be credited with the sum total of the norms it had earned from distributing its product to other sectors and to final buyers, and its own 'norm' would be that sum per unit of its output. It would then have to distribute that norm-revenue among its own suppliers in turn, crediting each with its norm per unit ($-worth) of delivery to it. It is as though farmers sold their grain at prices varying from one buyer to the other (say at $3 per unit delivery to the steel industry, $5 per unit delivered to the oil industry, etc.), thus earning a total of say, 10 million 'norm-$s' which they would then have to pay over to their own suppliers in strict proportion to the market value of inputs delivered to them. In such a system each sector would end up with a total norm-revenue equal to its own norm multiplied by its output, which it would finally distribute among its factors of production, again in strict proportion to the market value of the productive services they had absorbed from them. This last distribution would finally generate the 'mono-grain' or other 'factor-norms' (per unit of factor services) in the hands of factor-owners.

The workings of such an unusual arrangement might be more easily followed by visualizing a special currency of 'norm-$s' concentrated initially in the hands of final grain-buyers and paid by them to farmers, who would continue the circulation by paying their own suppliers,—always in proportion to the market values of their deliveries —until the process came to rest with all the norm-$s in the hands of factor-owners, thus generating the mono-grain-norms per unit factor service rendered. Such a norm circulation might take place in parallel with the familiar cost circulation in which buyers are *debited* by their suppliers uniformly in terms of cost-$s instead of sellers being uniformly *credited* as happens with norm-$s.

This norm circulation would of course end in different factor-norms if the initial norm-$s were issued to the economy by the final buyers of some product other than grain, say steel, with the remaining final buyers forbidden to credit their suppliers at all. Such a system would generate mono-steel or Stalinist norms consistent with the view that steel was the only final output of benefit to the economy while other goods and factors needed to be credited only to the extent that they contributed directly or indirectly to steel production. Indeed, we could imagine as many such 'monomaniac-use' systems as there were commodities offered to final buyers, each giving rise to its own set of monomaniac factor-norms,—a physiocratic system based on grain, a Stalinist[13] system based on steel, a mercantilist system based on cloth, etc. Each of these would deliver its own verdict on the relative weights (norms) to be attached to the factors.

We are, however, once more left without guidance as to which of these alternative norms, or what combination of them should serve as

---

[13] These expressions are of course derived from *stylized* versions of the historical value theories mentioned and cannot lay claim to historical authenticity.

the proper weighting of the factors. In this situation we are again thrown back on the 'functional' solution of mathematicians who suspend judgement by giving the final commodities algebraic weights (prices), say α, β, γ, etc., and express the single set of factor-norms as a set of functions of these,—leaving the matter there until such time as they feel able to give them numerical values in accordance with some principle yet to be discovered. This set of functions may be referred to as the 'upstream transformation' as it converts the prices of final commodities emerging at the end of the economic circuit or flow into values (norms) for the original factors absorbed at its source. Since the factor-norms are thus uniquely determined by the price-set of commodities, they could be described as the norm-implications of commodity prices.

1.9 The Eigenprice Synthesis

If we start with a totally arbitrary set of factor-norms, say all equal to unity, and use the 'downstream transformation' to convert them into commodity prices, we can certainly not regard the results as reflecting 'true' commodity values, since we have no reason to believe that the factor-norms from which we started were true reflections of the relative importance of the factors to the economy. Let us, however, assume for the moment that the derived commodity values *are* correct, and enquire what this would imply for the factors by subjecting them in turn to the second or upstream, transformation, thus converting them back into 'revised' factor-norms. These would of course turn out quite different from the all-unit set we had at first assumed, and therefore present us with a total set of factor- and commodity-prices which were inconsistent with one another. If factors and commodities were paid for in this way, some commodity-producers would get prices in excess of the total factor payments they had made (including the 'normal' uniform profit mark-up), thus earning unjustified profits, while others would not recoup all their factor-costs, thus incurring unjustified losses. Similarly it would follow that some factor-owners would be rewarded in excess of the contribution they had made to the production of final commodities, while others would be short-changed. A price system based on all-unit factor-norms would therefore be irrational in the economic sense of the term, and must be rejected.

How can we, then, arrive at a set of norms that would generate commodity-prices consistent with it? Such a set, when converted into prices downstream, would have to *convert back into itself* on subjecting these prices to the upstream transformation. In other words, the process of revising the initial factor-norms, i.e. subjecting them to the two transformations in this sequence, must end up with the same factor-norms from which we started, thus indicating that no further revision was possible or necessary and that we had arrived at what we shall call the factor-norms of the eigenprice-set. We can find this norm-set step by step, by starting from a completely arbitrary one whose first revision will yield a new set, different from the initial one. A second revision (applied to the revised set) will yield a third set differing from its predecessor, and so will every new revision in succession, until eventually the differences begin to converge towards zero and the revisions lead to a set whose further revision shows only negligible deviations from its predecessor, thus signalling that the process of revision is at an end. At this point we have found the factor-norms which, in conjunction with the commodity prices they imply, yield a rational price-set through which every producer would be paid exactly his costs (with the uniform margin added), and every factor-owner exactly according to his productivity (contribution to final output measured in the commodity-prices of the set). It is this set that we have named the 'eigenprices' of the economy. A concise definition of eigenprices would therefore identify them as the set of commodity-prices which is the price-effect of its own norm-implica-tion, and the set of factor-norms which is the norm-implication of its own price-effect.

In this section we wish to spare the reader numerical examples or mathematical formulae. We can, however, assure him, that given certain usual and perfectly plausible assumptions regarding the net-work of intersector flows in the economy, the revision process de-scribed above will eventually converge, and will moreover do so to a unique set of factor- and commodity-prices. These can be calculated for any economy by a mainframe computer using standard routines for the computation of the (dominant) eigenvectors and eigenvalues of certain matrices[14] derived from the economy's input–output tables.

[14] The speed of the convergence will grow as the ratio between the two largest eigenvalues of the revision matrix (product of the two transformations) departs from unity. Convergence will fail to arise in the exceptional case where this ratio is equal to unity, i.e. where the dominant eigenvalue of the matrix is a multiple root.

It is this mathematical terminology that we have borrowed in calling our new value-concept eigenprices.

In the process of calculating these prices the computer will also deliver a unique mark-up ratio to be applied to factor-costs before the full commodity cost prices are calculated. This ratio, which we shall name the economy's 'eigenyield', measures the final benefit accruing to the economy (in eigenprices) over and above the 'eigenrentals' (factor-norms) that must rationally be paid to the factors to create this benefit, thus yielding an indicator which, with suitable qualifications, may be taken to reflect its cost-effectiveness.

2

Numerical Illustrations

2.1 Cost-Fetishist Values

Labour-values

CONTRARY to an earlier impression among economists, including
some of outstanding distinction, we believe that the Marxian notion,
however one-sided and inadequate it may be, has a clear operational
meaning and can be given unambiguous quantitative expression. We
can do so by following a well-defined computational procedure applicable to any economic system composed of a finite number of
sectors or 'industries' (each producing a single commodity)[1] with the
aid of other commodities, labour, and other factors), provided only
that the intersector flows are measurable in independent homogeneous units. A three-sector model expressed in current $-values is shown
in Table 2.1 as a suitable illustration of annual flows from each sector
to all the others and to final uses (consumption, investment, defence,
etc.).

Table 2.1. *Intersector flows at current prices ($s)*

	Agriculture	Building	Clothing	Finals	Output
Agriculture	0	57	18	30	105
Building	74	0	9	60	143
Clothing	0	0	0	90	90
Labour	10	29	9		
Capital	30	1	9		
'Tax'	− 9	56	45		
Output	105	143	90		

To simplify the arithmetic we are counting as a sector's output only
that part of its production which is delivered to other sectors or final
users, thus excluding its self-consumed output and reducing all
figures in the main diagonal to zero. For the same reason we have
chosen figures and proportions which may fly in the face of realism,

---

[1] Multi-product sectors or 'joint production' would require complications which we
consider in Ch. 7; see also Appendix A.

except perhaps for a negative 'tax', i.e. a net subsidy in the case of agriculture. To fix homogeneous outputs in the mind, we may think of agriculture represented by *grain*, building by *steel*, and clothing by *cloth*. Thus the sector Building (which includes manufacturing) delivers $74m.-worth of steel to agriculture, while Clothing uses $18.-worth of grain and delivers its cloth exclusively to final users (consuming households). Capital combines all factors other than labour, including entrepreneurial profit, so that the residuals between output-values and total cost (in each column) must be imputed to tax payments net of subsidies going to government.

Table 2.2. *Intersector flows at mono-labour-costs*

	Mono-labour-costs p.u.	Agriculture	Building	Clothing	Finals	Output
Agriculture	1/3	0	19	6	10	35
Building	1/3	25	0	3	20	48
Clothing	1/5	0	0	0	18	18
Indirect labour-costs		25	19	9		
Direct labour (residual)		10	29	9		
Output		35	48	18		

If a $m.-worth of every commodity (i.e. each of the first three rows of Table 2.1) was measured in its proper labour-content (Marxian labour-value), this would result in a revalued scheme in which the gap between each total output-value and the sum of its sectoral inputs (i.e. its indirect labour-content) was exactly filled by the direct labour contribution as originally measured in Table 2.1, leaving no residue to be attributed to other factor contributions and no shortfall in neglect of any part of the direct labour known to have been spent in its production. Table 2.2 shows that this is achieved when the three output rows of Table 2.1 are revalued by multiplying them respectively by the coefficients 1/3, 1/3, and 1/5. These coefficients are therefore the proper measure of the Marxian labour-values, renamed here 'monomaniac labour-costs' or 'mono-labour-costs' for short. It is equally clear that these coefficients are unique and that any change in them would destroy the required identities, as the reader can easily satisfy himself by experimentally reducing, say, the first coefficient from 1/3 to 1/6, thus producing material cost-sums of 25, 9.5, and 6 respectively and thereby overstating the direct labour contribution to

Building and Clothing and understating it in the case of Agriculture even to the extent of turning it negative.

This completes our illustrative example of the characteristics of the full labour-costs and the, so far only intuitive, demonstration of their existence and values. In a later chapter we shall offer a general method for computation by means of linear algebra.

Capital values

By analogy with the argument above we could with equal ease illustrate mono-capital-costs for our three commodities, i.e. a set of multiplicative coefficients which when applied to the three rows of Table 2.1 would yield a sum of indirect capital-costs in each column that needed to be supplemented by exactly the 'capital' row of Table 2.1 to sum to the revalued output figures of Table 2.3. These coefficients, the full capital-contents or mono-capital-costs of commodities can be shown to be the unique set 2/5, 1/6, and 1/5 (Table 2.3).

Table 2.3.   *Intersector flows at mono-capital-costs*

	Mono-capital-costs p.u.	Agriculture	Building	Clothing	Finals	Output
Agriculture	2/5	0	23	7	12	42
Building	1/6	12	0	2	10	24
Clothing	1/5	0	0	0	18	18
Indirect capital-costs		12	23	9		
Direct capital (residual)		30	1	9		
Output		42	24	18 ◄		

Again it can easily be shown that the three mono-capital-costs cannot be varied without disturbing the fifth row of the scheme in Table 2.3 which replicates the capital row of Table 2.1; in other words these coefficients are indeed the unique monomaniac capital-costs of the three commodities and therefore correspond to a different form of cost-monomania from that of the labour-values, though still characterized by the wilful exclusion of all but one factor of production from any contribution to value-formation. Indeed, had we distinguished more than two original factors of production in our illustrative scheme, there could have been as many different cost-monomanias as there were factors, each yielding a different set of monomaniac commodity-valuations.

Composite factor-costs

So far we have been able to demonstrate the existence of commodity-valuations only in terms of alternative mono-factor-costs, such as the mono-labour- and mono-capital-costs reproduced for ease of reference to an accuracy of three decimals[2] in the rows of the cost-matrix below:

$$\begin{pmatrix} 0.333 & 0.333 & 0.200 \\ 0.396 & 0.165 & 0.196 \end{pmatrix}$$

As stated before, such monomaniac cost-valuations can give us as many commodity-costings as there are factors of production; but they cannot furnish any criteria for choice between them. Short of any doctrine or ideology that could determine such a choice we can obtain a *single* costing for our commodities only by imputing relative weights or norms to the separate factors purporting to measure their scarcity, utility, or any other index of preference or importance we may care to apply. Such a weighting, say (r_1, r_2), would give a unique single composite factor-costing for the three commodities of the type

$$0.333r_1 + 0.396r_2, \ 0.333r_1 + 0.165r_2, \text{ and } 0.200r_1 + 0.196r_2$$

Thus, if labour were weighted twice as heavily as capital, the composite factor-costings would be 1.062, 0.831, and 0.596.

To bring our costings into conformity with the traditional notion of 'full costs', however, we must in addition assume that they include a uniform mark-up of $\sigma(= 1/\phi - 1)$ per cent on all prime costs (materials and factor-costs), where ϕ is a uniform cost/turnover ratio, thus converting the above cost-matrix to the full-cost-matrix

$$1/\phi \begin{pmatrix} 0.333 & 0.333 & 0.200 \\ 0.396 & 0.165 & 0.196 \end{pmatrix} \tag{2.1}$$

and the composite full costs of commodities to

$$1/\phi\,(0.333r_1 + 0.396r_2), \ 1/\phi\,(0.333r_1 + 0.165r_2), \text{ and}$$

$$1/\phi\,(0.200r_1 + 0.196r_2).$$

We have seen, therefore, that under a non-monomaniac or pluralist system of valuation, the full costs of commodities may be established

[2] The figures used in the illustrative examples above were derived from computations carrying eight decimals in all. They were rounded in the examples to reduce the arithmetic to simple division, but must now be restored to a greater degree of accuracy.

clearly, but only in their (linear) dependence on the factor-norms
(r_1, r_2) for whose assessment we do not as yet possess any rational
criteria, and this is as far as cost-fetishism will take us.

2.2. Use-Fetishist Values

Commodity-norming

The valuation of commodities according to their *costs*, i.e. *their absorption of input-commodities and factors that are 'debited' to them*,
is so ingrained in our intuition through age-old habit and convention
that it takes a major conceptual effort to visualize and countenance
the opposite principle, that of *use* or *utility* as the sole measuring rod
of value. In the Marxian system, for instance, the value-in-use of a
commodity makes its appearance as hardly more than an *obiter dic-
tum*, a mere supplement to the cost-based value-in-exchange which is
defined as the full labour-cost discussed in the last chapter. It is only
the latter which is invested with an objective social existence independent of human subjectivity or individual whim. The former features merely as a *precondition* for the existence of value and is denied
any part in its determination.

As an 'experiment in thought', however, there is no logical reason
why we should not look at things from the other end of the telescope
and make the value of every commodity dependent on the *uses* it
serves. That means that commodities would be *credited* for every
$-worth of delivery they make to the production of other commodities
and to final uses, rather than being debited for every $-worth of
supplies they get from other lines and factors of production. The
credits so obtained would thus depend on the *destination* of each flow
(see Table 3.1 below) rather than on the sector of origin which deter-
mines its cost, and the list of credits attaching to the various sectors
and to factors would consist not of prices or costs, but of differently
conceived indices of economic worth which we shall call 'use-norms'
or 'norms' for short. These would function rather like honours or
merit marks awarded for various types of performance rather than
charges, black marks, or bills presented as a penalty for using up
resources, as is the case in cost accounting. In our simplified scheme
of Table 2.1, for instance, Agriculture would be awarded 57 steel-
norms for services to Building and 30 final norms for deliveries to

final users (the latter being measured in the grain-value so delivered itself). The Building industry, on the other hand, would get 74 grain-norms, 9 cloth-norms, and 60 final norms, while the Clothing industry would get only 90 final norms as it makes no contribution to other lines of production. The use-value or norm of each commodity in the given year would then be simply the sum of the credits obtained by it per unit of its output, while every $-worth of supplies or factor-services used up in its production, regardless of its origin, would be credited with this same norm. As a first step, of course, we need to find a rational method for determining the norms, and this is where we are again faced with the choice between monomanias and pluralist approaches which we encountered when *costing* goods.

The history of economic thought and policy provides some examples of use-monomanias, the wilful exclusion of all final deliveries but one from any credit for the nation's economic benefit. A stylized version of the physiocratic doctrine in eighteenth-century France, for instance, would only recognize grain (i.e. food) as a purveyor of benefit to the economy, excluding steel and cloth from any part in the creation of use-value except to the extent that they contributed to grain production. A Stalinist policy would cast steel in the same role, relegating grain and cloth to the status of handmaidens of steel without any value in their own right. Finally, a mercantilist school in a textile-exporting country might regard cloth as the be-all and end-all of economic activity, given that it was the only provider of export revenue to fill the coffers of the state.

Let us start with a physiocratic model in which all commodity-flows are valued in mono-grain-norms.[3] For convenience of reference we reproduce Table 2.1 as Table 2.4.

Table 2.4.   *Intersector flows at current prices ($s)*

	Agriculture	Building	Clothing	Finals	Output
Agriculture	0	57	18	30	105
Building	74	0	9	60	143
Clothing	0	0	0	90	90
Labour	10	29	9		
Capital	30	1	9		
'Tax'	− 9	56	45		
Output	105	143	90		

[3] We use the prefix 'mono' to distinguish the basis from the object of norming. Given that there are mono-grain norms of steel, cloth, and grain itself, and likewise for the other commodities, it might be difficult to avoid confusion between the mono-grain norm of steel and the mono-steel norm of grain unless the basis of valuation was clearly indicated by such a prefix.

A revaluation of these commodity flows in mono-grain norms entails multiplication of the first three columns of Table 2.4 and of each output by a set of coefficients which yields as a residual 'Finals' column the final output of grain as previously measured and no other benefit to the economy. Table 2.5 may be used to demonstrate that such a set exists and is unique, as any alteration in its components would result in the addition of final benefits denied by the physiocrats and/or fail to measure the whole of the final benefit conferred by Agriculture.

Table 2.5. *Intersector flows at mono-grain norms*[a]

	Agriculture	Building	Clothing	Finals	Output
Mono-grain norms	0.389	0.205	0	(Resid.)	
Agriculture	0	11.7	0	30	41.7
Building	29.2	0	0	0	29.2
Clothing	0	0	0	0	0
Factors and 'Tax'	12.5	17.5	0		
Output	41.7	29.2	0		

[a] Minor discrepancies are due to rounding.

The mono-steel norms, on the other hand, are a different set, as shown in Table 2.6 which results in a residual 'Finals' column bereft of all benefit except that derived from Building (i.e. steel). In both these cases the norms for clothing are equal to zero, since cloth makes no contribution to the other sectors' output and is deemed to confer no benefit in its own right. Only the mono-cloth norms show positive values throughout, the last of which must clearly be unity, since the whole of cloth output is taken to confer final benefit to the economy without any help from other sectors.

Table 2.6. *Intersector flows at mono-steel norms*[a]

	Agriculture	Building	Clothing	Finals	Output
Mono-steel norms	0.317	0.585	0	(Resid.)	
Agriculture	0	33.3	0	0	33.3
Building	23.3	0	0	60	83.3
Clothing	0	0	0	0	0
Factors and 'Tax'	10	50	0		
Output	33.3	83.3	0		

[a] Minor discrepancies are due to rounding.

To sum up, our mono-commodity norming entails the norms appearing in the columns of the matrix

Table 2.7.   *Intersector flows at mono-cloth norms*[a]

	Agriculture	Building	Clothing	Finals	Output
Mono-cloth norms	0.286	0.210	1	(Resid.)	
Agriculture	0	12	18	0	30
Building	21	0	9	0	30
Clothing	0	0	0	90	90
Factors and 'Tax'	9	18	63		
Output	30	30	90		

[a] Minor discrepancies are due to rounding.

$$\begin{pmatrix} 0.397 & 0.317 & 0.286 \\ 0.205 & 0.585 & 0.210 \\ 0 & 0 & 1 \end{pmatrix} \tag{2.2}$$

Factor-norming

The use-norming of factors, once commodity-norms are known (as in 2.2), presents no special difficulty: We know from Table 2.4 that $10m.-, $29m.-, and $9m.-worth of labour are spent in the service of Agriculture, Building, and Clothing respectively, and that the $48m.-worth of labour must therefore be awarded 10 grain-norms, 29 steel-norms, and 9 cloth-norms, making a total of $(10 \times 0.397 + 29 \times 0.205 + 9 \times 0)/48 = 0.208$ mono-grain-norms per unit labour. By the same method the mono-grain-norm of capital can be found to be $(30 \times 0.397 + 1 \times 0.585 + 9 \times 0)/40 = 0.301$ per unit. Similar procedures will establish the mono-steel-norms of the two factors to be 0.417 and 0.252 per unit respectively, and their mono-cloth-norms to be 0.375 and 0.447 per unit, so that a conspectus of the factor-norms would be given by the factor-norm matrix

$$\begin{pmatrix} 0.208 & 0.301 \\ 0.417 & 0.252 \\ 0.375 & 0.447 \end{pmatrix} \tag{2.3}$$

where the first column shows the alternatively based mono-commodity-norms of labour and the second those of capital.

We are thus presented with two alternative ways of factor-norming, but are given no clue as to which of them, or what combination of them would furnish the most rational single pair of factor-norms. A basis for such rationality could be provided only if the goods were allocated relative weights, say p_1, p_2, and p_3, which could then be transferred to the factor-norms of matrix (2.3), resulting in the composite factor-norms

$$r_1 = 0.208p_1 + 0.417p_2 + 0.375p_3$$
$$r_2 = 0.301p_1 + 0.252p_2 + 0.447p_3$$

(2.4)

for labour and capital respectively. In later chapters we shall give algebraic derivations for these formulae. Suffice it to say here, that in conventional terms r_1 and r_2 are probably best described as the average (and marginal) 'revenue productivities' of the two factors when commodity prices are fixed at p_1, p_2, and p_3. They show how the factor-norms could be derived (linearly) from any arbitrarily chosen set of commodity prices, but fail to give us any hint on how such a choice could be rationally made. This is as far as use-fetishism by itself can lead us.

2.3 Eigenprices: Numerical Illustrations

So far our ability to determine single cost prices for goods or use-prices (norms) for factors has been dependent on the arbitrary initial assumptions of a price-set for the opposite pole of the economic circuit, i.e. for factors as they transform themselves into goods, or for goods as they generate demand for factors. We must now enquire whether this remaining indeterminacy in the pricing process can be overcome, and cast about for criteria to determine the initial choice.

To start with, we shall test the arbitrary assumption that a $-worth of labour was 'worth' three times as much as a $-worth of capital, thus setting the initial factor-norms r_1, r_2 of Sect. 2.2 equal to 3 and 1 respectively, and the mark-up for full costing at 95 per cent (implying a cost-ratio ϕ of 0.514). In line with the transformation formulae (2.1) this would imply full costs of 2.71, 2.26, and 1.55 for the three commodities respectively, as may be seen from the first 'implied' line of Table 2.8. If these values are now accepted as proper commodity prices of departure they would, by virtue of formulae (2.4) imply factor-norms of 2.09 and 2.08 for labour and capital (see second 'implied' line of Table 2.8). By this token, therefore, our original assumption overvalued labour by nearly 70 per cent and undervalued capital by over 100 per cent, thus overstating the wage-rental ratio (relating labour to capital) by just under 200 per cent. If we had started from the arbitrary assumption of commodity-values equal to the previously implied costs (2.71, 2.26, and 1.55) in the second 'posited' line of Table 2.8 which, as we have seen, would have implied factor-norms of 2.09 and 2.08, the revised full costs of commodities (including the 95 per cent mark-up) would have been 2.96, 2.02, and 1.61 (see third 'implied' line of Table 2.8). In this case, therefore, our assumption would have overvalued grain and cloth by 9.2 and 3.9 per cent respectively, while undervaluing steel by nearly 10 per cent. If we restored the original estimate for grain in the revision by increasing the cost-ratio from 0.514 to 0.473, we would have ended up with costings of 2.20 and 1.75 for steel and cloth respectively, implying an initial undervaluation of the first by 8.9 per cent and of the second by 8.7 per cent, and it is clear that no tampering with the mark-up could reproduce the initial estimates for all three commodities at once.

Table 2.8.   *The computation of eigenprices by price-geared revisions* ($\phi = 51.43\%$)

	Goods prices[a]			Factor-norms[b]		
	p_1	p_2	p_3	r_1	r_2	
Posited				3	1	
	2.714	2.265	1.549			Implied
	2.714	2.265	1.549			Posited
Implied				2.0896	2.0799	
Posited				2.0896	2.0799	
	2.9562	2.0215	1.6061			Implied
	2.9562	2.0215	1.6061			Posited
Implied				2.0602	2.1172	
Posited				2.0602	2.1172	
	2.9658	2.0144	1.6089			Implied
	2.9658	2.0144	1.6089			Posited
Implied				2.0602	2.1195	
.	.	.	.	.	.	.
.	.	.	.	.	.	.
.	.	.	.	.	.	.
Posited				2.0646	2.1241	
	2.9740	2.0195	1.61325			Implied
	2.9740	2.0195	1.61325			Posited
Implied				2.0646	2.1241	

Note: Discrepancies due to rounding. It should be noted, however, that the set of eigenprices so found is determined up to a multiplicative constant only; for it is clear that if our arbitrary initial set (3,1) had been replaced by a multiple of itself (3k, k), each of the resulting eigenprices would have been multiplied by the same common factor.

[a] Implied values as per (2.2):

$$p_1 = 1/0.5143\,(0.333r_1 + 0.396r_2)$$
$$p_2 = 1/0.5143\,(0.333r_1 + 0.165r_2)$$
$$p_3 = 1/0.5143\,(0.200r_1 + 0.196r_2)$$

[b] Implied values as per (2.4):

$$r_1 = 0.208p_1 + 0.417p_2 + 0.375p_3$$
$$r_2 = 0.301p_1 + 0.252p_2 + 0.447p_3$$

The initial assumptions we have made thus entail price systems which reward some factor-owners for contributions they are not making to the final users of commodities, while overcompensating others, and compensate some producers (factor-users) in excess of the full costs (including normal profits) they have incurred, while short-changing others. Different initial assumptions would of course have resulted in rewards and penalties for factor-owners and/or producers that lacked economic justification in a similar way. No price system of this kind can be accepted as self-consistent or 'rational'.

To find a system free from these defects, we must evidently cast about for an initial estimate of factor-norms which, after an appropriate allowance for mark-up, *will generate commodity costs which in turn imply the initial factor-norms from which we started.* In the example of Table 2.8 such a set is found by continuing the process of price-geared revision ('downstream–upstream' transformation) through a number of iterations until both factor-norms and goods prices cease to be amenable to alteration by further revisions—in this case after as few as five iterations, when factor- and commodity-prices have both converged to stable values. Indeed, with factors normed at 2.06 and 2.12 and the cost-ratio set at 0.514, the prices of commodities will be 2.97, 2.02, and 1.61, and this would imply factor-norms equal to 2.06 and 2.12 respectively, as we have initially assumed. The full set of prices of goods and factors (2.97, 2.02, 1.61; 2.06, 2.12) thus forms a self-consistent set (given the cost-ratio of 51.4 per cent) in the sense that all commodities are priced at full cost when all factors are costed at full price, and none of these prices contains elements that cannot be economically justified.

As we shall see in a later chapter, this price system is unique up to a multiplicative constant (given our input–output structure) and may be regarded as in some way 'proper' to it. It will be termed the eigenprice system of the economy in question. Any deviation from it of the price system in actual operation must be taken as prima-facie evidence of irrationality, the existence of price elements which may be justified on historical, social, or moral grounds, but cannot claim a purely economic rationale. Chapter 3 will also offer an economic interpretation of the eigencost-ratio, ϕ, associated with the eigen-prices and implying a special form of social surplus, to be known as the economy's eigenyield.

Table 2.8 summarizes the experiments above, undertaken to show that an arbitrary initial choice of norms, prices, and mark-ups will in general result in inconsistent (i.e. 'irrational') price systems, while only one particular set will present a consistent structure—the economy's eigenprices. Table 2.8 also shows that these can be found by an iterative process starting from arbitrary assumptions and requiring in this instance only seven iterations. When starting out from different assumptions or requiring greater degrees of accuracy (say eight decimals), the iterations may need to be continued but, given certain plausible features of the input–output structure, will always converge in this way.

Table 2.9. *The computation of eigenprices and cost-ratio by cost-geared revisions*

Revision no.	Implied goods-costs[a]			Implied factor-norms[b]		Revision-ratios of factor-norms	
	c_1	c_2	c_3	r_1	r_2	r_1	r_2
0	1.395	1.164	0.7960	3^c	1^c		
1	0.7810	0.5340	0.4243	1.074	1.069	0.3580	1.069
2	0.4027	0.2735	0.2185	0.5443	0.5593	0.5067	0.5232
3	0.2071	0.1406	0.1124	0.2798	0.2878	0.5140	0.5146
4	0.1065	0.0723	0.0578	0.1439	0.1480	0.5145	0.5142
5	0.0548	0.0327	0.0297	0.0740	0.0761	0.5142	0.5142
Eigenprice[d] structure	0.1065	0.0723	0.0578	0.0740	0.0761		

Notes: The revision-ratios are the ratios between post- and pre-revision values in each case. The eigencost-ratio is the common revision-ratio obtained at the fifth cost-geared revision. Discrepancies are due to rounding errors.

[a] Implied values as per (2.1) without mark-up: $c_1 = 0.333r_1 + 0.396r_2$
$c_2 = 0.333r_1 + 0.165r_2$
$c_3 = 0.200r_1 + 0.196r_2$

[b] Implied values as per (2.4): $r_1 = 0.208c_1 + 0.417c_2 + 0.375c_3$
$r_2 = 0.301c_1 + 0.252c_2 + 0.447c_3$

[c] Arbitrary initial assumption

[d] Final revision of factor-norms and of goods costs divided by the common revision-ratio (eigencost-ratio). Since eigenprices are determined only up to a multiplicative factor, any multiple of the set obtained here is equally an eigenprice-set. The solution of Table 2.8, for instance, can be obtained by multiplying by the common factor 27.9 (but for rounding errors).

The experiment of Table 2.8 will be referred to as the 'price-geared' revision of norms since the transformations proceed from norms to commodity *prices* and back again. It assumes that the eigencost-ratio is already known ($\phi = 0.51427$). To compute eigenprices without this assumption and in a manner which simultaneously computes ϕ, we must proceed differently. In Table 2.9 the transformations proceed via commodity *costs* (i.e. without mark-up), thus showing at each step revised factor-norms compatible with commodities being weighted in accordance with the implied *costs* instead of the implied prices. At each of these 'cost-geared' transformations, therefore, the revised norms equal those that would emerge from the price-geared revision scaled down in the as yet unknown ratio ϕ. If, therefore, the end of the process is to be signalled by the fact that the post-revision price-geared norms equal their predecessors, the signal for ending the cost-geared revisions must be revised norms equal to a uniform scaling down in the ratio ϕ of their predecessors. Table 2.9 shows that in the four first revisions the two norms have non-uniform (*unequal*) revision-ratios. These do, however, rapidly converge towards equality as the iterations continue, until this equality is achieved with $\phi = 0.51427$ at the fifth revision. The eigencost-ratio is then identical with the common revision-ratio thus obtained, which will also be equal to each of the three revision-ratios for commodity costs. The eigenprices of Table 2.8 are merely uniform multiples of those of Table 2.9.

The reader should, however, be warned that when the calculation is done on the figures of Table 2.9 which are correct to four decimals only, the rounding errors will be substantial and compounded as the number of iterations increases, as the revision-ratios given in the table are taken from more precise calculations carrying eight decimals.

For future reference it is convenient to add here the results of similar calculations performed on other data in the first edition of this book (Table 2.10). We there assumed the same lay-out as in Table 2.1 for a different economy with three industries. With an input–output table of this kind and a cost-ratio of 90 per cent (computed by the method of Table 2.9), the two transformations corresponding to (2.1) and (2.4) become:

Table 2.10. *Intersector flows at current prices ($s)*

	Coal ind.	Power ind.	Service ind.	Finals
Coal industry	80	10	30	30
Power industry	20	25	25	20
Service industry	—	—	10	75
Capital	6	18	6	
Labour	39	27	17	
'Tax'	5	10	-3	
Output	150	90	85	

Downstream: $p_1 = 1/0.9 \times (0.17r_1 + 0.70r_2)$

$p_2 = 1/0.9 \times (0.30r_1 + 0.52r_2)$

$p_3 = 1/0.9 \times (0.25r_1 + 0.68r_2)$

Upstream: $r_1 = 0.17p_1 + 0.20p_2 + 0.63p_3$

$r_2 = 0.26p_1 + 0.13p_2 + 0.62p_3$

It is then easy to show that eigenrentals for capital and labour can both be unity,[4] and the eigenprices for the three commodities 0.97, 0.91, and 1.03 respectively; for unit eigenrentals will transform downstream into the eigenprices quoted, and these in turn will transform upstream into unit values (apart from rounding errors).

2.4 Standardization, Eigensurplus, and Eigenyield

Given that the eigenprices found for the three commodities in Table 2.8 (2.974, 2.019, and 1.613) are determined up to a multiplicative constant only, they could be scaled up or down in any fixed proportion without losing their characteristics as eigenprices, provided only that the two eigenrentals (1.038 and 1.068) are scaled up or down in a correlative proportion. The set is in fact one of relative prices only.

Table 2.11. *Intersector flows valued in standardized eigenprices*

	Standard eigenprice	Agriculture	Building	Clothing	Finals	Output
Agriculture	1.505	0	85.806	27.096	45.161	158.063
Building	1.023	75.225	0	9.211	61.408	145.844
Clothing	0.816	0	0	0	73.432	73.432
Costs (ξ)		75.225	85.806	36.307		
Labour	1.038	10.380	29.790	9.345		
Capital	1.068	32.047	1.068	9.614		
Factor cost (ω)		42.427	30.858	18.959		
Eigensurplus (τ)[a]		40.348	29.191	18.166		
Output		158.063	145.844	73.432		
Of which:						
Value added (υ)[b]		82.775	60.049	37.124		
Cost-ratio $\phi(=\omega/\upsilon)$[c]		0.512	0.514	0.511		
Eigenyield $\sigma(=\tau/\upsilon)$		0.951	0.946	0.958		

[a] Residual (τ = output – material costs – factor costs).

[b] $\upsilon = \omega + \tau$

[c] Small discrepancies are due to rounding. The correct result to four decimals is 0.5124 in each case (see Table 2.9).

We can, however, arrive at 'absolute' eigenprices by imposing an additional requirement, e.g. that the value of a chosen parameter of the economy (say total output, labour-costs, or the output of a particular industry) should be invariant to the transformation, i.e. should

[4] As we noted before, any set of factor- and commodity-prices proportional to the values given are eigenprices of the system. The particular multiples shown in the table have been so chosen as to equate the eigenvalue of the GNP (sum of final demands) to its current money value (125)

take on the same value in eigenprices as it does in current money value. It is convenient that the chosen parameter should be the economy's GNP, i.e. the sum of the 'finals' (final demands). This scaling to GNP which yields standard eigenprices is easily achieved by computing the ratio between the current GNP of Table 2.1 (180) and the GNP in the relative eigenprices of Table 2.8, and then scaling down the relative eigenprices in that ratio (0.506218). This yields the standard eigenprices listed in the first column of Table 2.11. At the same time we need to scale down the relative eigenrentals of the factors of production in the ratio 0.502761 in order to make the eigenvalue of the national income (sum of all factor-costs) equal to ϕ times the GNP, as required by the eigencost ratio 0.51427 found in Table 2.9, thus obtaining the standard eigenrentals listed in the same column.

The standard eigenprices so obtained, though called 'absolute' in contrast to the 'relative' prices of Tables 2.9 and 2.10, are only absolute prices as long as the physical unit of all factors and commodities is defined as the current $-worth of each. Dimensionally, they are pure numbers and represent the coefficients by which the current money prices need to be multiplied to yield the eigenprices per physical unit. It follows that a standard eigenprice below unity betokens that the money price of the commodity or factor is greater than its eigenprice (i.e. greater than the price which would *have had* to obtain if the observed final demand vector was to have been produced in conditions of perfect competition), in fact the commodity or factor is overpriced by the market in this sense. This may be caused by the existence of more than averagely strong monopoly elements in the producing industry, discriminative taxation of its inputs, excessive protection, or a variety of other causes which may be worth investigating if this signal is accepted. In our illustrative example (Table 2.11) it is evident that agricultural products are substantially underpriced, due perhaps to competitive sellers facing monopsony or to government subsidies keeping market prices down. Steel, the product of the building industry, appears to be slightly underpriced, but not significantly so, while clothing is overpriced by nearly 20 per cent. Standard eigenprices are thus prima-facie signals of price deviations from the competitive norm and, if of significant size, may fulfil a useful function for monopoly commissions or restrictive practices courts.

With the complete set of standard eigenprices as listed in the first column of Table 2.8 we can revalue the first five rows of Table 2.4.

as has been done in Table 2.11. We then find that the eigenvalues of commodity outputs exceed those of their inputs by a margin (τ) shown in the eighth row of the table as the eigensurplus. This measures the extent to which the economy has produced final eigenvalue (GNP) in excess of the eigencost it has incurred producing it, a surplus which can be spent by government or welfare organizations in accord with policy or need, e.g. by levying a uniform value added tax on each sector, which in this (somewhat fanciful case) could be as high as 95 per cent without prejudicing the production of the GNP by short-changing the production factors. It is a moot point whether this betokens a high degree of technical efficiency in the economy or a large measure of dictatorial constraints on the earnings of the factors of production, both of which appear to be underpaid (standard eigenrentals 1), though only slightly so.

It is noteworthy that eigenprices allow for a unique and uniform VAT-rate (eigenyield) for each sector,—a simple derivative of the eigencost-ratio which is implicit in the input–output relations of the economy and the structure of its final demand.

3

The General Theory of Eigenprices

3.1 The Basic Scheme in Algebraic Terms

For a rigorous definition of the concepts introduced in the last two chapters we must systematize our tableau économique and replace the arbitrarily chosen arithmetic by generalized schemata of an algebraic nature. We do so in (3.1) below, which illustrates an economy of n (= 3) production sectors using m (= 2) non-produced inputs or factors (say, capital and labour) in the shape of an input–output table of three quadrants. In the second (north-east) quadrant we show the sum of final uses, i.e. net exports, government and household consumption, fixed investment etc., together making up each sector's contribution to final uses y (the sectors' 'finals' for short) which, when added to its reprocessed output (row-sum of x's), make up its total output z. The sectors served by factor-inputs are identified by superscripts, as are the destinations of sectoral inputs, whose sector-origins are shown as subscripts, i.e. x_i^j stands for sector i's deliveries to sector j, y_i sector i's deliveries to end-users, and w_r^j factor r's absorption in the production of sector j.[1]

---

[1] As exercises of this kind are apt to result in a confusing proliferation of notational devices, a systematic directory of the most frequently occurring symbols for the convenience of readers appears as Appendix D. In stating origins and destinations of flows we replace the usual double-subscript notation by the subscript-superscript convention, which will enable us to write the constituent columns and rows of matrices unambiguously by quoting only the relevant affix in the proper position e.g. the jth column of matrix X as x^j, and its ith row as x_i'; the sectoral inputs of the rth factor can thus be written as w_r'. In particular, I stands for the unit matrix, i_r' and i^r for its rth row and column, and i' and i for the all-unit vectors (with 1 in all positions). For the rest we rely for clarity on the conventional notation, using lower-case letters for scalars, bold capital letters for matrices, and bold lower-case letters for vectors, with primes for rows (x') and unprimed for columns (x). In addition, the total row- and column-sums of vectors will be denoted by the corresponding lower-case Roman and Greek letters respectively:

$$X_i = x \qquad i'X = \xi$$
$$W_i = w \qquad i'W = \omega.$$

We retain the conventional use of the prime sign ($'$) to denote transposition of rows into columns or vice versa and the circumflex ($^\wedge$) for diagonal matrices.

The last row of (3.1) stands for residual surpluses and taxes (net of subsidies) entering into the formation of prices:

$$x_1^1 + x_1^2 + x_1^3 + y_1 = z_1$$

$$x_2^1 + x_2^2 + x_2^3 + y_2 = z_2$$

$$x_3^1 + x_3^2 + x_3^3 + y_3 = z_3 \qquad (3.1)$$

$$w_1^1 + w_1^2 + w_1^3 = w_1$$

$$w_2^1 + w_2^2 + w_2^3 = w_2$$

$$\tau^1 + \tau^2 + \tau^3 = \tau$$

All flows are assumed to be homogeneous,[2] each valued uniformly at a single price as actually traded during the given year inclusive of all price-related taxes,[3] so that the sum of any column equals the sum of the corresponding row, i.e.

$$\xi + \omega + \tau = x + y = z \qquad (3.2)$$

from which the traditional national income identity may be derived by simple summation,[4] i.e.

$$\omega'\mathbf{i} + \tau = \mathbf{i}'y \equiv y_0. \qquad (3.3)$$

Putting tableau (3.1) in matrix form (and generalizing the number of sectors and factors to n and m respectively), we can write

$$\begin{aligned}\mathbf{Xi} + \mathbf{y} &= \mathbf{z} \\ \mathbf{Wi} &= \mathbf{w},\end{aligned} \qquad (3.4)$$

where it is understood that each output z will depend on the productive inputs listed in the ith columns of matrices $\mathbf{X}$ and $\mathbf{W}$. Given that this dependence is of the usual proportional and 'limitational' kind involving fixed input-coefficients, we can write this as

---

[2] Our model so far does not allow for joint production of any sort; the extensions necessary for this will be discussed in Sect. 7.1 and Appendix A.

[3] It must be stressed that all flows in (3.1) are measured in *monetary* terms ($s at current prices). These may be regarded as surrogates for physical terms as long as their column-wise additivity is not lost sight of. This additivity lends to each flow a second, alternative dimension (norm-$s) based on equivalence-in-use, i.e. on an interpretation which physical flows do not admit. See Sect. 3.7.

[4] For the sake of simplicity we dispense with a fourth (south-east) quadrant for factor-inputs going directly into final uses (e.g. teaching, medical treatment, administration, etc.) by assuming that such inputs are routed through a special sector subsumed under services and relayed to final users as part of a sectoral contribution.

$$\begin{aligned} \mathbf{Az} + \mathbf{y} &= \mathbf{z} \\ \mathbf{Bz} &= \mathbf{w}, \end{aligned} \tag{3.5}$$

where the new symbols stand for the 'coefficient matrices' (of material and factor-inputs respectively):

$$\mathbf{A} = \mathbf{X}\hat{\mathbf{z}}^{-1} \text{ and } \mathbf{B} = \mathbf{W}\hat{\mathbf{z}}^{-1}. \tag{3.6}$$

The upper portion of (3.5) is clearly equivalent to $\mathbf{y} = (\mathbf{I} - \mathbf{A})\mathbf{z}$ and therefore yields the familiar formula for the output targets needed to create a prescribed 'final bill of goods' $\mathbf{y}$:[5]

$$\mathbf{z} = (\mathbf{I} - \mathbf{A})^{-1}\mathbf{y} \equiv \overline{\mathbf{A}}\mathbf{y}. \tag{3.7}$$

It should be stressed at this point that, while we do not deny the dependence of $\mathbf{A}$ and $\mathbf{B}$ on prevailing prices or other variables with feedback effects, it will be our assumption throughout this book that the coefficients observed in a given year have already undergone a process of adaptation to underlying preferences, aspirations, and constraints, whether perceived by atomistic producers in the light of market signals or directly selected by planners, policy-makers, or dictators. We shall therefore accept them as given and focus attention on the *ex post* evaluation of the static structure that is found to have resulted.

3.2 The Full-Cost Pricing of Commodities: Valuation by Cost

Suppose now that a cost-monomaniac value theory adopts the rth factor in (3.1) as the single cost-standard whose total (direct and indirect) absorption per unit of each product furnishes all products' cost-values $\mathbf{c_r}' = (c_r^1, c_r^2, \ldots, c_r^n)$.[6] For any product i these values must clearly satisfy the equation:

$$c_r^i + b_r^i + (a_1^i c_r^1 + a_2^i c_r^2 + \ldots + a_n^i c_r^i) = b_r^i + \mathbf{c_r}'\mathbf{a^i} \tag{3.8}$$

which defines cost-value on the given basis r as the sum of direct and indirect (in brackets) absorption of factor r per unit output of the

---

[5] We introduce here the 'inverted L' over the symbol of a matrix to denote its Leontief inverse, i.e. $(\mathbf{I} - \mathbf{A})^{-1} \equiv \overline{\mathbf{A}}$, which might be read as 'A Lin'.

[6] The products being valued are identified by the superscripts of c and the bases of valuation by the subscripts; thus c_r^j stands for the cost-value of commodity j on the cost-basis of (factor) r, i.e. with factor r being treated as the only value-forming factor.

product under valuation. Since this is true for all n products, it can be written in matrix form:

$$\mathbf{c_r}' = \mathbf{b_r}' + \mathbf{c_r}'\mathbf{A} \tag{3.9}$$

or explicitly as

$$\mathbf{c_r}' = \mathbf{b_r}'\overline{\mathbf{A}}. \tag{3.10}$$

If r stands for the factor 'homogeneous labour', the $\mathbf{c_r}'$ are evidently the Marxian labour-values as defined by imputation of all commodity-values to the single factor labour, with other factors arbitrarily excluded from any part in the formation of true value and their incomes ascribed merely to socially sanctioned exploitation.

It will be noted that the Leontief inverse $\overline{\mathbf{A}}$ acts here as a synthesizer in converting *direct* labour-costs $\mathbf{b}'$ into *full* (direct and indirect) labour-costs through simple post-multiplication. The latter are therefore seen to be quantifiable, subject only to our yardstick in quantifying the $\mathbf{b}'$, as the correct measure of homogeneous labour, and their numerical values can be obtained by a familiar computer process, given a knowledge of $\mathbf{A}$ and $\mathbf{b}'$.

Finally, of course, we can cast any of the $m - 1$ factors other than labour in the role of cost-basis, thus obtaining as many alternative sets of single-factor cost-values for our n products as there are factors. A conspectus of these would take the form of the cost-matrix

$$\mathbf{C} = \mathbf{B}\overline{\mathbf{A}}, \tag{3.11}$$

where each set is displayed in a row of n values, with each of the m factors in turn doing duty as the cost-basis as we move from row to row, and the typical element c_r^i denoting the cost of product i in terms of factor r. The first row might give the capital-values, the second the labour-values, the third the land- or import-values, etc. But ideology or doctrine apart, we have no criterion for accepting any of these as economically or logically superior to the others. Short of one-sided verdicts, we could arrive at single, unambiguous cost-values for our set of commodities only if we had prior valuations (norms) for the primary factors, say $\mathbf{r}' = (r_1, r_2, \ldots, r_m)$, which would allow us to let each of them enter into the formation of commodity-values with a preassigned relative weight. The composite cost-value of commodity i, say c^i, would then emerge as

$$r_1 c_1^i + r_2 c_2^i + \ldots + r_m c_m^i$$

or in matrix form:

$$\mathbf{c'} = \mathbf{r'C}. \tag{3.12}$$

To complete our full-cost pricing, however, we must allow for a uniform mark-up, say $100\,(1 - \phi)/\phi$ per cent to add the usual surplus (profit or tax) to factor-costs (3.12), thus yielding

$$\mathbf{p'} = 1/\phi \,.\, \mathbf{r'C} \tag{3.13}$$

for the composite full costs of commodities. The introduction of the profit rate $\sigma(= (1 - \phi)/\phi)$ presents us with one degree of freedom in addition to $\mathbf{r'}$, which will stand us in good stead in later stages of the analysis.

So far, however, we have no rational basis for choosing any set of factor-norms $\mathbf{r'}$ in preference to any other; and unless ideology, received doctrine, or some form of social ethics can lead us to such an a priori choice, we must continue our quest.

3.3 The Full-Price Costing of Factors: Valuation by Use

All value-measures reviewed in the last section were aggregations of cost elements derived from the side of factor supply, without regard to the utilities of products as determined by the demand for final goods. In the interests of a genuinely comprehensive and unified concept of value,[7] we must now abandon this type of cost-fetishism and turn—as a first step—to the opposite extreme, a one-sided view of value informed by utilities only and fully deserving the opprobrium of use-fetishism.

As in the case of cost-fetishism we shall start with the extreme, monomaniac, form of the disease, and assume that the final use of only *one* commodity, say y_k, is judged to be of true benefit to the economy, and that all other commodities are credited with usefulness only to the extent that they contribute to the satisfaction of the selected use, whether directly through contributions to the final use of

---

[7] Advocates of exclusively cost-based valuations such as Marx were of course aware that their value-in-exchange did not account for all the attributes attaching to the normal concept of value, and posited the existence of value-in-use as a parallel and complementary category. They did not, however, follow mainstream economists in their attempts to integrate both aspects of value in a single concept, and resigned themselves to living with a somewhat uncomfortable dichotomy.

commodity k, or indirectly by serving that production as an input. We are thus defining the 'k-based norms' $(v_k^1, v_k^2, \ldots, v_k^n)$ as follows:

$$z_i v_k = y_j + (x_i^1 v_k^1 + x_i^2 v_k^2 + \ldots + x_i^n v_k^n) \qquad (3.14)$$

giving expression to the fact that the total norm-credit awarded to the production of sector i must be equal to its *direct* credit for contributing to the final uses of k ($y_j = y_k$ if $j = k$, otherwise $= 0$) and to the *indirect* credit by providing inputs to k or to other sectors to the extent they themselves contribute to y_k (the bracketed expression). Dividing both sides of (3.8) by z_i we obtain the fully explicit definition

$$v_k^i = s_k + (d_i^1 v_k^1 + d_i^2 v_k^2 + \ldots + d_i^n v_k^n), \qquad (3.15)$$

where d are the delivery quotas of sector i allocated to the various i-consuming sectors of the economy $(d_i^r \equiv x_i^r/z_i)$, not to be confused with the input-coefficients $a_i^r (\equiv x_i^r/z_r)$ used in cost analysis earlier, the matrices $\mathbf{A}$ and $\mathbf{D}$ being defined as

$$\mathbf{A} = \mathbf{X}\hat{\mathbf{z}}^{-1} \text{ and } \mathbf{D} = \hat{\mathbf{z}}^{-1}\mathbf{X} \qquad (3.16)$$

respectively. The symbol s_k stands for the final-use quota y_k/z_k, thus implying $\hat{\mathbf{s}} \equiv \hat{\mathbf{z}}^{-1}\hat{\mathbf{y}}$

The definition (3.15) can be put more conveniently in matrix form:

$$\mathbf{v_k} = \hat{\mathbf{s}}\mathbf{i_k} + \mathbf{D}\mathbf{v_k}, \qquad (3.17)$$

where $\mathbf{i_k}$ stands for the kth column of the unit matrix, containing 1 in the kth place and zero everywhere else. Clearly (3.17) implies $(\mathbf{I} - \mathbf{D})\mathbf{v} = \hat{\mathbf{s}}\mathbf{i_k}$, and therefore the fully explicit matrix definition

$$\mathbf{v_k} = \overline{\mathbf{D}}\hat{\mathbf{s}}\mathbf{i_k} \qquad (3.18)$$

The vectors $\mathbf{v_k}$ above are thus shown to be the column vectors of the commodity-norm matrix $\mathbf{V}(\equiv \overline{\mathbf{D}}\hat{\mathbf{s}})$ in which each row lists the monomaniac use-norms of all commodities, with the basis of use-valuation shifting from one final good to the next as we move from row to row.

To obviate the arbitrary choice of a single commodity to serve as the use-base k, we could allow every commodity a contribution to the final uses of the economy with a (so far arbitrary) weight p, thus replacing $\mathbf{i_k}$ in (3.18) by a list of commodity prices $\mathbf{p}$, and obtain the general composite-norm equation:

$$\mathbf{v} = \overline{\mathbf{D}}\hat{\mathbf{s}}\mathbf{p} = \mathbf{Vp}. \tag{3.19}$$

This is the analogue of the explicit full-cost equation (3.12), with the important difference that commodity-valuations are now derived by aggregating contributions to final uses ($\mathbf{y}$) instead of summing calls on primary resources ($\mathbf{w}'$).

From here it is only a short step to the use-valuation (norming) of factors ($\mathbf{r}$) by the summation of their contributions to the several commodities they help to produce, i.e.

$$\hat{\mathbf{w}}\mathbf{r} = \mathbf{Wv} \tag{3.20}$$

or, after predivision by $\hat{\mathbf{w}}$ and defining the employment-quota matrix $\mathbf{E} \equiv \hat{\mathbf{w}}^{-1}\mathbf{W}$,

$$\mathbf{r} = \mathbf{Ev} = \mathbf{EVp} = \mathbf{E}\overline{\mathbf{D}}\,\hat{\mathbf{s}}\mathbf{p}. \tag{3.21}$$

Finally, transposing (3.21) for analogy with (3.12) and (3.13) we obtain

$$\mathbf{r}' = \mathbf{p}'\mathbf{V}'\mathbf{E}' = \mathbf{p}'\hat{\mathbf{s}}\overline{\mathbf{D}}'\mathbf{E}' \equiv \mathbf{p}'\mathbf{N}, \tag{3.22}$$

where $\mathbf{N}$ is the norm-matrix $\hat{\mathbf{s}}\overline{\mathbf{D}}'\mathbf{E}'$.

The meaning of the norm-matrix[8] $\mathbf{N}$ can be made clear by setting $\mathbf{p}'$ equal to a row of the unit-matrix, say $\mathbf{i}_k'$, which assumes that only the kth final yield $\mathbf{y}_k$ is credited with utility (measured in its own terms), while all others are deemed to make zero contributions to the final benefit accruing to the economy. This shows that the kth row of $\mathbf{N}$ records the norms of the m primary inputs (or factors) in terms of their contributions to the single final $\mathbf{y}_k$. Just as $\mathbf{C}$ was shown to be a conspectus of single-factor product costs, so $\mathbf{N}$ is now shown to be a conspectus of *single-yield* factor-norms. The traditional cost-monomania of *single-factor* theories of value has been stood on its head to turn into the use-monomania of *single-yield* theory, and if this is generalized by admitting *all* factors and yields to value-formation through preassigned relative weights $\mathbf{r}'$ and $\mathbf{p}'$, we generate shadow

---

[8] The idea of input–output analysis based on delivery quotas as well as input-coefficients and certain considerations deriving from it is not without antecedents. (See e.g. M. Augusztinovics, 'Methods of International and Intertemporal Comparisons of Structure', in A. P. Carter and A. Bródy (eds.), *Contributions to Input–Output Analysis*, North-Holland, Amsterdam, 1970.) The purpose of that exercise, however, is the quest for an aspect of economic structure invariant to the price system rather than the search for a system of universal pricing or valuation as such.

prices for products and factors as shown by the mappings or 'transformations' (3.13) and (3.22), i.e.

$$\mathbf{p}' = 1/\phi_* \cdot \mathbf{r}'\mathbf{C} \text{ and } \mathbf{r}' = \mathbf{p}'\mathbf{N}, \tag{3.23}$$

which will be termed the 'downstream' and 'upstream' transformations respectively.

Let us at this point explain, in anticipation of Sect. 3.5, that the two halves of (3.23) cannot both be true for any arbitrarily chosen set $\mathbf{r}'$. There is only one, unique set for which they will apply simultaneously,—the $\mathbf{r}'$ which forms part of the eigenprice-set $\mathbf{e}' = [\mathbf{p}', \mathbf{r}']$ and measures the factor-norms or eigenrentals, to be denoted by $\mathbf{r}'$.

3.4   Alternative Interpretations of Use-Norms

Yield-productivity

So far we have derived the factor-norms (rentals) by a process of conceptual inversion whereby a single selected commodity had its final supply (yield) cast in the role of ultimate determinant of use-value, to be traced upstream to the other end of the economy for analysis into derivative use-values (norms) attaching to the factors engaged in its production—just as, in more familiar types of analyses, the contributions of a single factor (e.g. labour) are traced downstream to be integrated into the cost-values of the end-products they help to create. To alleviate the strain that such an inversion must exert on our faculties of conceptualization, we offer a more direct interpretation, which can be made to follow immediately if we remind ourselves that the definitions of $\mathbf{A}$ as $\mathbf{X}\hat{\mathbf{z}}^{-1}$ and $\mathbf{D}$ as $\hat{\mathbf{z}}^{-1}\mathbf{X}$ (3.16) imply the relationships

$$\mathbf{D} = \hat{\mathbf{z}}^{-1}\mathbf{A}\hat{\mathbf{z}} \text{ and } \overline{\mathbf{D}} = \hat{\mathbf{z}}^{-1}\overline{\mathbf{A}}\mathbf{z}, \tag{3.24}$$

while those of $\mathbf{E}$ as $\hat{\mathbf{w}}^{-1}\mathbf{W}$ and $\mathbf{B}$ as $\mathbf{W}\hat{\mathbf{z}}^{-1}$ (3.20) and (3.6) imply

$$\mathbf{E} = \hat{\mathbf{w}}^{-1}\mathbf{B}\hat{\mathbf{z}}. \tag{3.25}$$

Accordingly, the norm-matrix $\mathbf{N}$ defined in (3.22) may be explained as

$$\mathbf{N} = \hat{\mathbf{s}}\overline{\mathbf{D}}'\mathbf{E}' = (\hat{\mathbf{y}}\hat{\mathbf{z}}^{-1})(\hat{\mathbf{z}}\overline{\mathbf{A}}'\hat{\mathbf{z}}^{-1})(\hat{\mathbf{z}}\mathbf{B}'\hat{\mathbf{w}}^{-1}) = \hat{\mathbf{y}}\overline{\mathbf{A}}'\mathbf{B}'\hat{\mathbf{w}}^{-1},$$

which, by virtue of (3.11) simplifies to

$$\mathbf{N} = \hat{\mathbf{y}} \mathbf{C}' \hat{\mathbf{w}}^{-1}. \qquad (3.26)$$

On the right-hand side of this equation the full-cost matrix $\mathbf{C}'$ is pre-multiplied by the diagonal matrix of yields ($\hat{\mathbf{y}}$), thus resulting in a conspectus of final yields valued at the single-factor cost based on each factor in turn ($\hat{\mathbf{y}} \mathbf{C}'$), i.e. a conspectus which might be called the yield-products of the factors. When this is post-divided by the total factor-uses ($\hat{\mathbf{w}}$), it will result in the sectoral yield-productivities of the factors at full-cost valuation.

We have thus analysed the total contribution of a unit of each factor evaluated in its own terms into such portions as may be debited to each of the sectors according to the yield generated by the direct and indirect use which that sector makes of the factors concerned.[9] The factor-norms simply measure the total credit accruing to each factor per unit when its sector credits are valued in the commodity-price system $\mathbf{p}'$, i.e. $\mathbf{p}' \mathbf{N}$, and are therefore unique projections or 'mappings' of the product prices assumed.

The generation of factor-norms—the norming circulation

Our inbred conceptions and traditions have made us conscious that in practice full commodity costs are generated by a mandatory flow of money-tokens requiring every sector to 'pay' for its inputs and to replace these outgoings fully by claiming in turn compensation for them at the uniform rate of its own costs for every unit product delivered to its clients. In this way the prices (rentals) of the factors of production are passed on to the final users of commodities who are ultimately responsible for their total discharge.

A similar money circulation under an imaginary, though fully practicable, régime would generate our factor-norms from given sets of commodity prices. Let us consider this norm-generating circulation

---

[9] The norm-values which the totality of all factors contributes to each of the end-uses are clearly the elements of the row-vector $\mathbf{w}' \mathbf{N}'$. But by virtue of (3.22) we have:

$$\mathbf{w}' \mathbf{N}' = \mathbf{w}' \mathbf{E} \overline{\mathbf{D}} \hat{\mathbf{s}} = \mathbf{i}' \hat{\mathbf{w}} \mathbf{E} \overline{\mathbf{D}} \hat{\mathbf{s}} = \mathbf{i}' \mathbf{W} \overline{\mathbf{D}} \hat{\mathbf{s}} = \boldsymbol{\omega}' \overline{\mathbf{D}} \hat{\mathbf{s}}.$$

Further, if the list of factors is complete in the sense of exhausting the current value of each product (i.e. if $\mathbf{i}' \mathbf{X} + \boldsymbol{\omega}' = \mathbf{z}' \mathbf{D} + \boldsymbol{\omega}' = \mathbf{z}'$ and therefore $\boldsymbol{\omega}' \overline{\mathbf{D}}' = \mathbf{z}$), the above chain of equations may be continued:

$$\mathbf{w}' \mathbf{N}' = \boldsymbol{\omega}' \overline{\mathbf{D}} \hat{\mathbf{s}} = \mathbf{z}' \hat{\mathbf{s}} = \mathbf{i}' \hat{\mathbf{z}} \mathbf{s} = \mathbf{i}' \hat{\mathbf{y}} = \mathbf{y}'.$$

Thus the total norm-value of all factors taken together equals the yield y_k of whichever sector k is selected as the use-valuation basis for the computation of norms, i.e.

$$w_1 n_k^1 + w_2 n_k^2 + \ldots + w_m n_k^m = y_k \text{ for all } k = 1, 2, \ldots, n.$$

in the simplest case of use-monomania where only one commodity, say good 1 (coal), ranks for final benefit, i.e. the point of departure is a commodity-price structure of (1, 0, 0), taking our cue from the arithmetic exercise of Table 3.1. The government or planning commission would then start by issuing to the coal industry (or coal bank) y units of a special currency, say 30 norm-$s (n$s). The coal bank would ascertain that it had been awarded 30 n$s for an output of 150 cost-$s (c$s), i.e. an initial norm of 0.20 n$/c$. It would then be required to unload this issue by paying into the banks of its supplying sectors and factors (capital bank and labour bank) a first-round distribution equal to their respective deliveries to the coal industry multiplied by that initial norm, leaving any residual profit or tax to be paid at the same rate (in this case, 5 c$s at 0.20 n$/c$, i.e. 1 n$) into a special 'tax bank', T. Alternatively we may say that the initial issue of 30 n$s must be completely unloaded to its input-providers (including the tax bank) in strict proportion to their deliveries to the coal industry. After the first-round distribution, every sector and every factor providing inputs to the coal industry would find a first-round n$-deposit in its bank from which it could compute its first-round norm, e.g. $16/150 = 0.11$ n$/c$ for the coal industry, $4/90 = 0.04$ n$/c$ for the power industry, $1/12 = 0.08$ n$/c$ for the tax bank, etc. It would now have to act exactly as the coal bank had done after the initial issue, i.e. unload the total of its n$-deposit in a second-round distribution to the banks of its own input providers (including the tax bank) at the rate of its own first-round norm per unit delivery, i.e. in strict proportion to their deliveries to itself. It is as though each sector owed its suppliers and production factors (including itself as a residual earner) a dividend in proportion not to capital invested, but to input-value contributed, where the total subject to distribution was not the net profit, but the gross dividend income received by the sector itself. The sector and factor banks (as well as the tax bank) would thus find a reflux of n$s from their first payments in the shape of second-round deposits returned to them by some or all of the sectors they had just paid. Only the factor and tax banks would be exempt from such refluxes as they are by definition free from suppliers to whom the n$-deposits would have to be unloaded, and can simply allow successive n$-deposits to accumulate in their vaults. The sector banks, however, would be obliged to *distribute* the successive n$-receipts of each round (always at the rate of their latest norm per unit delivery), and to do likewise with the sum of the resulting refluxes at the next round, until these refluxes had shrunk to negligible proportions. When this has happened, they will each be left without significant n\$-deposits and the whole of the initial issue of 30 n\$s will have found its way into the factor and tax banks. In each of these banks the cumulative total received divided by the total supply of the relevant factor will equal the factor-norms as defined throughout this exercise.

Table 3.1. *The generation of norms from Table 2.6*[a]

'Round'	Input	X			z	Distr.[b] δ	Incr.[c] γ δ/z	Cum[d] γ
	Coal	80	10	30	150	30	0.20	0.20
	Power	20	25	25	90	0	0	0
	Services	0	0	10	85	0	0	0
(0)	K	6	18	6	30	0	0	0
	L	39	27	17	83	0	0	0
	T	150	10	-3	12	0	0	0
	Sum	150	90	85	—	—	—	—
	Coal	16	0	0	150	16	0.11	0.31
	Power	4	0	0	90	4	0.04	0.04
	Services	0	0	0	85	0	0	0
(1)	K	1.2	0	0	30	1.2	0.04	0.04
	L	7.8	0	0	83	7.8	0.09	0.09
	T	1	0	0	12	1	0.08	0.08
	Sum	30	0	0	—	—	—	—
	Coal	8.54	0.44	0	150	8.97	0.06	0.37
	Power	2.13	1.11	0	90	3.24	0.04	0.08
	Services	0	0	0	85	0	0	0
(2)	K	0.64	0.80	0	30	1.44	0.05	0.09
	L	4.16	1.21	0	83	5.36	0.06	0.16
	T	0.53	0.44	0	12	0.97	0.08	0.16
	Sum	0.16	4	0	—	—	—	—
	Coal	4.78	0.36	0	150	5.14	0.03	0.40
	Power	1.20	0.90	0	90	2.10	0.02	0.10
	Services	0	0	0	85	0	0	0
(3)	K	0.36	0.65	0	30	1.01	0.03	0.12
	L	2.33	0.97	0	83	3.30	0.04	0.20
	T	0.30	0.36	0	12	0.66	0.05	0.22
	Sum	5.14	2.10	0	—	—	—	—
	Coal	2.74	0.23	0	150	2.98	0.02	0.42
	Power	0.69	0.58	0	90	1.27	0.01	0.11
	Services	0	0	0	85	0	0	0
(4)	K	0.21	0.42	0	30	0.62	0.02	0.14
	L	1.34	0.63	0	83	2.00	0.02	0.22
	T	0.17	0.23	0	12	0.40	0.03	0.25
	Sum	5.14	2.10	0	—	—	—	—
	Coal	1.59	0.14	0	150	1.73	0.01	0.43

Table 3.1.   (*cont.*)

'Round'	Input	X		z	Distr.[b] δ	Incr.[c] γ δ/z	Cum[d] γ
	Power	0.40	0.35	0	90	0.75	0.01	0.12
	Services	0	0	0	85	0	0	0
(5)	K	0.12	0.25	0	30	0.37	0.01	0.15
	L	0.77	0.38	0	83	0.15	0.01	0.24
	T	0.10	0.14	0	12	0.24	0.02	0.27
	Sum	2.98	1.27	0	—	—	—	—
	Coal	0.92	0.08	0	150	1.00	0.01	0.44
	Power	0.23	0.21	0	90	0.44	0.01	0.13
	Services	0	0	0	85	0	0	0
(6)	K	0.07	0.15	0	30	0.22	0.01	0.16
	L	0.45	0.23	0	83	0.68	0.01	0.25
	T	0.06	0.08	0	12	0.14	0.01	0.28
	Sum	1.73	0.75	0	—	—	—	—
	Coal	0.54	0.05	0	150	0.58	0.00	0.44
	Power	0.13	0.12	—	90	0.26	0.00	0.13
	Services	0	0	0	85	0	0	0
(7)	K	0.04	0.09	0	30	0.13	0.00	0.16
	L	0.26	0.13	0	83	0.39	0.00	0.25
	T	0.03	0.05	0	12	0.08	0.01	0.29
	Sum	1.00	0.44	0	—	—	—	—
	Coal	0.31	0.03	0	150	0.34	0.00	0.44
	Power	0.08	0.07	0	90	0.15	0.00	0.14
	Services	0	0	0	85	0	0	0
(8)	K	0.02	0.05	0	30	0.07	0.00	0.17
	L	0.15	0.08	0	83	0.23	0.00	0.25
	T	0.02	0.03	0	12	0.05	0.00	0.30
	Sum	0.58	0.26	0	—	—	—	—
	Coal	0.19	0.02	0	150	0.20	0.00	0.44
	Power	0.04	0.04	0	90	0.09	0.00	0.14
	Services	0	0	0	85	0	0	0
(9)	K	0.01	0.03	0	30	0.04	0.00	0.17
	L	0.09	0.04	0	83	0.13	0.00	0.17
	T	0.01	0.02	0	12	0.03	0.00	0.30
	Sum	0.34	0.15	0	—	—	—	—

[a] Minor discrepancies are due to rounding.
[b] Distribution due to suppliers.
[c] Incremental norm.
[d] Cumulative norm.

Clearly, the power- or service-based factor-norms could be generated in the same way as the coal-norms, by simply changing the initial issue of y_1 n\$s to the coal industry to one of y_2 n\$s to the power industry or one of y_3 n\$s to the service industry. The composite factor-norms based on arbitrary commodity prices p_1, p_2, and p_3 would require an initial issue of p_1, y_1, n\$s to the coal industry and $p_2 y_2$ n\$s and p_3y_3 norm-\$s to the other sectors respectively. In every case the initial issue will eventually 'settle' in the factor and tax banks and allow the factor-norms to be calculated by simple division.

A full-scale algebraic proof of this would be inordinately lengthy and tedious. Suffice it to say here that it would be based on the resolution of the $\overline{\mathbf{D}}$-term in the definition of factor-norms (3.22) into the infinite geometric series $\mathbf{I} + \mathbf{D} + \mathbf{D}^2$ ... whose separate terms show the successive 'rounds' of the process described.

In Table 3.1 we content ourselves with an arithmetic illustration of the process based on the figures of Table 2.10, which yields the factor-norms 0.17 and 0.25 after nine rounds (the figures are 0.1689 and 0.2536 without rounding) and would approach the true values 0.17 and 0.26 very rapidly if the process were continued, while the cumulative results of 0.44, 0.14, and 0 approach the commodity-norms established in the same exercise.

The norm generated after nine rounds in the tax bank (0.30) would be a factor-norm only if the payments into that bank corresponded to genuine factor contributions rather than mere residuals or rents. The figure must be considered devoid of meaning for the time being.

3.5 Eigenprices: Algebraic Definition

It is undoubtedly one of the signal achievements of mainstream economics to have overcome the uncomfortable dichotomy between value-in-exchange (cost-based) and value-in-use (utility-based) which Marxian and related systems have to live with. The synthesis of these two archetypal value-forming principles into a single concept of value or competitive price lies at the heart of Marshallian and neoclassical economics as it has been accepted and taught even at the most elementary level (supply and demand) for over a century now. Previous chapters of this book have explored particular approaches to the two principles in turn, culminating in the two statements of (3.23) which elucidate the transmission of costs and utilities from one end of the economy to the other (i.e. from goods to factors and vice versa), and which we repeat here for ease of reference:

$$\mathbf{p}' = 1/\phi_* \cdot \mathbf{r}'\mathbf{C} \text{ and } \mathbf{r}' = \mathbf{p}'\mathbf{N}. \tag{3.27}$$

It now remains for us to merge them into a single concept of value reflecting the operation of both principles in equal measure.

What we propose is a simple merging or synthesis of the two principles which, for want of anything better, we shall call the system of eigenprices, thus recruiting the German prefix for 'own' or 'proper' which has by now become common international coinage in linear algebra and would appear to claim neither too much nor too little for this new and untried tool of analysis.[10]

Starting from the first equation of (3.27), we note that it defines a transformation or mapping from factor-rentals $\mathbf{r}'$ to a correlative set of commodity prices, $\mathbf{p}'$. We may now enquire how this resultant set would map back into factor-rentals when subjected to the transformation defined by the second equation of (3.27). To ascertain this, we must map $\mathbf{r}'$ into itself by going through the two stages $\mathbf{p}'(r)$ and $\mathbf{r}'(p)$ in sequence, thus producing

$$\mathbf{r}'[\mathbf{p}'(r)] = \mathbf{r}'(1/\phi_* \cdot \mathbf{r}'\mathbf{C})\mathbf{N} = 1/\phi_* \cdot \mathbf{r}'\mathbf{F}, \qquad (3.28)$$

where $\mathbf{F}$ stands for the cost-norm-matrix $\mathbf{CN}$[11]. The result of this reflexive mapping will in general deviate from $\mathbf{r}'$, unless our first choice of $\mathbf{r}'$ has hit upon a very particular set known as an eigenvector or latent vector of $\mathbf{F}$. Yet any discrepancy between $\mathbf{r}'$ and $1/\phi_* \cdot \mathbf{r}'\mathbf{F}$ must be taken as a prima-facie inconsistency or derogation from rationality in the factor-rental set we have selected: some or all of them deviate from the properly valued contributions (norms) of the factors (as derived from the properly costed commodities they produce), and some or all of the commodity prices implied deviate from the properly normed factors absorbed in the production of these commodities. In fact, the economy is beset by extra-normal profits or losses for factor-owners and commodity-producers implicit in a price system which is distorted by just the sort of extra-economic incubus (monopoly power, extortion, administrative *fiat*, etc.) which it is the purpose of any rational price system to eliminate.

A fully consistent and rational factor- and product-price system ($\mathbf{r}', \mathbf{p}'$) would have to be such that each was the proper mapping of

[10] Expressions like 'intrinsic', 'implicit', or 'endogenous' probably claim too much, without necessarily conveying more precise information.

[11] The matrix F will be recognized as the conspectus of the factor-norms of all possible single-yield bases weighted in proportion to the single-factor costs of the base-yield commodities, i.e. its typical element f_k^j will equal $\mathbf{c_k}'\mathbf{r}^j$ or $c_k^1 r_j^1 + c_k^2 r_j^2 + \ldots + \ldots$.

the other as per (3.27) and therefore mapped back into itself, i.e. it would have to satisfy the two equations

$$\mathbf{r}' \equiv \mathbf{r}'(\mathbf{p}) = \mathbf{p}'\mathbf{N} \text{ and } \mathbf{p}' = 1/\phi_* . \mathbf{r}'\mathbf{C}, \qquad (3.29)$$

thus leading to the requirements

$$\mathbf{r}' = 1/\phi_* . \mathbf{r}'\mathbf{CN} \text{ and } \mathbf{p}' = 1/\phi_* . \mathbf{p}'\mathbf{NC},$$

or equivalently

$$\mathbf{r}'(\phi_* \mathbf{I} - \mathbf{F}) = 0 \text{ and } \mathbf{p}'(\phi_* \mathbf{I} - \mathbf{P}) = 0. \qquad (3.30)$$

where $\mathbf{F}$ and $\mathbf{P}$ stand for the cost-norm and norm-cost matrices $\mathbf{CN}$ and $\mathbf{NC}$ respectively.[12] To solve these equations in a non-trivial way, the scalar ϕ_* must be chosen to make the system's determinate vanish, i.e. it must be an eigenvalue or latent root of the matrices $\mathbf{F}$ and $\mathbf{p}$,[13] which makes $\mathbf{r}'$ and $\mathbf{p}'$ into the corresponding eigenvectors of the two matrices, to be known as the eigenprices of the economic system defined by $\mathbf{X}$, $\mathbf{y}$, and $\mathbf{W}$ of scheme (3.1) or (3.4), a set which may be written $\mathbf{e}' = (\mathbf{p}', \mathbf{r}')$, where $\mathbf{p}'$ stands for (commodity) prices and $\mathbf{r}'$ for (factor-)rentals.[14]

3.6 Eigencost and Eigenyield

Definition and meaning

The meaning of the suggested price system can be further clarified by restating the requirements as

---

[12] The first of these ($\mathbf{F}$) is the conspectus of cost-weighted norms (see n. 11) and the second that of norm-weighted costs, with every valuation-base featuring as an alternative weighting system in both cases.

[13] The requirement of economic sense (reality and non-negativity) imply, moreover, that it is the *dominant* (algebraically largest) latent root that must be chosen, along with the latent vector corresponding to it. Given (3.29), it can be shown that ϕ_* will satisfy both equations of (3.30) since $\mathbf{r}'\mathbf{C}$ can be substituted by $\phi_* \mathbf{p}'$ in the first requirement, thus yielding $\phi_* \mathbf{r}' = \phi_* \mathbf{p}'\mathbf{N}$, while the second is derived by multiplying both sides by $\mathbf{C}$. Moreover, as long as $\mathbf{F}$ is semi-positive and indecomposable, the eigenvector $\mathbf{r}'$ associated with its dominant root is bound to be positive, and therefore all eigenprices $\mathbf{p}'$ are at least non-negative.

[14] The use of latent roots and vectors in pricing models is not new. These tools have found application both in the exegesis of classical price systems and in the construction of novel concepts, and are implicit in some types of value theory conceived long before the mathematics of linear algebra had become naturalized in the discipline of economics. See F. Seton, 'The Transformation Problem', *Review of Economic Studies*, June 1957.

$$\mathbf{p}' = 1/\phi_* \cdot \mathbf{p}'\mathbf{NC} = 1/\phi_* \cdot \mathbf{r}'\mathbf{C} = 1/\phi_* \cdot \mathbf{r}'\mathbf{B}\overline{\mathbf{A}}, \qquad (3.31)$$

where the vector $\mathbf{r}'\mathbf{B}$ will be recognized as the eigenprice-value of the primary inputs (value added) per unit output of each sector, and therefore $\mathbf{r}'\mathbf{BA}$ as their full (direct and indirect) factor costs, i.e. the value added by the sectors in terms of the norms $\mathbf{r}'$ which themselves reflect factor scarcities in relation to final demand. The coefficient $1/\phi_*$ thus states the uniform proportion in which these value added measures must be blown up to give the eigenprices of the sectoral products, i.e. the uniform *ad valorem* VAT-coefficient. Its reciprocal, ϕ_*, therefore measures the uniform proportion of the eigenprice of products returned to factor-owners after the deduction of the notional value added tax, i.e. the factor-cost-ratio of each and every product in terms of eigenprices, to be termed the eigencost-ratio of the system. Correlatively, the ratio $\sigma_* (\equiv 1/\phi_* - 1)$ will measure the proportion of eigenprice withheld from the factors of production as such and accruing either to government in the shape of VAT or as an equivalent unilateral transfer to agents not acting in the capacity of the factors specified in the model (such as monopoly, extortion, deception, or pricing errors by central agencies). The incubus is therefore analogous to the Marxian surplus, defined as accruing to capitalists over and above the costs of materials (constant capital) and labour (variable capital) which they have to bear, except that our concept of eigensurplus is in no way bound up with a one-factor theory of value or any notion of class-exploitation.

This analogy becomes even closer when it is recalled that, as in the case of the Marxian surplus, the eigenprices $(\mathbf{p}', \mathbf{r}')$ will ensure the distribution of the incubus among producers in strict proportion to the total factor-cost (value added) contributed by each, the latter thus playing the same role as Marx's 'variable capital' (wage-costs) from which the surplus is extracted through a uniform rate of exploitation (ϵ). Our eigensurplus ratio σ_*, however, could be identified as exploitation only in so far as it was not channelled through VAT to a government deemed to act in the social interest, but accrued to an unproductive club of sectoral entrepreneurs contributing no factor with a positive norm under the operative system of eigenprices. Even to that extent, however, the victims of this exploitation would not necessarily be wage-earners, and its beneficiaries not necessarily class-bound owners of the means of production. Instead, they would be holders of monopolies or special bargaining power capable of enforcing tariff protection, excessive wage-incomes, extortionate rent or interest, or any other form of uneconomic reward.

It might be more fruitful, however, to look on the ratio σ^* as a measure of the excess value that the system is capable of yielding over and above the necessary rewards of its production factors when properly remunerated (normed) in accordance with their scarcities relatively to final demand. It is in fact in a special sense an indicator of cost effectiveness in the use of all specified factors taken together, and thus comes near to a standard of systemic merit in Professor Bergson's sense.[15] It falls short of such a standard, however, as it could attain a high value not merely owing to high factor-productivities, but also owing to excessive coercive powers exercised by public or private bodies in depressing the rewards of some or all productive factors, e.g. by systematic anti-consumptionist policies, or excessive forced investment, or defence policies. Nevertheless, as a crucial characteristic of a system's operation which enables unbiased comparisons to be made, the eigensurplus-ratio remains an indicator of considerable interest for the assessment of economic performance. The latent root of the norm-cost matrix $\mathbf{F}$ from which it is derived is thus a measure of the proportion of disposable value flows which, apart from direct taxation, is returned to the factors as the proper reward for creating that value. It is only the surplus remaining available over and above this which (again direct taxation apart) can be used in a discretionary manner according to social policy or need, rather than according to work. The eigensurplus-ratio should therefore also have a certain appeal to Marxists in spite of its radical departure from their value theories by assessing—in a thoroughly bourgeois manner of course—the extent to which a system is able to pass from the realm of necessity to the realm of freedom, i.e. from the socialist principle of distribution according to work to the communist prescription of distribution according to need.

If this surplus is to measure the *total* share of GNP diverted to social policy in this manner, the factor contributions W in scheme (3.1) would of course need to be recorded *net* of all direct taxes levied on the factors (income tax, profits tax, corporation tax, etc.). To the extent that they are recorded *gross* of such taxes, the eigenyield will measure only that part of the surplus which is extracted from factor-

---

[15] A. Bergson, *Productivity and the Social System—the USSR and the West*, Harvard University Press, Cambridge, Mass., 1978.

contributions through the operation of the price system, i.e. that part which would be automatically withdrawn from distribution according to work if the correct system of eigenprices were in operation. Additional withdrawals would still be possible, but only by interference in the income stream in the shape of direct taxation or confiscation net of unilateral transfers in the other direction (wage subsidies or family income supplements paid to workers, operating subsidies to companies or individual profit-earners, etc.). In practice, the sectoral distribution of such taxes would be extremely difficult to ascertain and we shall therefore need to content ourselves with the computation of the net-of-tax eigenyield which measures the system's capacity for discretionary appropriations without resorting to unilateral transfers of income.

An eigencost-ratio below unity (implying a positive eigensurplus) thus betokens some degree of pre-tax expropriation of the providers of primary inputs in favour of the community, government, or other beneficiaries (foreign countries, the future, etc.). It implies that the economic system is more than paying its way. Conversely, a ratio above unity (i.e. a negative eigensurplus) would imply a degree of subsidization of current factors by non-factor agents, possibly by the government drawing on the past (consuming capital), the future (increasing national debt), or on foreign countries (current external deficit); it would characterize an economic system unable or unwilling to pay its way out of its own resources as they become available to it here and now, unless it was prepared to depress factor rewards sufficiently below the rational level. An intersystem comparison of eigensurplus-ratios, undertaken with due caution, may therefore still be of considerable interest.

Finally, it should be recognized that any quantitative expression for the net-of-tax eigensurplus actually computed from a concrete scheme as displayed in (3.1) can only be relative to the factor-base specified in that model. It will measure the proportion of economic yield (national income) accruing to any agent other than the owners of the specified factors and may therefore include returns to proper factors of production which for one reason or another had to be omitted from the specified base. Such reasons may be lack of statistical data on some factors that are in principle measurable, or conceptual difficulties in the way of measuring others held to be contributing to the productive effort to an unquantifiable extent (entrepreneurship, technical know-how, X-efficiency, etc.).

Eigensurplus and residual inputs

The eigensurplus as defined above may be interpreted as the eigen-valuation of the residual tax or profit row in our basic scheme (3.1) when its components are formally treated as the productive contributions of a notional factor and given a positive eigen-norm g on a par with genuine factors. This may be seen by repeating the algebraic derivation of eigenprices with the south-west (third) quadrant of the basic scheme and all related matrices ($\mathbf{W}$, $\mathbf{B}$, $\mathbf{E}$, $\hat{\mathbf{W}}$, etc.) augmented by the row $\boldsymbol{\tau}'$, now annexed to the normal factor-input rows $\mathbf{w}'$:

$$\mathbf{W_a} = \begin{pmatrix} \mathbf{W} \\ \boldsymbol{\tau}' \end{pmatrix}, \ \mathbf{B_a} = \mathbf{W_a}\hat{\mathbf{z}}^{-1} = \begin{pmatrix} \mathbf{B} \\ \boldsymbol{\rho}' \end{pmatrix}, \ \hat{\mathbf{w}}_\mathbf{a} = \begin{pmatrix} \hat{\mathbf{W}} & 0 \\ 0' & \tau \end{pmatrix}, \ \mathbf{E_a} = \hat{\mathbf{w}}_\mathbf{a}^{-1} \mathbf{W_a} = \begin{pmatrix} \mathbf{E} \\ \boldsymbol{\tau}'/\tau \end{pmatrix}$$

$$\text{and } \mathbf{r_a}' = [\mathbf{r}', g] \tag{3.31}$$

and therefore

$$\mathbf{C_a} = \mathbf{B_a}\overline{\mathbf{A}} = \begin{pmatrix} \mathbf{C} \\ \boldsymbol{\rho}'\overline{\mathbf{A}} \end{pmatrix}, \ \mathbf{N_a} = \hat{\mathbf{s}}\overline{\mathbf{D}}'\mathbf{E_a}' = (\mathbf{N}, \hat{\mathbf{s}}\overline{\mathbf{D}}' \cdot \boldsymbol{\tau}/\tau).$$

These augmentations transform the matrix $\mathbf{F}$ (whose latent root furnishes the eigencost-ratio ϕ_*) into the larger matrix:

$$\mathbf{F_a} = \mathbf{C_a}\mathbf{N_a} = \begin{pmatrix} \mathbf{C} \\ \boldsymbol{\rho}'\overline{\mathbf{A}} \end{pmatrix}(\mathbf{N}', \hat{\mathbf{s}}\overline{\mathbf{D}}'\boldsymbol{\tau}/\tau) = \begin{pmatrix} \mathbf{F} & \cdot & \cdot \\ \boldsymbol{\rho}'\overline{\mathbf{A}}\mathbf{N} & \cdot & \cdot \end{pmatrix} \tag{3.32}$$

whose characteristic equation raises the latent root to unity (owing to the inclusion of $\boldsymbol{\tau}'$ among genuine factor-costs) and defines the new inclusive factor-norms $\mathbf{r_a}'$ as

$$\mathbf{r_a}'(\mathbf{I} - \mathbf{F_a}) = 0 \text{ or } \mathbf{r_a}' = \mathbf{r_a}'\mathbf{F_a}; \text{ i.e. } [\mathbf{r}', g] = [\mathbf{r}', g]\begin{pmatrix} \mathbf{F} & \cdot & \cdot \\ \boldsymbol{\rho}'\overline{\mathbf{A}}\mathbf{N} & \cdot & \cdot \end{pmatrix}. \tag{3.33}$$

The first element on the right-hand side establishes the equality:

$$\mathbf{r}' = \mathbf{r}'\mathbf{F} + g\boldsymbol{\rho}'\overline{\mathbf{A}}\mathbf{N} \text{ or } (1 - \phi_*)\mathbf{r}' = g_*\boldsymbol{\rho}'\overline{\mathbf{A}}\mathbf{N}. \tag{3.34}$$

Post-multiplying both sides by the column-vector of factor-uses $\hat{\mathbf{w}}$, we finally obtain:[16]

$$(1 - \phi_*)\,\mathbf{r}\hat{\mathbf{w}} = g\boldsymbol{\rho}'\overline{\mathbf{A}}\mathbf{N}\hat{\mathbf{w}}, \text{ or } (1 - \phi_*)\,\mathbf{r}'\mathbf{w} = g_*/\boldsymbol{\tau}'\overline{\mathbf{A}}\mathbf{N}\mathbf{w} = g_*\boldsymbol{\tau}. \tag{3.35}$$

---

[16] By virtue of n. 9 above we have $\mathbf{Nw} = \mathbf{y}$ and therefore $\boldsymbol{\rho}'\overline{\mathbf{A}}\mathbf{Nw} = \boldsymbol{\rho}'\overline{\mathbf{A}}\mathbf{y} = \boldsymbol{\rho}'\mathbf{z}$ (see 3.7). Finally, from the definition of $\boldsymbol{\rho}'$ as $\boldsymbol{\tau}'\mathbf{z}^{-1}$, it follows that $\boldsymbol{\rho}'\mathbf{z} = \boldsymbol{\tau}'\mathbf{i} = \tau$.

The last statement, which assumes standardized norming, shows clearly that the eigensurplus, expressed here as the proportion $(1 - \phi_*)$ of national income in eigenprices, equals the sum of residuals $\boldsymbol{\tau}'$ valued at their standardized norm g_* as it emerges from their treatment as the contributions of a notional productive factor.

This demonstration clarifies an important point, so far only implicit in our argument. The existence of the eigensurplus in our interpretation of the term is conditional on the existence of a genuine residual row $\boldsymbol{\tau}'$ not attributable to any of the productive factors specified in the basic scheme.[17] This in turn precludes the measurement of any of the factor-inputs $\mathbf{w}'$ (e.g. profits) as a mere residual, since this would by definition banish all non-factor residuals from the economy, unless these were identified with taxes or subsidies included in the price of commodities.

3.7   The Scaling of Eigenprices

Equations (3.30) which define the system of eigenprices of products and factors $(\mathbf{p}', \mathbf{r}')$ identify them as the dominant eigenvectors of the matrices $\mathbf{P}$ and $\mathbf{F}$. As is well known, however, eigenvectors are defined only up to a multiplicative constant. In fact, we have merely defined the *structure* or *scale-model* of eigenprices without as yet specifying their absolute values or scale. This absolute scaling is bound to be arbitrary and can follow any number of principles, such as keeping certain aggregates or ratios of the current-price *tableau* invariant to the revaluation.[18] We might for instance fix the scale so that the total eigensurplus comes to equal the current value of a residual 'tax'-row, in line with some notion that the revaluation into eigenprices ought merely to redistribute the surplus without altering its size. The macro-aggregate we have chosen to keep invariant to the transformation in the present exercise, however, is the sum of all yields (finals) supplied by the industrial sectors of (3.1), in fact the GNP $y_0 (= \Sigma y)$. This has the advantage of yielding eigenprices with a weighted mean equal to unity,[19] thus making them more readily com-

---

[17] I am indebted to Mr M. F. Scott of Nuffield College, Oxford, for alerting me to the need to enter this caveat.

[18] The analogous problem in the context of Marxian values and 'production prices' is discussed more exhaustively in Seton, 'The Transformation Problem'.

[19] $\mathbf{p}_*'\mathbf{y} = \mathbf{i}'\mathbf{y} = y_0$ implies $\mathbf{p}'(\mathbf{y}/y_0) = 1$.

parable with current prices (=1) by simply noting their deviation from that mean.

Scaled in this way, we call eigenprices 'standardized' and denote them by $\mathbf{e}_*' = [\mathbf{p}_*', \mathbf{r}_*']$. Their reciprocals, which measure current prices per unit-worth of eigenprices, will thus enable us to spot relative underpricing ($1/p_* < 1$) or overpricing ($1/p_* > 1$) of products or factors by the current price system with the greatest ease. In the same way, the eigenrentals would emerge standardized to replicate the factor-costed national income, i.e.

$$\mathbf{f}_*'\mathbf{w} = \phi_* y_0.$$

When the original tableau (3.1) is thus transformed by the revaluation of each and every flow in standardized eigenprices (denoted by appending a subscript asterisk to the symbols (y_*, w_*, z_* etc.) we can use it directly for the comparison of important structural ratios (investment ratios, foreign trade dependence, factor-shares, or branch contribution to GNP) across different systems, as has been done in Part III, without the need to impose alien or arbitrarily chosen price structures on the systems to be compared. The standardized eigenprices implicit in each system provide us with an objectively determined yardstick independent of those arbitrary choices to which the results of comparisons are so often unduly and notoriously sensitive.

It must be stressed, however, that given the inevitable arbitrariness remaining in the scaling factor, the absolute eigenvalues of economic flows still cannot serve as a basis for intersystem comparisons, unless we are prepared to indulge in some form of price-grafting, such as the initial acceptance of universally valid world prices for some or all final products and the derivation from them of internal factor-norms and product costings leading to shadow prices for both traded and non-traded goods and factors, in partial conformity with certain prescriptions leading to project appraisal in developing countries.[20] This, however, is a possible application of eigenprice calculations whose legitimacy and results are beyond the scope of this book and remain to be explored elsewhere.

[20] See Ian M. D. Little and James A. Mirrlees, *Manual of Industrial Project Analysis in Developing Countries*, i and ii, OECD, Paris, 1969.

3.8 A Quasi-Market Generation of Eigenprices

The definition of eigenprices (3.30) readily suggests a procedure for generating them by a process of iterative adjustment starting from an intial market-based or freely chosen price system in any economy.

Based on an initial list of factor-rentals r_0', we allow the normal (cost-generating) money circulation to generate the correlative factor-costs (ex-profit) of commodities in the first round, say $p_1' = r_0'C$. We then accept these as the basis for a new round of norm-generating circulation, distributing the cost-\$s (c\$s) accordingly to final users and instructing economic agents to behave as described in Sect. 3.4. This will generate the revised factor-norms of the first round $r_1' = p_1'N$. These are then accepted as the charges per unit factor in a second round of goods-costing circulation. The process of alternating norm-and cost-generating circulations must then be continued, leading to successive revisions of the norms of the previous round:

$$r_{k+1}' = p_{k+1}'N' = r_k'CN = r_k'F$$

until the revised norms assume a stable proportionate structure no longer subject to significant revision in further rounds, i.e.

$$\lim_{k \to K} r_{k+1} = \phi_* r_k',$$

i.e. until

$$r_k'(\phi_* I - F) = 0.$$

When this point has been reached, the norms of the latest round are sufficient approximations to the eigenprices of factors (r') and the constant proportionality factor ϕ approaches the eigencost-ratio of the system. As the signal that this has been achieved, we may accept the convergence of the revision-ratios $r_{k+1}\hat{r}_k^{-1}$ to a single figure ϕ_*.

Table 3.2 shows the results of alternating norm- and cost-generating circulations applied to the figures of Table 2.10, with initial factor-prices set at 0.5 and 2 per \$ of capital and labour respectively. As can be seen, a close approximation to the correct (non-standardized) eigenprices and eigencost-ratio is attained in as few as five rounds.

The same result could be achieved by starting from any other initial set of factor- or goods-prices, notably from actual market prices for final goods ($p_0' = i'$), although a latent root as close to unity as we have assumed may in some cases slow down or obfuscate the ratios in the last two columns to show self-reversing discrepancies (0.89, 0.93, followed by 0.93, 0.89, etc.) for some successive rounds before ultimately settling down to equality. This, however, affects only the efficacy of the process of generating eigenprices proposed here, and not the basic principles underlying their definition.

Table 3.2. *The generation of eigenprices*

'Round' k	r_k'	$= p_k'N$		$p_{k+1}' = r_k'C$			$\phi' = r_{k+1}' \hat{r}_k^{-1}$	
0	0.5	2		1.49	1.19	1.49	—	—
1	1.43	1.47	→	1.27	1.19	1.36	2.86	0.74
2	1.31	1.33	←	1.15	1.08	1.23	0.92	0.90
3	1.19	1.20	←	1.04	0.98	0.11	0.91	0.90
4	1.07	1.09	←	0.94	0.89	1.01	0.90	0.91
5	0.97	0.99	←	0.86	0.81	0.92	0.91	0.91
.	.	.	←	.	.	.	.	.
.	.	.		.	.	.	.	.
.	.	.		.	.	.	.	.
1	1			0.87	0.82	0.93		0.91

3.9 Dimensional Balance and the Lack of Price Invariance

As long as the monetary units in which the input–output table is expressed are regarded as nothing more than surrogates for physical units our verbal definition of norms as yield-productivities (sect.3.4) or outputs per unit of factor-inputs appears to be at variance with the algebraic definition of the norm-matrix N (3.22) as a product of dimensionless quotas. Indeed, the former interpretation suggests a lack of dimensional balance when the yield-productivity of any commodity is defined as a sum of other yield-productivities weighted by commodity-prices and the final-output quota (3.15). Moreover, given that the elements of the cost-matrix C (based on factor-inputs of, say, labour and land) vary in dimension from labour-time/money output (hr/$) to land area/money output (ha/$) as we move from one row to the next, the elements of the product matrices P and F (NC and CN) appear to be meaningless congeries of heterogeneous units (e.g. ½hr/$ + ½ha/$)), and the dimension of its eigenvalue, the eigencost-ratio ϕ, is similarly left in limbo.[21]

---

[21] I am indebted to Professor I. Steedman of Manchester University for pointing this out to me and thereby alerting me to the need for something like this section in any exposition of eigenprices.

This brings to light a perplexity which appears to have dogged our understanding of value-flows in input–output analysis for some time and cannot be resolved if the $-yardstick is taken for a simple surrogate for physical units of unvarying dimension along each row of the matrix. In the author's view the two-sidedness of our value-concept (cost and use) makes it incumbent on us to interpret each input–output flow differently according as it is considered a cost-flow (as determined by the sector of origin) or a use-flow (as determined by the sector of destination). In the first case the elements of each row are commensurable as outputs of grain, steel, or cloth (og, os, oc), while in the second case the elements of each column become commensurable as inputs into grain, steel, or cloth (ig, is, ic). In fact, the dimensions of the matrices X and W must be viewed alternatively as

$$\mathbf{X} = \begin{pmatrix} \text{og} & \text{og} & \text{og} \\ \text{os} & \text{os} & \text{os} \\ \text{oc} & \text{oc} & \text{oc} \end{pmatrix} \text{ or} = \begin{pmatrix} \text{ig} & \text{is} & \text{ic} \\ \text{ig} & \text{is} & \text{ic} \\ \text{ig} & \text{is} & \text{ic} \end{pmatrix}$$

$$\mathbf{W} = \begin{pmatrix} 1 & 1 & 1 \\ k & k & k \end{pmatrix} \text{ or} = \begin{pmatrix} \text{ig} & \text{is} & \text{ic} \\ \text{ig} & \text{is} & \text{ic} \end{pmatrix}.$$

It is the whole crux of use-norming (valuing by use rather than cost) that both the concept and the dimension attaching to economic flows must be varied in this way. Failure to do so by regarding input-columns as dimensionally incommensurable would deprive us of any criterion of equivalence-in-use on a par with the criteria of equivalence-in-cost afforded by the commensurablity of output-rows, and would imprison us in the grip of cost-fetishism,—that beguiling and addictive form of half-vision from which we should at all times try to escape.

If the above dual-dimension hypothesis is accepted, the basic matrices **C** and **N** will show the following dimensional pattern element for element:

$$\mathbf{C} = \begin{pmatrix} \dfrac{1}{\text{og}} & \dfrac{1}{\text{os}} & \dfrac{1}{\text{oc}} \\ \dfrac{k}{\text{og}} & \dfrac{k}{\text{os}} & \dfrac{k}{\text{oc}} \end{pmatrix} \quad \mathbf{N} = \begin{pmatrix} \dfrac{\text{og}}{1} & \dfrac{\text{og}}{k} \\ \dfrac{\text{os}}{1} & \dfrac{\text{os}}{k} \\ \dfrac{\text{oc}}{1} & \dfrac{\text{oc}}{k} \end{pmatrix}$$

This justifies both the cost interpretation of **C** and the productivity interpretation of the norm-matrix **N**, besides making it clear that their product in any order will yield matrices **P** and **F** composed entirely of pure numbers, with the eigenvalue (ϕ_*) and eigenvectors ($\mathbf{p'}, \mathbf{r'}$) equally dimensionless.

The norms are thus factor-productivities and the eigenprices pure numbers (even when scaled to GNP), i.e. conversion coefficients turning current prices into absolute eigenprices of the same dimension

It should be noted in conclusion that a change in current (market-) commodity- and factor-prices would not in general leave eigenprices unchanged even if physical flows remained unaffected, as the matrices **P** and **F** would undergo complicated non-similar transformations.[22] We cannot therefore claim that eigenprices share the putative advantage of certain other diagnostic price systems (e.g. Marxian production prices) of being invariant to current prices. They reflect both the physical (technological) and the financial (price) characteristics of an economy. This is clear from the fact that they redistribute the surplus equally between sectors, thus being dependent on a parameter which requires a price system for its determination, since physical flows by themselves cannot define a surplus.

---

[22] A similarity-transformation is one that leaves eigenvalues unchanged.

PART II

Eigenprices: Historical Parallels, Special Cases, and Extensions

4

Reduced Models

4.1 Production of Commodities by Means of Primary Factors Only (Feedback-Free Models)

THE classical models in use before input–output analysis burst on the scene, and still in the minds of economists for most theoretical purposes, dispense with intersectoral feedback effects and treat the production process as a direct transformation of primary (non-produced) inputs into final commodities. What happens to our eigenprices and related concepts in such a degenerate subsystem?

The formal modification required is the reduction of the intersectoral coefficient and quota matrices to zero, i.e. $\mathbf{A} = \mathbf{D} = 0$, and the consequent reduction of their Leontief inverses to the unit matrix, i.e. $\overline{\mathbf{A}} = \overline{\mathbf{D}} = \mathbf{I}$, with the diagonal matrix of end-use quotas $\hat{\mathbf{s}}(=\hat{\mathbf{z}}^{-1}\hat{\mathbf{y}})$ similarly reduced to $\mathbf{I}$. This simplifies both cost- and norm-matrices as defined in (3.11) and (3.22) to[1]

$$\mathbf{C} = \mathbf{B} \text{ and } \mathbf{N} \equiv \mathbf{M}' = \mathbf{E}'. \tag{4.1}$$

Not surprisingly, therefore, the full costs reduce to direct costs and the yield-norms to factor-quotas; i.e. the yield-product of every factor in terms of a given product becomes simply its allocation to that product, and its yield-productivity the proportion (quota) of the factor so allocated. Accordingly, the factor-valuation (cost-norm) matrix defined in (3.27) becomes

$$\mathbf{F} = \mathbf{BM}'. \tag{4.2}$$

The eigencost-ratio is thus the eigenvalue of all possible quota-weightings $\mathbf{b}'^r\mathbf{m}^j$ or $\mathbf{m}_j'\mathbf{b}^r$ (with r taking on all factor-, and j all product-labels).

In particular, if the number of sectors (but not necessarily factors) is reduced to one, the sectoral allocation quotas of every factor, and

---

[1] As the reader will notice, we denote the basic matrices in feedback-free models by the letters immediately preceding in the alphabet those of the full models.

therefore all norms, will trivially rise to unity, i.e. the average (and marginal) physical product becomes one.[2] In these conditions the factor quota matrix $\mathbf{M}'$ reduces to the all-unit vector $\mathbf{i}'$, while the factor-coefficient matrix $\mathbf{B}$ turns into the column vector $\mathbf{b}$. In consequence, the factor-valuation matrix $\mathbf{F}$ (3.27) becomes a 'dyadic' matrix $\mathbf{bi}'$ whose eigenvector and dominant eigenvalue can be shown to be $\mathbf{i}'$ and $\mathbf{i}'\mathbf{b}$ respectively

$$\mathbf{i}'\mathbf{i}'\mathbf{bI} - \mathbf{bi}' = \mathbf{i}'\mathbf{b} - \mathbf{i}'\mathbf{Bi}' = 0. \tag{4.3}$$

The latter $\mathbf{i}'\mathbf{b}$ is of course the reduced system's eigencost-ratio ϕ (3.27), thus shown to be the simple sum of all factor input-coefficients—or the single coefficient b, if we drive trivialization to the extreme of reducing also the number of factors to one. We have thus established that, in the traditional one-good—one-factor model, our eigencost-ratio is represented by the single input-requirement per unit output, and the eigensurplus-ratio σ correspondingly by the expression $1/b - 1$, i.e. the excess of output per unit input over the factor's marginal productivity (its due reward). This result, trivial though it is, accords well with our intuitive understanding of the more complex general scheme.

We can, however, get little or no help from this particular model for a better understanding of eigenprices themselves; for the model trivializes these out of existence by positing a world in which marginal costs (in terms of all factors) and marginal products are all identically equal to one. It follows that *any* commodity price we may choose will equate the marginal revenue products of all factors to that one price and at the same time ensure that it also measures the commodity's marginal cost, once the factors are all equally priced. The principle of reciprocal marginality (PRM), i.e. self-consistent product and factor-pricing in conformity with marginal costs and marginal revenue-productivities respectively, is therefore automatically operative in this model at current prices, and we need not do any repricing to achieve it.[3]

---

[2] This trivial result becomes obvious when it is revalled that the physical unit of both product and factor is defined in dollar terms; i.e. \$1-worth of each factor adds \$1-worth to the product, since inputs and outputs must have the same total dollar value.

[3] In other words, any system of uniform prices (per dollar's worth) for product and factors can serve as an eigenprice system, including the all-unit vector $\mathbf{i}'$, i.e. the current price system itself.

We fare somewhat better in this respect when we turn to the alternative non-feedback model characterized by a single factor serving the production of n different goods. Here it is best to start by expressing the product prices p with the aid of the norm-cost matrix $\mathbf{P}$ as per (3.30). The latter can be obtained by commuting the matrix (4.2), i.e.

$$\mathbf{P} = \mathbf{M}'\mathbf{B} \qquad (4.4)$$

which under the assumptions of the model reduces to the dyadic matrix $\mathbf{mb}'$. By analogy with (4.3), the eigenvector and dominant eigenvalue of this can be shown to be $\mathbf{b}'$ and $\mathbf{b}'\mathbf{m}$ respectively:

$$\mathbf{b}'(\mathbf{b}'\mathbf{mI} - \mathbf{mb}') = (\mathbf{b}'\mathbf{m} - \mathbf{b}'\mathbf{m})\mathbf{b} = 0. \qquad (4.5)$$

Thus the eigencost-ratio ϕ is now the weighted mean of the input-coefficients $\mathbf{b}'$ (with the end-use quotas for weights), while the eigenprices of the products become identical with their direct factor requirements per unit (marginal costs). The eigenprice of the factor (r) can then be chosen at will, provided only that the n products are priced at $\mathbf{rb}'$. In this case, therefore, the principle of reciprocal marginality is not realized by the current price structure, since the marginal costs of products (in terms of the single factor) are no longer unity, but equal to their factor requirements per unit (multiplied by the factor-price $\mathbf{r}'$). The two 'halves' of the principle of reciprocal marginality (see Chapter 5) could be stated explicitly as

(1) $\mathbf{p}'$ to be = marginal cost (including mark-up) = $1/\phi_* \cdot \mathbf{rb}'$
(2) $\mathbf{r}$ to be = marginal revenue-product = $\mathbf{p}'\mathbf{m}$,

whence $\phi_* \mathbf{p}' = \mathbf{p}'\mathbf{mb}'$ or $\mathbf{p}'(\phi_* \mathbf{I} - \mathbf{mb}') = 0$. as stated before.

4.2 Production of Commodities by Means of Commodities Only (Factor-Free Models)[4]

The concentration on intrasectoral flows in the production process to the exclusion of primary factors is the preserve of a particular school of theoreticians influenced at several removes by the Marxian schemes of 'production and reproduction' and greatly helped by the new tools forged in Leontief's busy input—output workshop. The device on their banner is complementarity rather than substitutability,

---

[4] Leontief case considered only.

with the attendant *penchant* for that quasi-engineering approach to economics that has earned them the suspicion, and sometimes revulsion, of their mainstream colleagues. Accused of apostasy from the Round Table of King Arthur to the Square Table of King Wassily,[5] they are seen as having abandoned the quest for the Holy Grail in favour of a search for illumination of a radically different sort.

We can, however, throw a bridge to their world by the simple deletion of the third quadrant (**W**) from our scheme of things (3.1) and its replacement by a direct emanation of the intersectoral flows, giving formal expression to the idea that value added is dependent not on any importation of inputs from outside the sectoral system, but on a spontaneous secretion of the material inputs themselves—typically proportional to them in size—as if a surplus product had been created by crystalline accretion as a reward for the effort and ingenuity of the labour of combining them.[6]

In effect, this alters our cost-forming equation (3.9), $\mathbf{c_r}' = \mathbf{c_r}'\mathbf{A} + \mathbf{b_r}'$ by replacing the second term on the right-hand side by $\alpha\mathbf{c_r}'\mathbf{A}$, where α measures the surplus-forming power of the system (or of labour). This substitution defines a rate of surplus, independently of any valuation base (standard factor) r, by the homogeneous equation

$$\mathbf{c}' = \mathbf{c}'\mathbf{A} + \alpha\mathbf{c}'\mathbf{A} = (1 + \alpha)\,\mathbf{c}'\mathbf{A} \qquad (4.6)$$

which may be written more explicitly as

$$\mathbf{c}'\left(\frac{1}{1 + \alpha}\,\mathbf{I} - \mathbf{A}\right) = 0. \qquad (4.7)$$

This equation shows that our eigencost-ratio, as extracted from this particular model, is a simple function of the von Neumann maximal growth-rate α;[7] i.e.

$$\phi_* = 1/(1 + \alpha), \qquad (4.8)$$

[5] Reference is here to Professor Wassily Leontief, of course.

[6] In many instances labour is itself assimilated to the network of intersector flows along with an input column of wage-goods consumed by workers, to complete the analogy with production sectors in the 'closed version' of the Leontief analysis.

[7] J. V. Neumann, 'A Model of General Economic Equilibrium', *Review of Economic Studies*, 8(1945/6), 1–9; previously published in German in K. Menger (ed.), *Ergebnisse eines Mathematischen Seminars*, Vienna, 1938. The underlying assumption that every product is involved in every production process ('no whales or wranglers') is spelled out in the accompanying comment to von Neumann's English-language paper by D. G. Champernowne (pp. 10–18).

while the full-cost vector c' turns into a particular form of diagnostic prices described by East European analysts as the 'N-income price system'[8]—a variant of Marxian-type 'channel-prices' which ensures that every sector earns the same rate of value added (wages + profits + tax-revenue, etc.), or, in other words, that any revenue remaining available after settling expenses on material inputs is distributed (or imputed) in proportion to the material costs borne by the earning sector, regardless of any factor contributions from which it has benefited. If the matrix A is fashioned on Leontief's 'closed model' (i.e. incorporates a row for labour and a column for consumption out of wages), these prices correspond to the classical Marxian 'production prices'.[9]

Our product norms v, which in this instance are genuine duals of the full-cost values c', derive from the symmetric notion that the residual outputs left over for final use after the sectors' total input requirements have been met stand in a uniform ratio χ to these requirements, and can therefore be expressed by

$$v = Dv + \chi Dv \text{ or } \left(\frac{1}{1+\chi} I - D\right) v = 0. \tag{4.9}$$

Since D is 'similar' to A (see (3.24)), its eigenvalue $1/(1 + \chi)$ will equal $1/(1 + \alpha)$, and χ is therefore equal to the von Neumann growth rate α. The product-norms v will then turn out identical with the sectoral contributions to Sraffa's 'representative commodity',[10] defined as the current output-mix measured in such physical units as would make the structure of total inputs Xi into an exact scale-model of the output structure z necessary to supply it, thus allowing the multi-product system to be treated for crucial purposes as if it were a single-sector model measured in terms of the representative commodity.

We cannot of course identify either c' or v with our eigenprices, as the absence of factor-costs deprives the principle of reciprocal marginality of the meaning we have given it in the body of this paper.

[8] B. Sekerka, O. Kýn, and L. Hejl, 'Price Systems Computable from Input–Output Coefficients', Research Paper no. 15 of the Mathematical Economics Laboratory of the Czechoslovak Academy of Sciences, Prague, 1967: 10; also in paper submitted to the Fourth International Conference on Input–Output Techniques, Geneva, 8–10 Jan. 1968.

[9] See e.g. A. Bródy, 'Three Types of Price Systems', *Economics of Planning*, 5 (1965), 58–66.

[10] P. Sraffa, *The Production of Commodities by Means of Commodities*, CUP, 1960: 24.

5

The Link with Marginal Analysis

5.1 A Linear-Programming Approach

WE can now begin to throw a bridge to the more traditional marginal-ist theory of value by sketching out a possible derivation of full cost and use-norm prices as dual solutions of standard linear-programming problems.[1]

Given a set of n final demands $\mathbf{y}$ and m factor-prices $\mathbf{r}'$ the produc-tion problem is the task of choosing the cheapest factor-mix $\mathbf{w}'$ to produce a final bill of goods that is sufficient in the sense of not falling short of the final demand that the community is known to be making on any of the n sectors, i.e.

$$\min_{w} \mathbf{r}'w \text{ subject to } \mathbf{w} > \mathbf{C}y. \qquad (5.1)$$

The dual of this—the marketing problem—would be the one facing a trader offering to sell the community its desired assortment of products $\mathbf{y}$ at the most lucrative set of product prices $(\mathbf{c}')$ that is realistic in the sense of not implying a higher charge for any product than the cost of the factor-mix necessary to produce it, i.e.

$$\max_{c} \mathbf{c}'y \text{ subject to } \mathbf{c}' < \mathbf{r}'\mathbf{C}. \qquad (5.2)$$

The primal and dual constraints may be condensed into the single statement

$$\mathbf{c}'y < \mathbf{r}'\mathbf{C}\mathbf{w} < \mathbf{r}'w. \qquad (5.3)$$

---

[1] We have not so far succeeded in formulating the primal–dual pairs (5.1)/(5.2) and (5.4)/(5.5) in precise conformity with the standard paradigms. Their exact nature and mutual relationship is therefore still in doubt, and must be left to mathematical friends and critics for verification as unfinished business. However, intuition and the 'conical' character of the sets involved (in the sense of positive homogeneity of degree one) en-courage us to stand by the interpretation offered with some degree of confidence. We are greatly indebted to Professor Terence Gorman of Nuffield College for impressing on us the need to enter this caveat, but wish to exempt him from any responsibility for the way in which we have interpreted it in this footnote.

and since the first and last terms of this inequality must reach their upper and lower limits respectively, the two problems will be solved simultaneously only when all three terms of (5.3) are equal, and in particular only when

$$\mathbf{r}'\mathbf{C}w = \mathbf{c}y.$$

A sufficient condition for this to hold is clearly that

$$\mathbf{c}' = \mathbf{r}'\mathbf{C},$$

i.e. that, given the factor-prices $\mathbf{r}'$, the product-prices charged be equal to the cost prices as defined in (3.11). As is well known, however, the dual solutions of a linear-programming problem measure the improvements achievable in the primal objective function (at optimum) by relaxing each of the primal constraints in turn. The cost prices $\mathbf{c}'$ are thereby shown to be the factor-cost savings obtainable from lowering the final demand for each commodity by one unit—in other words, they are the marginal costs of the products under the conditions assumed.

To find a similar linear-programming approach to the factor-norms $\mathbf{r}'$, we must recast the primal–dual pair of programs by shifting from the original to what might be called the 'conjugate' problem.[2] The pre-established data are now product-prices $\mathbf{p}'$ and factor availabilities $\mathbf{w}$, and a supply problem may be defined as the task of selecting the most valuable final output-mix $\mathbf{y}$ that is feasible in the sense of requiring no more than the factor-endowments available, i.e.

$$\max_{y} \mathbf{p}'y \text{ subject to } \mathbf{y} < \mathbf{N}\mathbf{w}. \tag{5.4}$$

The dual to this, which might be called the 'take-over' problem, would be to find the most economic purchase prices for the factors ($\mathbf{r}'$) that are acceptable in the sense of offering no less for any factor combination than the price of the product that could be produced with its aid, i.e.

$$\min_{n} \mathbf{r}'w \text{ subject to } \mathbf{r}' > \mathbf{p}'\mathbf{N} \tag{5.5}$$

At optimum, the two objective functions must again come up fully to the constraints, for which a sufficient condition will evidently be

[2] i.e. from the 'input-planning–output-pricing' scheme to the output-planning–input-pricing' problem.

$$\mathbf{r}' = \mathbf{p}'\mathbf{N}$$

thus revealing our use-norms (3.22) as the increases in the primal objective function ($\mathbf{p}'\mathbf{y}$) achievable by adding extra units to each of the factor endowments $\mathbf{w}'$, in fact as the marginal revenue productivities of the factors.

With full-cost product-pricing thus leading us from factor-rentals to marginal product-costs and full-price factor-costing from product-prices to marginal factor-productivities, it will be clear that our eigen-prices, which lead from either to the other and back again, will represent the unique price structure that fulfils the double condition (1) that all factor-rentals equal marginal revenue productivities (in terms of product-prices), and (2) that all product-prices equal marginal costs (in terms of factor-rentals), thus obeying what might be called the principle of reciprocal marginality (PRM) and justifying their characterization as quasi-competitive. The operational meaning and application of PRM is spelled out in somewhat greater detail in Sect. 5.2 below.

5.2 The Principle of Reciprocal Marginality Generalized

The principle of reciprocal marginality (PRM) explained at the end of Sect. 5.1 can be extended from the Leontief model governed by limitational input-coefficients to the general case of non-linear production and transformation functions as used or implied in traditional neoclassical economics. Here the link between output-mix $\mathbf{z}$ input-use $\mathbf{w}$ is provided by functions of the general form

$$t(\mathbf{z}, \mathbf{w}) = b(\text{constant})$$

whose number could be smaller than that of products (n) or factors (m). If the number is equal to m, the functions could in general be made explicit with respect to each w_j in turn, thus specifying a fixed requirement for each factor deriving solely from the output-mix $\mathbf{z}$ and independent of the quantities of other factors used. If the number is below m, on the other hand, there is some scope for factor substitution. In what follows we shall allow the maximum scope for this by positing only one such transformation function, assumed sufficient to specify all possible input- and output-mixes in the sense that, given

w, any output-mix **z** obeying $t = b$ could be produced, and, given **z**, any factor-mix **w** obeying $t = b$ would be sufficient to produce it.

The first PRM condition—that inputs be priced in accordance with their marginal revenue productivities—can then be formulated by computing the maximal sales revenue obtainable at given product-prices **p′** and factor-endowments **w**, i.e. by solving the constrained extremal problem

$$\max_{z} s \equiv \mathbf{p'z}, \text{ subject to } t(\mathbf{z}, \mathbf{w}) = b.$$

The maximizing **z** obtained by standard Lagrangian methods, say $\zeta(\mathbf{p'}, \mathbf{w})$ when substituted in the sales function

$$\mathbf{p'}\zeta(\mathbf{p'}, \mathbf{w})$$

furnish what has in a different context been called the 'maximum-value' or 'indirect-utility' function of the system $\hat{s}$ [3] and the condition requires that the factor rentals **r′** be equated to the derivatives of this function with respect to w_j, i.e.

$$r_j = \frac{\partial \hat{s}}{\partial w_j}(\mathbf{p'}), \text{ for } j = 1, 2, \ldots, m \text{ or } \mathbf{r'} = \hat{s}_w(\mathbf{p'}).$$

This provides the non-linear transformation rules for n product-prices into m factor-rentals corresponding to the linear transformation of prices into norms in equation (3.22) which we have called the upstream transformation.

To formulate the corresponding downstream transformation we need only remind ourselves of the conjugate problem of finding the cheapest factor-mix **w** to satisfy the given demand-structure **z**, i.e.

$$\min_{w} e = \mathbf{r'w}, \text{ subject to } t(\mathbf{z}, \mathbf{w}) = b.$$

Again, the minimizing **w**, say $\omega(\mathbf{r'}, \mathbf{z})$, can be obtained by standard Lagrangian methods and substituted in e, to furnish the so-called 'expenditure function',[4] to be renamed more appropriately the 'minimum expenditure function':

[3] See e.g. A. Dixit, *Optimization in Economic Theory*, OUP, 1976: 24 ff., and W. M. Gorman, 'Tricks with Utility Functions', in M. Artis and R. Nobay (eds), *Essays in Economic Analysis*, CUP, 1976: 211 ff.

[4] See Dixit, *Optimization in Economic Theory*, or Gorman, 'Tricks with Utility Functions'.

$$\check{e} = \mathbf{r}'\boldsymbol{\omega}(\mathbf{r}', \mathbf{z})$$

whose derivatives (with respect to $\mathbf{z}$) will in turn furnish the downstream transformation rules (or second PRM conditions)

$$p_i = \frac{1}{\phi_*} \frac{\partial \check{e}}{\partial z_i}(\mathbf{r}'), \text{ for } i = 1, 2, \ldots, n \text{ or } \mathbf{p}' = \check{\mathbf{e}}_z(\mathbf{r}')$$

corresponding to the linear transformation (3.13).

If the two sets of transformations applied in series (i.e. the reflexive transformation) possess a fixed point, that point is the vector of eigenrentals and eigenprices we are looking for, i.e. the eigenrentals are the solutions $\mathbf{r}'$ of

$$\mathbf{r}' = \hat{s}_w \left[\frac{1}{\phi_*} \check{\mathbf{e}}_z(\mathbf{r}') \right]$$

a system of m equations in $m + 1$ unknowns $(\mathbf{r}', \phi)$ whose consistency can be assured by the proper choice of ϕ. Simultaneously, the eigenprices of products $\mathbf{p}'$ will emerge from

$$\mathbf{p}' = \frac{1}{\phi_*} \frac{\partial \check{e}}{\partial z_i} [\hat{s}_w(\mathbf{p}')]$$

in the same way.

The generalization we have proposed furnishes the clue to what is perhaps the most illuminating interpretation of the concept of eigenprices: These prices invert the conceptual train of thought of Paretian economics, which leads from given prices and rentals to optimal quantity-mixes (maximizing utility or revenue and minimizing costs), by starting out from quantity-mixes (as observed in input—output flows) and leading to the price and rental systems which would need to have served as the underlying price-base to yield these flows as the outcome of Pareto-optimizing behaviour (i.e. equating marginal revenues to factor-rentals and marginal costs to product-prices). In other words, eigenprices could be thought of as the view that an economy must implicitly be taking of the values of its products and resources for it to have combined them in the observed quantities in pursuit of a Pareto optimum.

The concept would of course be invalidated if it were shown that an economy had systematically or on principle rejected such optima in favour of output- and/or input-combinations that suited its aspirations and endowments less well than could have been achieved. Short of this, however, eigenprices should reflect the economy's own implicit view of the relative urgency of wants and scarcity of resources which informs its activities, and the structural and performance ratios measured in these terms must by that token appraise relative effort, sacrifice, or benefit from the angle of most relevance to those who operate it or suffer under its sway.

6

Partial Eigenprices

6.1 Specific Uses

AN obvious extension of eigenprices is the definition of a subspecies generated by narrowing down the final-use contribution (y) that is to serve as the basis for norming to one of the several sub-categories of final use (say α, β, etc.), such as consumption, investment, or defence, which may be singled out as the only one whose benefit is to be reflected in the valuation system. Such 'partial' eigenprices will clearly deviate from the total eigenprices discussed so far, but may be appropriate for special functions or diagnoses relating to an economy. Unfortunately, their exact relation to each other and to total eigenprices is a highly complicated one, not amenable to straightforward formalization in algebraic terms; but a start may be made by offering rigorous definitions of the subspecies in its own right and exploring their possible links with other price-concepts familiar in the literature, though established in different contexts.

It is clear that norming based exclusively on the partial final-use category α, in an economy reduced to two sectors (without loss of generality), will generate product-norms ($\mathbf{v}^\alpha$) defined by equations

$$d_1^1 v_1 \alpha + d_1^2 v_1^\alpha + p_1 \alpha_1 m_1 = v_1^\alpha$$
$$d_2^1 v_1^\alpha + d_2^2 v_2^\alpha + p_2 \alpha_2 m_2 = v_2^\alpha$$

or

$$\mathbf{D} \mathbf{v}_\alpha + \hat{\boldsymbol{\alpha}} \mathbf{S} \mathbf{p} = \mathbf{v}^\alpha, \tag{6.1}$$

where $\mathbf{p}$ stands for product-prices (so far arbitrarily imputed), and $\hat{\boldsymbol{\alpha}}$ for the ratios of partial to total final use in each sector, such that $\hat{\boldsymbol{\alpha}} + \hat{\boldsymbol{\beta}} \ldots = \mathbf{I}$. By making this explicit with respect to the product-norms, we obtain

$$\mathbf{v}_\alpha = \overline{\mathbf{D}} \hat{\boldsymbol{\alpha}} \hat{\mathbf{S}} \mathbf{p} \quad \text{or} \quad \mathbf{v}_\alpha = \mathbf{p}' \hat{\boldsymbol{\alpha}} \hat{\mathbf{S}} \overline{\mathbf{D}}, \tag{6.2}$$

an equation that corresponds to (3.19) as established for the total case, with $\hat{S}$ replaced by $\hat{S}$. Given these product-norms, the factor-norms $\mathbf{S}_\alpha'$ emerge as

$$\mathbf{r}_\alpha' = v_\alpha \mathbf{R}' = \mathbf{p}' \hat{\alpha} \hat{\mathbf{S}} \overline{\mathbf{D}} = \mathbf{p}' \hat{\alpha} \mathbf{N} \qquad (6.3)$$

as they did in the total case (see (3.22)), except for the substitution of $\hat{s}$ by $\hat{\alpha}\hat{s}$ and this establishes an upstream transformation for the partial case. There is no reason why the opposite, downstream, transformation should be anything but the familiar costing procedure of (3.6), whether in the total or the partial case, and we therefore have

$$\mathbf{p}_\alpha' = 1/\phi_\alpha \cdot r_\alpha' \mathbf{C}' \qquad (6.4)$$

where ϕ_α is now the 'α-eigencost ratio'.

To achieve the complete consistency between product- and factor-prices, which is the distinguishing mark of the genus eigenprice, we need only combine equations (6.3) and (6.4), signalling the new-found consistency by substituting $\mathbf{r}_\alpha'$ for the provisional norms n_α', and $\mathbf{P}_\alpha'$ for the provisional prices $\mathbf{p}'$ in (6.3), i.e.

$$\mathbf{r}_\alpha' = \mathbf{p}_\alpha' \hat{\alpha} \mathbf{N} = 1/\phi_\alpha \cdot \mathbf{r}_\alpha' \mathbf{C} \hat{\alpha} \mathbf{N} \equiv 1/\phi_\alpha \cdot \mathbf{r}_\alpha \mathbf{F}_\alpha. \qquad (6.5)$$

The α-eigenprices and α-eigencost ratio are therefore the eigenvector and dominant eigenvalue of the matrix $\mathbf{C}\hat{\alpha}\mathbf{N}$, while the total eigenprices were similarly related to the matrix $\mathbf{CN}(\equiv \mathbf{F})$. The only change is thus the reduction of all norms in the ratio that the selected use-category bears to the total final use of each product.

A particular variant of partial eigenprices, where the norm-base is the portion of final use entering the trade balance, i.e. export net of import, is worthy of special attention. We may call them 'foreign-trade-geared' or 'external' eigenprices, and can define them in accordance with (6.5) by the simple device of replacing $\hat{\alpha}$ by $\hat{\epsilon}$:

$$\mathbf{r}_\epsilon' = 1/\phi_\epsilon \cdot \mathbf{r}_\epsilon' \mathbf{C} \hat{\epsilon} \mathbf{N} \text{ or } \mathbf{r}_\epsilon'(\phi_\epsilon \mathbf{I} - \mathbf{C} \hat{\epsilon} \mathbf{N}) = 0, \qquad (6.6)$$

where $\hat{\epsilon}$ is the ratio of net export to the total final use of each sector's product.

The last-quoted formulation enables us to relate external to total eigenprices in the particular case where net exports absorb a *uniform* proportion ϵ of the final use of each product. The diagonal matrix $\hat{\epsilon}$ then changes into the unit matrix multiplied by a scalar $(\epsilon \mathbf{I})$, and (6.6) can be written

$$\epsilon \mathbf{r}_\epsilon'(\phi_\epsilon/\epsilon' \cdot \mathbf{I} - \mathbf{F}) = 0.$$

This is clearly identical with the definition of total eigenprices (3.30), with prices $\mathbf{r}'$ turning into $\mathbf{r}_e'$ and the total eigencost ratio from ϕ_* into ϕ_ϵ/ϵ. In this particular case, therefore, external eigenprices can be shown to be equal to total eigenprices scaled up by the net export ratio, while the external eigencost ratio is correspondingly scaled down. Clearly, such a rescaling makes sense only when applied to eigenprices that have already been scaled or standardized in the first place (see Sect. 3.6), a fact to which we draw attention by starring the relevant symbols in the equations:

$$\mathbf{r}_e' = 1/\epsilon \cdot \mathbf{r}_*' \text{ and } \phi_\epsilon = \epsilon\phi_*. \tag{6.8}$$

The resulting external prices $\mathbf{r}_e'$, however, are no longer standardized themselves, since their internal product with the sectoral value added elements $\boldsymbol{\omega}$ would no longer be equal to the total national income ω_0, as required by standardization (see Sect. 3.6), but would reach the higher level $(1/\epsilon)\mathbf{r}_*'\boldsymbol{\omega}$, i.e. $(1/\epsilon)\omega_0$. In order to achieve proper 'scaling to national income', therefore, the external rentals of (6.8) would themselves need to be scaled down in the proportion ϵ, i.e.

$$\mathbf{r}_e^{*\prime} = \epsilon\mathbf{r}_e' = \mathbf{r}_*' \tag{6.9}$$

The same is true of the external eigenprices of commodities $\mathbf{p}_e'$, which can be derived from the partial eigenrentals as

$$\mathbf{p}_e' = 1/\phi_e \cdot \mathbf{r}_e'\mathbf{F}_e = 1/\epsilon\phi_* \cdot \mathbf{r}_e'\epsilon\mathbf{F} = 1/\epsilon\phi_* \cdot \mathbf{r}_*'\mathbf{F} = 1/\epsilon \cdot \mathbf{p}_*'. \tag{6.10}$$

As they stand these would overvalue the GNP ($\mathbf{p}_*'\mathbf{y}$) by the factor $1/\epsilon$ and must therefore be scaled down by the factor ϵ, in the same way as the external eigenrentals, i.e.

$$\mathbf{p}_e^* = \epsilon\mathbf{p}_e' = \mathbf{p}_*'. \tag{6.11}$$

Thus we conclude that, in the particular case of an export ratio (ϵ) applying *uniformly* to all products, external prices remain equal to total eigenprices, and only the eigencost ratio is affected in the proportion ϵ, as shown in (6.8).

6.2 Specific Factors

The cost-analogue of restricting the eigenprice base to specific final *uses* is clearly a similar restriction in respect of the *factors* or the types of their renumeration that are to be accounted as costs.

This has particular relevance when important parts of government revenue are raised by drawing on factor incomes *after* they have accrued and entered input–output statistics, i.e. by imposing direct taxes or levies on wages, profits, rental incomes, etc. If the true rewards of factors are to be measured in such cases, the pre-tax factor input matrix ($\mathbf{W}$) in scheme (3.1) and the corresponding matrices of coefficients ($\mathbf{B}$) and costs ($\mathbf{C}$) must in each sector be reduced in a proportion a equal to the ratio of pre-tax to post-tax income ($= 1 - t$, where t is the average rate of direct taxation).

Allowing discrimination in tax rates between production sectors, but not factors, the downstream transformation (3.13) would be:

$$\mathbf{p_a}' = 1/\phi_a \cdot \mathbf{r_a}'\hat{a}\mathbf{C}, \qquad (6.12)$$

where $\hat{a}$ is the diagonal matrix of post-tax to pre-tax value added in the various sectors, $\mathbf{p_a}'$ and $\mathbf{r_a}'$ the product- and factor-prices generated by this tax regime, and ϕ_a the post-tax eigenratio yet to be computed.

With the upstream transformation $\mathbf{r}' = \mathbf{p}'\mathbf{N}$ unaltered except for the subscript, a, the partial eigenrentals $\mathbf{r_a}'$, are the solutions of

$$\mathbf{r_a}' = 1/\phi_a \cdot \mathbf{r_a}'\hat{a}\mathbf{F} \quad \text{or} \quad \mathbf{r_a}'(\phi_a\mathbf{I} - \hat{a}\mathbf{F}) = 0. \qquad (6.13)$$

ϕ_a and $\mathbf{r_a}'$ are thus the eigenvalue and eigenvector of the matrix $\hat{a}\mathbf{F}$, instead of those of $\mathbf{F}$, which would generate the *total* eigenvalues ϕ and $\mathbf{r}'$.

We can compare the two systems most clearly (but not explicitly) by juxtaposing the two characteristic equations:

$$\text{post-tax: } \mathbf{r_a}'\hat{a}(\phi_\alpha\hat{a}^{-1} - \mathbf{F}) = 0$$

$$\text{pre-tax: } \mathbf{r}'(\phi_*\mathbf{I} - \mathbf{F}) = 0. \qquad (6.14)$$

If we drive simplification to the point where direct tax rates are uniform as between sectors, thus reducing the matrix $\hat{a}$ to $a\mathbf{I}$ (where a is a scalar), we can perform an explicit comparison by rewriting the post-tax equation as

$$a\mathbf{r_a}'(\phi_a/a \cdot \mathbf{I} - \mathbf{F}) = 0. \qquad (6.15)$$

This makes it clear that the relationship between the post- and pre-tax values in such a case would be

$$\mathbf{r_a}' = \mathbf{r}^*/a \text{ and } \phi_a = a\phi_*. \qquad (6.16)$$

In other words, the eigenrentals are scaled up, and the eigencost-ratio scaled down, in proportion to post- and pre-tax ratio $a(=1-t$, where t is the average tax rate), assuming always that prices and rentals are scaled or 'standardized' to start with. If, however, the resulting partial eigenrentals $\mathbf{r_a}'$ are themselves to be standardized, they must again be scaled down in the ratio a, thus remaining equal to the standardized total eigenprices ($\mathbf{r_a^*} = \mathbf{r^*}$). Just as before, therefore, the restriction of value-forming factors to a *uniform* proportion of total value added in each sector will leave the standardized total eigenprices unaffected, and will merely scale down the eigencost ratio in the same proportion (a). A change in eigenprices will be brought about only if the base-factor varies as a proportion of total value added from sector to sector.

6.3 Marxian Labour-Values

In an extreme case we might eliminate all factors other than labour and thus approximate the Marxian labour-values, although for a *complete* assimilation to these concepts we would need to add a number of further steps. In particular, we would need to dispense with the use-norming of factors and restrict ourselves to a downstream transformation like (6.12) with the diagonal $\hat{a}$ interpreted as the ratio of wages to total value added, even though this would leave the factor-rentals $\mathbf{r_a}'$ still to be determined.

For this determination the Marxian system allows us two options.

1. We could accept the verdict of the market (or of the price bureau in centrally planned economics) and value the factors in current money prices as recorded in the original input–output scheme, thus equating $\mathbf{r_a}'$ with the first row of the unit-matrix $\mathbf{i_1}'$, where the first element is unity and all others zero. With $\hat{a}$ measuring wage to value added ratios this would amount to accepting actual wage payments as the proper measure of labour contributions per unit output, i.e. $\mathbf{a}' = w\mathbf{i_1}'$ (where w is the average money wage per hour), while disqualifying all other factor contributions by setting ϕ_a equal to 1. This converts our downstream transformation to

$$\boldsymbol{\lambda_i} = w\mathbf{i_1}\mathbf{C} = w\mathbf{i_1}\mathbf{B}\overline{\mathbf{A}} = \mathbf{b_1}\overline{\mathbf{A}} = \mathbf{b_1}\overline{\mathbf{A}}, \tag{6.17}$$

where w is set equal to 1 in line with the Marxian practice of measuring labour contributions in terms of labour-hours themselves, and $\mathbf{b_1}$

is the first row of the factor-input coefficient matrix **B**, a definition that replicates the previously established formula (3.10) for the case where $\mathbf{b_r}' = \mathbf{b_1}'$ and refers to the factor-inputs of labour. This is the straightforward, *first* definition of the Marxian labour-values, which I have elsewhere called the definition *by imputation* ($\boldsymbol{\lambda}_i$). [1]

2. The second option would base itself on an alternative definition '*by alienation*' ($\boldsymbol{\lambda}_a$), also due to Marx. Here we drive cost-fetishism to the ultimate extreme by valuing labour contributions as the cost of labour-power (in terms of consumption out of wages) marked up by a rate of exploitation (ψ), uniformly applied to all product costings. This assumes that, in addition to the *material* input-coefficients **A**, we also know the consumption coefficient matrix **H** whose n columns are the consumption purchases (out of wages) of workers engaged in the various production sectors per unit output, so that the total prime-cost inputs in real terms are $\mathbf{G}(\equiv \mathbf{A} + \mathbf{H})$ products per unit output, and the global (direct and indirect) prime costs are the columns of the synthesized matrix $\mathbf{G\overline{A}}$. To this must be added in each sector the column of exploited (unpaid) labour inputs $\psi\mathbf{H}$, thus defining the Marxian values as

$$\boldsymbol{\lambda}_a' = \boldsymbol{\lambda}_a'(\mathbf{G\overline{A}} + \psi\mathbf{H\overline{A}}) = \boldsymbol{\lambda}_a\mathbf{A\overline{A}} + \boldsymbol{\lambda}_a'\mathbf{H\overline{A}} + \psi\boldsymbol{\lambda}_a'\mathbf{H\overline{A}}. \quad (6.18)$$

Those familiar with the Marxian theory will recognize on the extreme right-hand side the familiar analysis of value into constant capital, variable capital, and the surplus ($\mathbf{c} + \mathbf{v} + \mathbf{s}$), all measured in terms of labour-value themselves, and the constant ψ as the Marxian 'rate of exploitation'.

The last equation enables us to define the Marxian values in a manner that parallels the definition of eigenprices, i.e.

$$\boldsymbol{\lambda}_a'\left(\frac{1}{1 + \psi}\mathbf{I} - \mathbf{H\overline{A}}\right) = 0. \quad (6.19)$$

where the eigenvalue $1/(1 + \psi)$ is obviously akin to the eigencost ratio ϕ_*, but the matrix furnishing that eigenvalue (and the corresponding eigenvector $\mathbf{v}_a$) is the matrix of direct and indirect (synthesized) consumption coefficients of labour $\mathbf{H\overline{A}}$ instead of the norm-cost matrix $\mathbf{P}(= \mathbf{NC})$ which furnishes eigencost and eigenprices (ϕ and $\mathbf{p}'$).

---

[1] F. Seton, 'The Question of Ideological Obstacles to Rational Price Setting in Communist Countries', in A. Abouchar (ed.), *The Socialist Price Mechanism*, Duke University Press, Durham, NC, 1977: 10–39.

It is possible to show that, given certain assumptions implicit in the Marxian system, the two definitions of value (λ_i' and λ_a' in (6.17) and (6.19)) are equivalent. The crucial assumptions derive from the doctrine that under capitalism the real wage is never more than a subsistence ration. This implies

1. that all households consume the same product-mix per unit output, say **h**, and the columns of the consumption-input matrix **H** will only differ by constant factors measuring the amount of labour used per unit output in the various production sectors, i.e.

$$\mathbf{H} = \mathbf{h l'}; \tag{6.20}$$

2. that households need to consume all their wages and cannot save (in terms of value); that is, that the value of the uniform consumption-basket **h** is equal to the portion of the total labour contribution that is paid for. In other words,

$$\lambda_a' \mathbf{h} = \frac{1}{1 + \psi} \equiv \text{the Marxian cost ratio } \phi_m. \tag{6.21}$$

Given the two implications (6.20) and (6.21), we can write the definition *by alienation* (6.19) as

$$\lambda_a' \left(\frac{1}{1 + \psi} \mathbf{I} - \mathbf{h l'A} \right) = \frac{1}{1 + \psi} \lambda_a' \mathbf{h} \lambda_i' = \frac{1}{1 + \psi} (\lambda_a' - \lambda_i') = 0. \tag{6.22}$$

In other words, $\lambda_a' = \lambda_i' \equiv \lambda'$ and the equivalence of the two Marxian definition is proved.

A straightforward comparison of eigenprices **p'** and Marxian labour-values λ' would thus take the form

$$\mathbf{p'}(\phi \mathbf{I} - \mathbf{NC}) = 0 \tag{6.23}$$

$$\lambda' \left(\frac{1}{1 + \psi} \mathbf{I} - \mathbf{H \overline{A}} \right) = 0.$$

It is clear, therefore that eigenprices would turn into labour-values if the household consumption of workers per unit output **H** could be accepted as the true use-norms of factors (**NB**), and the global (direct and indirect) absorption of material inputs ($\overline{\mathbf{A}}$) as the true 'costs' of commodities (**C**). In this case the eigencost-ratio would turn into the ratio in which wage payments (i.e. unexploited labour) stood to total value added (i.e. the total contribution of labour), i.e. $\phi = 1/(1 + \psi)$.

Eigenprices must, however, deviate from labour-values to the extent that the issue is not prejudged in this way, and both norms and costs are derived from the transformation (or production) functions under which the economy actually operates.

A similar reduction of the eigenprice system, this time focusing on the eigencost ratio, will serve to make explicit its relationship to the Marxian rate of exploitation (ψ) and the latter's derivative cost-ratio ϕ_m, i.e. the proportion of paid to total (paid and unpaid) labour. In line with the single-factor model of the Marxian scheme, we must set

$$\mathbf{W} = \mathbf{w_1}'; \ \mathbf{B} = \mathbf{W}\hat{\mathbf{z}}^{-1} = \mathbf{b_1}'; \ \hat{\mathbf{w}} = w_1 = L \text{ (total labour)} \qquad (6.24)$$

and

$$\mathbf{E} = \hat{\mathbf{w}}^{-1}\mathbf{W} = \mathbf{w_1}'/L = \mathbf{e_1}'. \qquad (6.25)$$

The cost matrix $\mathbf{C}$ is thereby reduced to the row-vector of labour-values:

$$\mathbf{C} = \mathbf{B}\overline{\mathbf{A}} = \mathbf{b_1}'\overline{\mathbf{A}} = \boldsymbol{\lambda}' \qquad (6.26)$$

and the norm-matrix, in line with (3.26), to the column-vector of final products valued in eigenprices per unit labour in use, i.e.

$$\mathbf{N} = \hat{\mathbf{y}}\mathbf{C}'\hat{\mathbf{w}}^{-1} = \frac{1}{L}\hat{\mathbf{y}}\boldsymbol{\lambda} = \mathbf{y}_\lambda/L. \qquad (6.27)$$

Since $L(= \mathbf{b_1}'\mathbf{z})$ is by virtue of (3.7) equal to $\mathbf{b_1}\overline{\mathbf{A}}\mathbf{y}$ and therefore equals $\boldsymbol{\lambda}_\mathbf{y}'$ or Σy_λ, the last expression in (6.27) represents the structure of final demand in terms of eigenprices, an obvious weighting system for any set of commodity-prices $\mathbf{p}'$ to be transformed into the single factor-norm (or revenue productivity) of labour $\mathbf{r_1}'$ (see (3.23)). It follows from the last two equations that the cost-norm matrix $\mathbf{F}$ ($=\mathbf{CN}$) whose dominant furnishes the eigencost-ratio reduces to a scalar (which is its own dominant), i.e.

$$\phi_* = \text{dom. } \mathbf{CN} = \boldsymbol{\lambda}'\mathbf{y}_\lambda/L = \overline{\lambda}. \qquad (6.28)$$

The eigencost-ratio thus reduces to a weighted mean or average of the labour-values with the eigenpriced final demands serving as weights.

To contrast this with the Marxian cost-ratio, we need only remind ourselves of the Marxian assumption (6.21):

$$\phi_m = \boldsymbol{\lambda}'\mathbf{h},$$

a weighted sum of the same labour-values that figure in the single-factor eigencost-ratio (6.28), but with weights now reduced from the *total* final supply of each sector per unit GNP to the supply for wage-financed consumption per unit output of each sector and the weights expressed in currently priced instead of labour-valued supplies.

We may therefore identify the Marxian value system as a special subspecies of eigenprices reduced to 'partial' coverage on both the factor- and the final-use side (Sects. 6.1 and 6.2), in which, moreover, the norming of the single factor is based on untransformed weighting of commodity-prices and which to that extent falls short of complete consistency.

6.4 OECD Shadow Prices for Project Appraisal

These prices, occasionally dubbed 'Little–Mirrlees', in deference to the authors of the relevant OECD Manual,[1] have now acquired so much influence that some exploration of their kinship with eigenprices, particularly of the external variety (Sect. 6.1), seems to be called for. Although the use of foreign trade or 'border' prices, which lies at the basis of the Manual, strongly suggests such a kinship, it will turn out to be a fairly remote and even deceptive one. Nevertheless some attention to it, however summary and impressionistic, will increase our understanding of both the price systems under comparison.

It should be understood from the outset that the purpose of the OECD prices is not the construction of a generalized or self-consistent system, but the provision of relatively simple tools enabling project-appraisers who are not necessarily sophisticated economists to find short cuts to difficult decisions, vastly more sensible and productive of economic benefit than could be achieved by reliance on market prices. In that the Manual brilliantly succeeds, and its success is by no means tarnished by the lack of internal consistency on which we shall have to dwell. After all, consistency is often a very minor virtue, the panoply of the intellectually timid or the fig-leaf of the sexless, and its absence may betoken no more than a healthy contempt for

---

[1] I. M. D. Little and J. A. Mirrlees, *Manual of Industrial Project Analysis in Developing Countries*, ii, *Social Cost Benefit Analysis*, OECD, Paris, 1969; henceforth referred to as 'the Manual'.

redundant clothing on the part of those who have no such defects to hide.

In the second place, it should be understood that the Manual's reliance on the border prices of foreign trade[2] is in no way intended to make foreign trade or the acquisition of foreign currency into the be-all and end-all of an economy. It merely identifies the most direct and simple indicators of the terms on which an economy can substitute one product for another. In an economy too small to affect world prices by its own demand and supply behaviour (such as the Manual assumes), these terms can most readily be ascertained by consulting the foreign trade prices payable for imports or exports of commodities at the country's borders, without the inconvenience and risk of error involved in complicated input-output calculations. It is then a relatively easy matter to compute price ratios for 'non-traded' goods and factors on this directly ascertainable basis.

In offering a formalization of border prices ($\mathbf{u}'$) in this section, we would not wish to commit the authors of the OECD Manual to this particular interpretation of their brainchild. We have, however, based our own applied study of the system (commissioned by one of these authors via the OECD)[3] on this interpretation, and have not been made aware of any protest in this respect.

We start by dividing the economy into a department of, say, three sectors (subscript $0 = 1, 2, 3$) producing 'non-tradables' which are neither exported nor imported, and one of the two sectors (subscript $x = 4, 5$) producing 'tradables' whose predominant origin or destination is foreign and whose border prices are π_4 and π_5 respectively. We also distinguish two domestic factors, a and b, whose 'border prices' v_a and v_b are determined by aggregation of tradable border prices, as are those of the non-tradable sectors $\mathbf{u}_0' = (u_1, u_2, u_3)$. Of course, the choice of 3, 2, and 2 for the number of sectors and factors is in substitution for the abstract numbers n_0, n_x, and m for expository purposes only, and implies no departure from generality. The conspectus of intersector flows in such an economy takes the form shown in (6.29).

---

[2] The term 'border prices' is not used in the Manual itself, which prefers a variety of less descriptive expressions like 'shadow prices' or 'accounting prices', but it has been widely adopted by subsequent commentators as a handy and fairly accurate label.

[3] Seton, *Shadow Wages in Chile*, OECD, Paris, 1972, and 'Shadow Wages in Chile', in R. S. Eckaus and P. N. Rosenstein-Rodan (eds.), *Analysis of Development Problems*, North-Holland, Amsterdam 1973.

$$
\begin{array}{l|l|l}
 & x_1^1 + x_1^2 + x_1^3 & + x_1^4 + x_1^5 & + y_1^a + y_1^b + j_1 = z_1 \\
\text{Non-tradables} & x_2^1 + x_2^2 + x_2^3 & + x_2^4 + x_2^5 & + y_2^a + y_2^b + j_2 = z_2 \\
(0) & x_3^1 + x_3^2 + x_3^3 & + x_3^4 + x_3^5 & + y_3^a + y_3^b + j_3 = z_3 \\
\hline
\text{Tradables} & x_4^1 + x_4^2 + x_4^3 & + x_4^4 + x_4^5 & + y_4^a + y_4^b + j_4 = z_4 \\
(x) & x_5^1 + x_5^2 + x_5^3 & + x_5^4 + x_5^5 & + y_5^a + y_5^b + j_5 = z_5 \\
\hline
\text{Factors} & w_a^1 + w_a^2 + w_a^3 & + w_a^4 + w_a^5 & = w_a \\
 & w_b^1 + w_b^2 + w_b^3 & + w_b^4 + w_b^5 & = w_b
\end{array}
$$

$$(6.29)$$

or, in matrix terms,

Non-tradables	$X_0^0 i$	$+ X_0^x i$	$\mathbf{y_0^0} + \mathbf{y_0^b} + j_0 = z_0$
Tradables	$X_x^0 i$	$+ X_x^x i$	$\mathbf{y_x^0} + \mathbf{y_x^b} + j_x = z_x$
Factors	$W^0 i$	$+ W^x i$	$= w$

where previously used symbols retain their meaning, while $(\mathbf{y^a},$ $\mathbf{y^b}) \equiv \mathbf{Y}$ stand for the products bought by the two factors out of their rewards for current productive services, and j represent final uses not held to be in the line of factor rewards. It goes almost without saying that the y-variables will in practice be very difficult to ascertain, but the crucial column listing the wage-goods consumed by labour should be amenable to estimation from workers' family budget data, so that the method of the Manual is quite easily applicable to the one main (and possibly only) factor of production in respect of which the Manual recommends its special procedure. In what follows, however, we shall assume, for the sake of completeness and consistency, that the procedure is, conceptually at least, applicable to all the factors distinguished in (6.29), thereby departing from the detailed simplifications of the Manual.

With the border prices of tradables ($\boldsymbol{\pi_x}$) culled from foreign trade statistics and adjusted for trade and transport costs to and from the border, the border-price contents[4] of non-tradables ($\mathbf{u_0'}$) and of factors ($\mathbf{v'}$) are implicitly defined by the Manual or its commentators[5] as follows

$$\mathbf{u_0'}\mathbf{X_0^0} + \boldsymbol{\pi'}\mathbf{X_x^0} + \mathbf{v'}\mathbf{W^0} = \mathbf{u_0}\hat{\mathbf{z}}_0$$

[4] The expression 'border-price content' seems more appropriate than 'border prices' or 'derived border prices' when applied to non-tradables or factors.

[5] See above n.3.

$$\mathbf{u_0'y_0} + \boldsymbol{\pi}\mathbf{Y_x} = \mathbf{v'\hat{w}} \tag{6.30}$$

Post-multiplying the first of these equations by $\mathbf{\hat{z}_0^{-1}}$ and the second by $\mathbf{\hat{w}^{-1}}$, we obtain the usual restatement of the scheme in terms of input-coefficients:

$$\mathbf{u_0'A_0^0} + \boldsymbol{\pi'}\mathbf{A_x^0} + \mathbf{v'B^0} = \mathbf{u_0'}$$

$$\mathbf{u_0'H_0} + \boldsymbol{\pi'}\mathbf{H_x} = \mathbf{v'}, \tag{6.31}$$

where the only new symbols are $\mathbf{H}$, standing for factor consumption per unit factor-use ($\equiv \mathbf{Y\hat{w}^{-1}}$).

The reader will easily recognize in the first equation of (6.31) an exact replica of our costing procedure (3.9), this time restricted to non-tradables, with border-prices tradables entering into the cost-structure on a par with factors, and factors themselves being priced at $\mathbf{v'}$, a set of rentals defined by the second equation.

It should be noted here that in defining the shadow prices of tradables the Manual departs from the cost-aggregation principle applied to the case of non-tradables (i.e. $\mathbf{u_x'}$ is not defined by $\mathbf{u_x'X_0^x} + \boldsymbol{\pi'}\mathbf{X_x^x} + \mathbf{v'W^x} = \mathbf{u_x'\hat{z}_x}$), but sets them equal to directly observable 'border prices' culled from foreign trade statistics (i.e. $\mathbf{u_x'} = \boldsymbol{\pi'}$). In consequence, there is nothing to ensure that the prices of domestically produced tradables are in any way related to domestic costs, even to those calculable in terms of border-price-related non-tradable or factor-prices. The equality of prices with average (or marginal) costs is thus clearly violated in the tradables domain, and the principle of price determination for particular products becomes dependent on the domain to which they have been allocated. Given that the Manual gives only impressionistic guidance on the criteria for this allocation (predominant origin or destination of the product), the structure of the shadow prices emerging could easily become dependent on the free-hand judgement of the project-appraiser or on his assiduity in combing foreign trade statistics for usable border prices to help in the exercise.[6]

---

[6] This search will often be complicated or frustrated by disparities in the definition or breakdown of productive sectors between input–output data and foreign trade statistics (e.g. tariff data), the latter being typically available only in such detailed breakdowns (by quality, weight, chemical composition, etc.) as to require painstaking and uncertain aggregation procedures before even a semblance of harmonization can be achieved.

Moreover, as the second equations of (6.30) and (6.31) show, the factor-prices are equated to the 'border-price contents' of the purchases made by factor-owners out of their current incomes, and are thus aimed to reflect only the economic *costs* of factor utilization without regard to the productivities of the factors in terms of final goods. There is no reference to the 'use' component of value implicit in the norms that enter into eigenprices; and this, in conjunction with the almost exclusive attention paid to labour among the factors of production, brings the recommendations of the Manual much more into line with the Marxian cost-fetishist and factor-monomaniac position than is widely appreciated.

Nevertheless, the Manual injects an element of valuation by use through a number of adjustments recommended for the calculation of shadow-wages, which allow for the fact that some of the wages paid by a project reflect a raising of consumption levels in line with what is socially desirable in low-income countries and therefore do not constitute a cost to the economy in the true sense of the term. These adjustments, with their hint at an unspecified, but implicitly assumed, social welfare function, could with every justification be cited in the Manual's defence against the accusation of cost-fetishism.

To find explicit expressions for the border prices of all products and factors we need only solve equations (6.31) and substitute in the first the value of v' found from the second, thus obtaining

$$\mathbf{u_0}'(\mathbf{A_0^0} + \mathbf{H_0}\mathbf{B^0}) + \boldsymbol{\pi}'(\mathbf{A_x} + \mathbf{H_x}\mathbf{B^0}) = \mathbf{u_0}'. \tag{6.32}$$

By writing $\mathbf{G_0}$ and $\mathbf{G_x}$ for the two bracketed expressions, we obtain finally:

$$\mathbf{u_0}' = \boldsymbol{\pi}'\mathbf{G_x}(\mathbf{I} - \mathbf{G_0})^{-1}, \tag{6.33}$$

where

$$\mathbf{G_0} \equiv \mathbf{A_0^0} + \mathbf{H_0}\mathbf{B^0}$$

and

$$\mathbf{G_x} \equiv \mathbf{A_x^0} + \mathbf{H_x}\mathbf{B^0}. \tag{6.34}$$

The last two statements will enable us to specify the steps necessary to convert border prices into total eigenprices as defined in (3.30)

1. The absorption of tradables by sectors producing non-tradables must be subsumed under factor-inputs $\mathbf{W^0}$ (possibly as part of the

absorption of complementary imports). This dispenses with the 'domain' superscript and subscript x and 0, and eliminates the matrix $\mathbf{X_x^0}$, thus converting the first equation of (6.31) into

$$\mathbf{u'A} + \mathbf{v'B} = \mathbf{u'} \tag{6.35}$$

and the second into

$$\mathbf{u'H} = \mathbf{v'}. \tag{6.36}$$

The solution of the two converted equations $(\mathbf{HB\overline{A}})$, when scaled up to allow for uniform profit, is therefore

$$\mathbf{u'} = 1/\phi \cdot \mathbf{u'HB\overline{A}} = 1/\phi \cdot \mathbf{u'HC} \tag{6.37}$$

thus making the prices $\mathbf{u'}$ into an eigenvector of the matrix $\mathbf{HC'}$ (corresponding to the dominant ϕ).

2. The matrix $\mathbf{H}$ must be assumed to have the dyadic form $\mathbf{hv'}$ embodying the assumption that the common human biology of all factor-owners forces each of them to consume a subsistence-basket of uniform composition $\mathbf{h}$ (per unit output), or at least that only the consumption of such baskets can properly be regarded as their factor-reward, while any deviation from it is the result of 'discretionary' expenditure unrelated to *necessary* rewards for productive services. The difference between the total rewards paid out to various factors (i.e. between the columns of $\mathbf{H}$) is therefore solely one of scale, as determined by the difference between their costs (given by the vector $\mathbf{v'}$).

3. The proper valuation of the final uses of all commodities (per unit output) must be unity ($\mathbf{u'y} = 1$), and that of the subsistence-basket h (per unit output), that proportion of the national income which is mortgaged to the necessary reward of factors i.e.

$$\mathbf{u'h} = \phi. \tag{6.38}$$

The assumptions of this and the preceding note lead to the equation

$$\mathbf{u'} = 1/\phi \cdot \mathbf{u'hv'c} = \mathbf{v'C} \tag{6.39}$$

thus replacing the costing equation (3.5).

4. Finally, when replacing costs by full-cost prices, and requiring product-prices and factor-rentals to be mutually consistent (signalled by the replacement of $\mathbf{u'}$ and $\mathbf{v'}$ by $\mathbf{p'}$ and $\mathbf{r'}$), we arrive at the two eigenprice-generating transformations:

$$\mathbf{p}' = 1/\phi \ . \ \mathbf{r}'\mathbf{C} \text{ and } \mathbf{r}' = \mathbf{p}'\mathbf{N} \qquad (6.40)$$

as per (3.27), which uniquely determine the previously arbitrary factor-rentals $\mathbf{v}'$ by equating them to the eigenvector of $\mathbf{CN}(\equiv \mathbf{F})$ corresponding to the dominant ϕ_*.

The four steps outlined above serve to establish a remote but discernible kinship between eigenprices and OECD border-price valuations, differentiating the latter from the former in the main by virtue of their separate treatment of tradable products as original factor-inputs subject to special pricing rules, and by the cost-fetishist valuation of other factors independently of use or productivity considerations. They also make it clear that the kinship, however remote it may be, is as much with total eigenprices as with partial, external eigenprices, which, in spite of their orientation towards foreign trade, are neither in practice nor in theory any nearer OECD prices than eigenprices in their most general definition.

7

Extensions

7.1 The Problem of Joint Production[1]

REALITY and statistical practice will often force us to abandon the convenient fiction of homogeneous industries (producing one commodity only) which has served us well for expository purposes so far. In many cases this restrictive assumption can be relaxed without damage to the concept or computability of eigenprices. Indeed, a restatement of the model to accommodate a generalization of this sort allows a more succinct definition through which some facets of eigenprices can be put into sharper relief.[2]

In this restatement the sectors absorbing inputs as represented by the columns of the input–output matrix X can no longer be identified as the 'industries' named in the row-headings, but must be redefined as heterogeneous 'activities' whose outputs are themselves various mixes of commodities $(z', z^2, \ldots, z^n)$, thus supplementing the matrix of input-flows X by a conformable matrix of outputs Z in lieu of the single output-vector z of the previous analysis. Activity r is then defined by the set of commodity- and factor-inputs x^r and w^r as before, and a correlative vector of commodity-outputs z^r, measured in current money values, all of which can be varied in the same proportion in step with the 'level of intensity' at which the activity is undertaken. Each activity may be presumed to take its label (r) from the commodity whose output is the largest among the elements of z^r. We assume that there is one and only one such activity for every commodity listed, whose intensity is then measured by the quantity (current money value) of that commodity in z^r. This assumption

[1] The treatment adopted here is virtually identical with the model of my article in *Economic Systems Analysis*, 1/2 (1989), 273–83. I am grateful to the editor of that journal, Dr A. Bródy, for permission to draw on this work and lift a number of statements and paragraphs from it for inclusion in this section.

[2] A more pragmatic method is explained and put to good use in this book by Professor A. E. Steenge in Appendix A. The method adopted here puts greater emphasis on conceptualization and is *protanto* less concerned with preserving 'industries' in the intuitive sense of sectors whose inputs and outputs must at all times be non-negative.

ensures that the number of activities equals that of commodities, thereby making their conspectuses X and Z into square $n \times n$ matrices. (The case where the number of goods exceeds that of activities, i.e. where some subsidiary products are not the main products of any other industry, thus making X and Z into non-square matrices, will not be treated here, though also amenable to eigenprice calculations in approximative form).

The basic scheme of (3.1), when laterally summed, becomes

$$Xi + y = Zi \qquad (7.1)$$

$$Wi = w,$$

a statement from which the original version can be derived by substituting the diagonal matrix of single-product outputs $\hat{z}$ for the matrix of multi-product outputs Z, thus allowing the scheme to imply the familiar input-coefficients $A = X\hat{z}^{-1}$ and $B = W\hat{z}^{-1}$ for goods and factors respectively. In the present scheme these are not directly visible, though a generalized form of A and B (XZ^{-1} and WZ^{-1}) will shortly make its appearance in the guise of 'homogenized'-sector columns defined as inputs of activity-sets.

These sets are weighted sums (linear combinations) of the activities producing the Z-columns, with weights equal to the 'levels of intensity' at which they enter as constituents of the homogenized sectors (each producing one commodity only). This can be seen by recalling that weighted sums of the output-columns of Z are formed by post-multiplying Z by the column-vector of weights; if that column-vector is the rth column of Z^{-1} the resulting product will by definition be i^r, the rth column of the unit-matrix, in which only one unit of the rth commodity appears while all other outputs are reduced to zero. In other words, the columns of Z^{-1} show the weights at which the original activities need to be combined in order to yield homogenized sectors producing one unit of each commodity in turn.

The fact that many of these weights are bound to be negative calls for an additional refinement of interpretation. We may think of the weights (columns of Z^{-1}) as changes in the activity-targets forming part of a pre-established production-plan, a historical document of no further concern to us, i.e. as a re-targeting of activities. If the plan is to be changed to allow one more unit of commodity r to be produced without any other change, the necessary re-targeting is shown by the rth column of Z^{-1}. With this interpretation the appearance of a negative weight poses no special problem, as it only means that the level of the activity concerned is to be *reduced* rather than increased in the re-targeting. This is a change of plan implementing a decision to forgo part of the planned production of certain goods in order to save the planned inputs of certain others, a negative activity which need not cause us any conceptual discomfort. The re-targeting needed to produce one more unit of commodity r (and no other change) will entail changes of $(\mathbf{XZ}^{-1})\mathbf{i}^{\mathbf{r}}$ and $(\mathbf{WZ}^{-1})\mathbf{i}^{\mathbf{r}}$ in commodity- and factor-inputs respectively, and in this sense the new **A**- and **B**-matrices are still amenable to the same interpretation as the originals.

Returning now to (7.1) we can start the derivation of eigenprices by defining the unit-costs of commodities $\mathbf{c}'$ in their dependence on any arbitrary set of factor-prices $\mathbf{r}'$ by the cost-balancing equations

$$\mathbf{c}'\mathbf{X} + \mathbf{r}'\mathbf{W} = \mathbf{c}'\mathbf{Z}, \tag{7.2}$$

simplifying to

$$\mathbf{c}' = \mathbf{r}'\mathbf{WY} = \mathbf{r}'\mathbf{C}, \tag{7.3}$$

where $\mathbf{Y}$ is the matrix $\mathbf{Z}-\mathbf{X}$ listing in each column the net output of the column-good (net inputs negative) and $\mathbf{C}$ is the generalization of the matrix $\mathbf{B\overline{A}}$ of the previous analysis.[3] By allowing each sector the uniform rate of surplus on factor-cost σ, the full costs of goods $\mathbf{p}$ become

$$\mathbf{p}' = 1/\phi \cdot \mathbf{r}'\mathbf{WY}, \tag{7.4}$$

where ϕ is the uniform cost-ratio.

This equation represents the downstream transformation corresponding to (3.6) in the single-product industry case.

A similar generalization must be applied to the norm-defining equations (3.8), which now become norm-balancing equations

$$\mathbf{Xv} + \mathbf{Y}'\mathbf{p} = \mathbf{Zv}, \tag{7.5}$$

thus defining commodity norms as

$$\mathbf{v} = \mathbf{Y}^{-1}\mathbf{Y}'\mathbf{p}, \tag{7.6}$$

where $\mathbf{p}$ is any arbitrary set of product prices and $\mathbf{Y}$ again the net-output matrix $\mathbf{Z}-\mathbf{X}$. This equation is the generalized version of (3.13),

---

[3] $\mathbf{A} = \mathbf{XZ}$ implies $\mathbf{I} - \mathbf{A} = (\mathbf{Z} - \mathbf{X})\mathbf{Z}^{-1} = \mathbf{YZ}^{-1}$ and $\overline{\mathbf{A}} = \mathbf{ZY}^{-1}$. This in turn implies $\mathbf{B\overline{A}} = \mathbf{WZ}^{-1}\mathbf{ZY}^{-1} = \mathbf{WY}^{-1}$.

i.e. of $\mathbf{v} = \mathbf{Vp} = \bar{\mathbf{D}}\hat{\mathbf{s}}\mathbf{p}$ since $\bar{\mathbf{D}} = \hat{\mathbf{z}}^{-1}\mathbf{X}$ becomes $\mathbf{Z}^{-1}\mathbf{X}$ while $\bar{\mathbf{D}} = \mathbf{Y}^{-1}\mathbf{Z}$ and $\hat{\mathbf{s}}$ becomes $\mathbf{Z}^{-1}\mathbf{Y}'$.

The commodity norms can now be converted into factor norms by means of an equation identical with (3.20), i.e.

$$\hat{\mathbf{w}}\mathbf{r} = \mathbf{Wv} \text{ or } \mathbf{r} = \mathbf{Ev} = \mathbf{EY}^{-1}\mathbf{Y}'\mathbf{p} = \mathbf{N}'\mathbf{p}, \tag{7.7}$$

where $\mathbf{E}$ is the matrix of factor quotas $\hat{\mathbf{w}}^{-1}\mathbf{W}$, and finally by transposition

$$\mathbf{r}' = \mathbf{p}'\mathbf{N} = \mathbf{p}'\mathbf{YY}'^{-1}\mathbf{R}', \tag{7.8}$$

where the present N is the generalization to the multi-product sector worlds of the norm matrix N introduced in (3.22) for the single-product sector case. Equation (7.7) thus corresponds to the upstream transformation converting product-prices into factor-norms.

The consistency requirement between product-prices (7.4) and factor-norms (7.7) on which eigenprices are based, as explained in Sect. 2.1, can thus be put in the form

$$\mathbf{p}'(\mathbf{I} - \mathbf{NC}) = \mathbf{r}'(\mathbf{I} - \mathbf{CN}) = 0, \tag{7.9}$$

a statement identical with (3.26) provided $\mathbf{C}$ and $\mathbf{N}$ are redefined in line with footnote 3 and (7.7), i.e. by replacing the inverse output-vector $\hat{\mathbf{z}}^{-1}$ (diagonalized) by the inverse mixed-output matrix z^{-1} in all coefficient matrices ($\mathbf{A}, \mathbf{B}, \mathbf{D}, \hat{\mathbf{s}}$).

With this multi-product version of eigenprices it becomes somewhat easier to justify their claim to simultaneous equality with full costs and utilities. The cost identity emerges directly from (7.4) as

$$\mathbf{p}' = \mathbf{r}'\mathbf{C}, \tag{7.10}$$

while the use identity can be derived by reversing the definition of commodity-norms (7.5) to give

$$\mathbf{p}' = \mathbf{v}'\mathbf{Y}'\mathbf{Y}^{-1}, \tag{7.11}$$

where the multiplier will be recognized as the matrix of net outputs of activities per unit final use of each commodity. The right-hand side of (7.11) therefore values the final output of goods at the use-values gained after deducting those lost in absorbed inputs when undertaking the set of activities producing them in unit quantities, i.e. it measures the net gain in use-value achieved by the production of each commodity. The eigenvalues of the factors $\mathbf{r}'$ are of course defined in terms of use-norms only (7.7) since factor inputs are by definition non-produced.

7.2 Warranted Supply and Factor Employment

The interpretation of the left-hand dominant eigenvector of the norm-cost matrix $\mathbf{P}$ $(= \mathbf{NC})$ as a form of rational price system (eigenprices) naturally prompts the search for a correlative interpretation of the right-hand eigenvector of the same matrix. In other words, if the equation

$$\mathbf{p}'(\phi\mathbf{I} - \mathbf{P}) = 0 \text{ or } \mathbf{p}'\mathbf{NC} = \phi\mathbf{p}' \qquad (7.12)$$

defines eigenprices, what are the economic variables defined by the dual system, say $\mathbf{q}$, as in (7.13)?

$$(\phi\mathbf{I} - \mathbf{P})\mathbf{q} = 0 \text{ or } \mathbf{NCq} = \phi\mathbf{q}. \qquad (7.13)$$

With the primal solution identified as a set of prices, the dual solution must be a set of final supplies ('finals'), suggesting the provisional term 'eigenfinals' by analogy.

To approach a reasonable interpretation of these, we note that

$$\mathbf{C}\tilde{\mathbf{y}} = \mathbf{B}\overline{\mathbf{A}}\mathbf{q} = \mathbf{B}\tilde{\mathbf{z}} = \mathbf{W}\hat{\mathbf{z}}^{-1}\mathbf{z} = \mathbf{W}\mathbf{i} = \tilde{\mathbf{w}}, \qquad (7.14)$$

and therefore

$$\mathbf{NCq} = \mathbf{N}\tilde{\mathbf{w}} = \hat{\mathbf{s}}\overline{\mathbf{D}}'\mathbf{E}'\tilde{\mathbf{w}} = \hat{\mathbf{s}}\overline{\mathbf{D}}'\mathbf{W}'\hat{\mathbf{w}}^{-1}\tilde{\mathbf{w}} = \hat{\mathbf{s}}\overline{\mathbf{D}}'\mathbf{W}'\mathbf{i} = \mathbf{V}'\tilde{\omega}. \qquad (7.15)$$

The left-hand side of (7.13) thus measures the factor employments $\tilde{\omega}$ each valued at the commodity-norm of the sector it serves, i.e. the cost of factor services when properly valued at their use-productivities, and therefore the incomes duly at the disposal of factor-owners for the purchase of goods. If it is further assumed that factor-owners (the 'population') and government exert final demands of identical commodity-structure, i.e. that the population demands a uniform proportion ϕ of each final, equation (7.13) expresses the final supply-structure $\mathbf{q}$ that will be demanded by the economy as a whole. The eigenfinals $\mathbf{q}$ could therefore be described as the warranted supply structure in the sense of being the only pattern of supply that will 'create its own demand' under the conditions specified.[4]

In parallel with this we can define **g** as the structure of factor-employment which, under the same conditions, will create commodity-demands whose input-requirements of factors are equal to the employment-structure assumed, i.e. as the employment-structure assuring its own demand, since by virtue of (7.13) and (7.15)

$$\mathbf{CNg} = \phi\mathbf{Cq} = \phi\mathbf{g} \text{ or } (\phi\mathbf{I} - \mathbf{Q})\mathbf{g} = 0. \tag{7.16}$$

It can be shown, moreover, that the eigenfinals must be equal to the eigenpriced *actual* finals of the system, i.e. $\mathbf{q} = \hat{\mathbf{y}}\mathbf{p}$; for $\hat{\mathbf{y}}\mathbf{p}$ can easily be seen to be the right-hand dominant eigenvector of $\mathbf{P}(= \mathbf{NC})$. In fact, by virtue of (3.16), (3.24), and (3.25) we can write[5]

$$\mathbf{NC}\hat{\mathbf{y}}\mathbf{p} = \hat{\mathbf{y}}\mathbf{C}'\hat{\mathbf{w}}^{-1}\mathbf{C}\hat{\mathbf{y}}\mathbf{p} = \hat{\mathbf{y}}\mathbf{C}'\mathbf{N}'\mathbf{P} = \hat{\mathbf{y}}\mathbf{C}'\mathbf{r} = \hat{\mathbf{y}}\phi\mathbf{p} = \phi\hat{\mathbf{y}}\mathbf{p},$$

$$(\phi\mathbf{I} - \mathbf{P})\hat{\mathbf{y}}\mathbf{p} = 0. \tag{7.17}$$

In a similar way we can show that a warranted employment structure **g** would be equal to the eigenpriced *actual* structure $\hat{\mathbf{w}}\mathbf{r}$, as $\hat{\mathbf{W}}\mathbf{r}$ is the right-hand eigenvector of **F**; for by virtue of (3.26) and (3.23) we have

$$\mathbf{F}\hat{\mathbf{w}}\mathbf{r} = \mathbf{CN}\hat{\mathbf{w}}\mathbf{r} = \mathbf{C}\hat{\mathbf{y}}\mathbf{C}'\hat{\mathbf{w}}^{-1}\hat{\mathbf{w}}\mathbf{r} = \mathbf{C}\hat{\mathbf{y}}\mathbf{C}'\mathbf{r} = \phi\mathbf{C}\hat{\mathbf{y}}\mathbf{p}, \tag{7.18}$$

and, from the definitions of **C**, **W**, **R**, and **V**:

$$\phi\mathbf{C}\hat{\mathbf{y}}\mathbf{p} = \phi\mathbf{B}\overline{\mathbf{A}}\hat{\mathbf{y}}\mathbf{p} = \phi\mathbf{W}\overline{\mathbf{D}}\hat{\mathbf{z}}^{-1}\hat{\mathbf{y}}\mathbf{p} = \phi\mathbf{W}\mathbf{V}\mathbf{p} = \phi\hat{\mathbf{w}}\mathbf{R}\mathbf{V}\mathbf{p}$$

$$= \phi\hat{\mathbf{w}}\mathbf{N}'\mathbf{p} = \phi\hat{\mathbf{w}}\mathbf{r} \tag{7.19}$$

and, merging the last two equations:

$$(\phi\mathbf{I} - \mathbf{F})\hat{\mathbf{w}}\mathbf{q} = 0.$$

Results like the foregoing (7.17) must, however, be interpreted with some care, since the multiplication of each y by its eigenprice **p** to

---

[4] The assumption of identical demand structures for population and government is of course highly implausible. It could only be dropped by replacing the uniform ratio ϕ in (7.12) and (7.13) by a set of ratios $\hat{\phi}$ different *inter se* and rendering generalized eigenprices and eigenfinals as the left- and right-hand vectors annihilating $(\hat{\phi} - \mathbf{P})$ rather than $(\phi\mathbf{I} - \mathbf{P})$. This, however, would require a knowledge of $\hat{\phi}$ from exogenous forces or some theory of 'rational' patterns of profitability which goes beyond the scope of this book. But see Sect.7.5 below.

[5] I owe this proof to Dr E. Dietzenbacher of the University of Groningen.

form $\hat{\mathbf{y}}\mathbf{p}$ creates a new set of y ($\mathbf{q}$) and therefore a norm-matrix $\tilde{\mathbf{N}}(=\hat{\mathbf{q}}\mathbf{C}'\hat{\mathbf{w}}^{-1})$ and norm-cost matrix $\tilde{\mathbf{P}}(=\tilde{\mathbf{N}}\mathbf{C})$, say $\tilde{\mathbf{N}}$ and $\tilde{\mathbf{P}}$, different from the ones from which the eigenprices $\mathbf{p}'$ were originally derived. We must therefore resist the temptation of regarding eigenprices as correction factors converting actual into rational final supplies ('creating their own demand') in the same way in which they convert actual into rational prices (eigenprices).

7.3 Eigenyield and the Structure of Final Use

In Sect. 3.5 we discussed the eigencost-ratio ϕ which emerges as the dominant eigenvalue of norm-cost and cost-norm matrices $\mathbf{P}(=\mathbf{NC})$ and $\mathbf{F}(=\mathbf{CN})$, and the associated eigenyield $\sigma(=1/\phi-1)$. We concluded that the latter can, with certain qualifications, be interpreted as an index of cost effectiveness, and that therefore economic decision-makers might well be interested (other things remaining equal) in increasing it, i.e. lowering the eigencost-ratio ϕ as much as possible without prejudicing other desiderata. If we deny them direct influence on the technological coefficients ($\mathbf{A}$, $\mathbf{B}$, and $\mathbf{C}$) and the delivery quotas ($\mathbf{D}$), the only instrument available to them is the pattern of final use (y) which could be manipulated by government expenditure and fiscal policy or by the direct *fiat* of planners in a centrally planned economy.

The nexus between y and the dominant eigenvalue of $\mathbf{P}$ and $\mathbf{F}$ is established by the norm-matrix $\mathbf{N}$ which is a constituent factor of both and can be equated to $\hat{\mathbf{y}}\mathbf{C}'\hat{\mathbf{w}}^{-1}$ (3.26), thus making $\mathbf{P}$ equal to

$$\hat{\mathbf{y}}\mathbf{C}'\hat{\mathbf{w}}^{-1}\mathbf{C} \equiv \hat{\mathbf{y}}\mathbf{M} = \mathbf{P}, \qquad (7.20)$$

where $\mathbf{M}$ is newly defined as the symmetric singular matrix $\mathbf{C}'\hat{\mathbf{w}}^{-1}\mathbf{C}$. The formal question we therefore have to address is the extent and direction in which changes in y will affect the dominant eigenvalue of $\mathbf{P}$.

We can establish this with the aid of an important theorem in perturbation theory[6] which states that a small disturbance of a matrix $\mathbf{P}$ (converting $\mathbf{P}$ into $\mathbf{P}+d\mathbf{P}$) will cause its dominant eigenvalue ϕ to change by

---

[6] See e.g. A. S. Deif, *Advanced Matrix Theory for Scientists and Engineers*, Wiley, New York, 1982, Theorem 1, p. 207. The theorem only holds if $\mathbf{P}$ has n distinct (non-multiple) roots.

$$d\phi = \mathbf{p}'d\mathbf{P}\mathbf{q}, \tag{7.21}$$

where $\mathbf{p}'$ and $\mathbf{q}$ are the left-hand and right-hand dominant eigenvectors of $\mathbf{P}$ respectively.

Since $\mathbf{P} = \hat{\mathbf{y}}\mathbf{M}$ (7.20), the effect of a small increase dy of any element in y, say y_r, can be expressed as $d\mathbf{P} = \mathbf{E_r}\mathbf{M}$, where $\mathbf{E_r}$ is a matrix containing dy in the rth place of the main diagonal and zero everywhere else (such that premultiplication by it betokens an increase of y_r by dy and no other change). It follows then by virtue of (7.21) that

$$d\phi = \mathbf{p}'\mathbf{E_r}\mathbf{M} = \mathbf{p}'dy\mathbf{i_r}'\mathbf{M}\mathbf{q} \tag{7.22}$$

and, since $\mathbf{M} = \hat{\mathbf{y}}^{-1}\mathbf{P}$,

$$d\phi = \mathbf{p}\,dy(\mathbf{i_r}'\mathbf{P}\mathbf{q}/y_r) = p_r dy(\mathbf{i_r}'\phi\mathbf{q}/y_r) = \phi dy(p_r\tilde{\mathbf{q}}_r/y_r). \tag{7.23}$$

Denoting the bracketed term by k_r (the 'rth criterion'), we can write the proportional perturbation of ϕ as

$$d\phi/\phi = k_r dy, \text{ where } k_r \equiv p_r \mathbf{q}_r/y_r = p_r^2 \text{ (by virtue of 7.6).} \tag{7.24}$$

A shift of dy \$ from final supply s to final supply r would therefore change ϕ in the ratio $(k_r - k_s)$, i.e. it would reduce the eigencost ratio if and only if $k_r < k_s$, in other words if and only if $p_r < p_s$. Our criterion for a favourable (eigencost-reducing) shift in the final bill of goods would thus appear to amount to an injunction to shift as far as possible to sectors whose products have lower rather than higher eigenprices[7], until a state is reached where there is no more scope for such shifts because all eigenprices are equalized.

This criterion-rule immediately prompts the question whether such repeated shifts in the structure of final use towards its warranted state could eventually achieve a structure through which the eigencost-ratio was *minimized*. The problem is greatly complicated by the fact, already referred to in the last paragraph of Sect. 7.2, that each such shift will alter the norm-cost matrix $\mathbf{P}(= \hat{\mathbf{y}}\mathbf{C}'\hat{\mathbf{w}}^{-1}\mathbf{C})$ and thereby both the system of eigenprices ($\mathbf{p}'$) and the warranted use-structure $\tilde{\mathbf{y}}(= \hat{\mathbf{p}}\mathbf{y})$ to which the shift is intended to lead. Indeed, the ideal structure will only be realizable if the technology in operation fulfils prior

---

[7] i.e. to goods that are 'overpriced' in terms of the current price structure.

conditions shaping the matrices $\mathbf{C}$ and $\mathbf{P}$ to a very specific pattern; for there must exist a $\mathbf{y}$ such that:

$$\phi\mathbf{y} = \mathbf{Py} = \hat{\mathbf{y}}\mathbf{C}'\hat{\mathbf{w}}^{-1}\mathbf{Cy} = \hat{\mathbf{y}}\mathbf{C}'\mathbf{i} \quad^8 \tag{7.25}$$

and therefore

$$\mathbf{C}'\mathbf{i} = \phi\hat{\mathbf{y}}^{-1}\mathbf{y} = \phi\mathbf{i}. \tag{7.26}$$

Thus the columns of $\mathbf{C}$ must all sum to ϕ, the dominant eigenvalue of $\mathbf{P}$, and it follows at once that the column-sums of $\mathbf{P}$ itself must all be unity, since

$$\mathbf{i}'\mathbf{P} = \mathbf{i}'\hat{\mathbf{y}}\mathbf{C}'\hat{\mathbf{w}}^{-1}\mathbf{C} = (\mathbf{Cy})'\hat{\mathbf{w}}^{-1}\mathbf{C} = \mathbf{w}'\hat{\mathbf{w}}^{-1}\mathbf{C} = \mathbf{i}'\mathbf{C} = \phi\mathbf{i}'$$

or equivalently $\mathbf{i}'(\phi\mathbf{I} - \mathbf{P}) = 0.$ (7.27)

The last equation shows that the left-hand eigenvector of $\mathbf{P}$, and therefore the eigenprices appropriate to the 'cost-minimizing' situation would have to be unity throughout.

In the ideal situation we are contemplating, therefore, the criteria $\mathbf{k}'$ will equal $\mathbf{p}'$, i.e. will have the same value (unity) for all sectors, and no further shift in y could reduce the eigencost-ratio any further. Given that at the same time all prices would coincide with eigenprices $(\mathbf{p}' = \mathbf{i}')$, the situation, if realizable, could be described as the formal optimum in respect of both prices and quantities.

It is, however, a formal optimum only, as it must be remembered that the original pattern of supply from which we had started ($\mathbf{y}$) had been chosen by the sovereign in the economy (consumers, planners, etc.) as the one corresponding most closely to desiderata formulated on social or political grounds. Every departure from y by way of a shift in production targets must therefore entail a shift towards a less desired assortment. A careful balance would need to be struck between the gain in cost-effectiveness from such departures and the loss in satisfaction incurred. These considerations might well severely limit the distance between y and q that can be travelled. Nevertheless minor adjustments in output targets guided by the criteria k may well be possible and desirable.

---

[8] By substituting for $\mathbf{Cy}$ from (7.22).

7.4 Eigenyield and Price Deviance

When comparing the current price system of different economies it is convenient to extract in each case a statistic which measures its departure from eigenprices — the 'price deviance', d, in the case of commodity prices, and the 'rental deviance', e, in the case of factor-norms. With eigenprices scaled to GNP current price- and norm-coefficients are by definition equal to unity (Sect.2.3), and the deviances in question will therefore be $p_r - 1$ and $r_r - 1$ for any individual sector **r**. The deviances for the economy as a whole can be defined as the root-mean square of all sectoral deviances weighted by their importance in GNP at commodity prices or national income at factor-cost, (y_r/y_0 and w_r/w_0), i.e.

$$d^2 = \Sigma y(p-1)^2/y_0 \text{ and } e^2 = \Sigma w(r-1)^2/w_0. \tag{7.28}$$

It follows that

$$d^2y = \Sigma y(p^2 - 2p + 1) = p'\hat{y}p - 2y_* + y_0 \tag{7.29}$$

and $\qquad e^2w = \Sigma w(r^2 - 2r + 1) = r'\hat{w}r - 2w_* + w_0,$

where the symbols with subscripts $_0$ and $_*$ denote totals in current and eigenprices respectively. Given the scaling of eigenprices and eigen-rentals, i.e. $y_* = y_0$ and $w_* = w_0$, the equations simplify to

$$y_0(d^2 + 1) = p'\hat{y}p \text{ and } w_0(e^2 + 1) = r'\hat{w}r. \tag{7.30}$$

It only remains therefore to find a nexus between $p'\hat{y}p$ and $r'\hat{w}r$, a task which requires some tedious algebra:

$p'\hat{y}p = 1/\phi p'\hat{y}C'r$ by virtue of (3.26)

$\qquad = 1/\phi p'\hat{y}\hat{z}^{-1}\overline{D}'W'r$ since $C = B\overline{A} = W\hat{z}^{-1}\overline{A} =$

$$W(\hat{z} - X)^{-1} = W\overline{D}\hat{z}^{-1} \quad (7.31)$$

$\qquad = 1/\phi p'\hat{s}\overline{D}'W'r = 1/\phi p'V'R'\hat{w}r = 1/\phi p'N\hat{w}r =$

$1/\phi r'\hat{w}r$ by virtue of (7.32).

Taking equations (7.30) and (7.31) together, we find that

$$y_0(d^2 + 1) = 1/\phi w_0(e^2 + 1) \text{ or } \phi = (w_0/y_0)(e^2 + 1/d^2 + 1). \tag{7.33}$$

We have thus established that the eigencost-ratio depends on the current cost-ratio (w_0/y_0) and a factor varying directly with the rental deviance, e, and inversely with the price deviance, d.

This result provides support for the presumption that, given current cost-ratios and rental deviances, economies will benefit from lower eigencost-ratios to the extent that their price systems approach the 'rational' ideal of eigenprices. We might therefore expect free enterprise economies, with their prices a better approach to competitive levels, to show lower eigencost-ratios than centrally planned economies with prices imposed by planners without knowledge of or regard to competitive levels. This effect is, however, swamped by a current cost-ratio (w_0/y_0) often drastically depressed by a price structure that underprices mass-consumption goods through subsidization in relation to investment or defence goods, and we should not be surprised if the eigencost-ratios of different countries showed a hierarchy completely out of step with their competitiveness, whether intuitively perceived or calculated as their departure from eigenprices (price deviances).

7.5 Eigenprices in Disequilibrium

Our definition of eigenprices so far has been derived from economies assumed to be in equilibrium; for given the technology ($\mathbf{A}, \mathbf{B}$) and the allocation of factors ($\hat{\mathbf{W}}, \mathbf{I}$), a single set of final uses ($\mathbf{y}$) in the defining equation uniquely determined the eigenprices of commodities:

$$\mathbf{P}'(\phi\mathbf{I} - \mathbf{P} = \mathbf{p}'(\phi\mathbf{I} - \hat{\mathbf{y}}\mathbf{C}'\hat{\mathbf{w}}^{-1}\mathbf{C}\mathbf{E}') = 0. \qquad (7.34)$$

There was no need to identify the vector $\mathbf{y}$ in this equation as either the bill of final *demands* or the *supply* of final goods and services, as it was tacitly assumed that there would be no discrepancy between the two. In Sect. 7.2, for instance, any change in $\mathbf{y}$, such as an addition to demand by $d\mathbf{y}$ to $\overline{\mathbf{y}}$ was assumed to bring about a consequential change in the norm-cost matrix from P to $\overline{\mathbf{P}}(=\overline{\mathbf{y}}\mathbf{C}'\hat{\mathbf{w}}^{-1}\mathbf{C}\mathbf{E}')$, thus changing eigenprices and eigenrentals to take account of the improved technology and/or factor allocation required to meet the increased demand. It is for this reason that changes in $\mathbf{y}$ brought about by increased *demand* for one or more final goods could not in their effects on eigenprices be distinguished from equal changes in *supply*.

The matter is quite different if we allow disequilibrium situations to arise. Suppose an increase in demand from $\mathbf{y}$ to $\bar{\mathbf{y}}$ takes place without a matching change in technology ($\mathbf{C}$) or factor employment ($\hat{\mathbf{w}}$, $\mathbf{E}$). We cannot then interpret the set of eigenprices and eigenrentals mechanically derived from (7.34) by substituting $\hat{\bar{\mathbf{y}}}$ for $\hat{\mathbf{y}}$ as the proper eigenprices of the new system, since $\mathbf{r}'$ no longer measures the *actual* revenue productivities of the factors (or $\mathbf{p}'$ those of the commodity inputs); for we know that the resources available are only capable of producing $\mathbf{y}$, not $\bar{\mathbf{y}}$. To measure the new revenue productivities the total sectoral outputs $\mathbf{z}$ would have to be adjusted to the new demands by increasing them from $\bar{\mathbf{A}}\mathbf{y}$ to $\bar{\mathbf{A}}\bar{\mathbf{y}}$, thus requiring a change in factor employment from $\mathbf{w}(= \mathbf{B}\bar{\mathbf{A}}\mathbf{y})$ to $\bar{\mathbf{w}}(= \mathbf{B}\bar{\mathbf{A}}\bar{\mathbf{y}})$, unless the technologies ($\mathbf{A}$, $\mathbf{B}$) improved sufficiently to meet the new demand without additional factor inputs. As long as no such changes occur, the solution of (7.34) with only $\hat{\mathbf{y}}$ replaced by $\hat{\bar{\mathbf{y}}}$, say $\bar{\mathbf{p}}'$ and $\bar{\mathbf{r}}'$, far from reflecting the revenue productivities as they *really* are, measure only those *required* to produce $\bar{\mathbf{y}}$ with technologies and factor-employments capable of producing only $\mathbf{y}$, and are therefore more properly referred to as 'shadow eigenprices' and 'shadow norms'. They are simply the left-hand eigenvectors of the matrix $\mathbf{P}(= \hat{\mathbf{y}}\mathbf{M})$ in which $\hat{\mathbf{y}}$ may take on different values without the consequential changes in $\mathbf{M}$.

The right-hand eigenvectors of the same matrix, to be known as the shadow eigenfinals, can again be interpreted as the warranted supply of the economy (as they were in Sect. 7.1), with the proviso that demand changes are accompanied by appropriate changes in the revenue productivities of factors and commodity inputs occurring spontaneously without shifts in technology or factor allocations. In this case, however, the shadow eigenfinals $\bar{\mathbf{q}}$ are genuine duals of the prices $\bar{\mathbf{p}}'$, since they are the right-hand eigenvectors of the same matrix that has $\bar{\mathbf{p}}'$ as its left-hand eigenvector (in contrast to the actual eigenprices and eigenfinals whose relationship is more complicated).

This opens the way to establishing a direct link between the (shadow) eigenprice of a commodity, say r, and a characteristic of its output volume which might be described as its scarcity as induced by the structure of the economy as a whole. With q_r identified as the warranted supply the latter could be defined as

$$\sigma_r \equiv q_r/y_r - 1, \tag{7.35}$$

an expression which varies from an upper limit of ∞ (for $y = 0$) to reach the value zero when there is no scarcity ($y_r = q_r$), and a lower limit of -1 when supply is unlimited ($y_r = \infty$).

Further, given that q_r equals y_r valued at its eigenprice $p_r y_r$ (7.6) or $\bar{p}_r y_r$ when account is taken of the complications of Sect. 7.4, the ratio on the right-hand side of (7.29) is seen to equal $\bar{p}_r$, thus establishing that

$$\bar{p}_r \equiv \sigma_r + 1. \tag{7.36}$$

In fact, the (shadow) eigenprice of a commodity measures not merely its cost and utility, but can also serve as an index of its scarcity in relation to the output warranted by the overall structure of supply and demand.

Perhaps this interpretation has greater import for the eigenprice system in the context of production factors, whose eigenrentals or norms have so far only been derived from the utility-side, since they are by definition not produced by commodity- or factor-inputs and cannot therefore be valued from the cost-side as commodities are, to establish the identity of the two valuations which is, after all, the hallmark of eigenprices. If a factor, r, is fully employed, thus allowing w_r to be interpreted as its total availability as well as its total use, a proper measure of its scarcity would be

$$\sigma_r \equiv g_r / w_r - 1, \tag{7.37}$$

which by virtue of (7.7) equals $\bar{r}_r - 1$, thus showing the (shadow) eigenrental to equal the index of scarcity

$$\bar{r}_r \equiv \sigma_r + 1. \tag{7.38}$$

This goes a considerable way towards making good the deficiency of the so far only one-sided definition of factor-rentals ($\mathbf{r}$ or $\bar{\mathbf{r}}$) by bringing supply-constraints into play as co-determinants of their values on a par with demand factors (utility), with the scarcity of factor resources replacing costs which can only be invoked in that role in the case of commodities.

8

A Tentative Verdict on Eigenprices

8.1 A Summary of Basic Characteristics

THE many ramifications and parallels of eigenprices we have passed in review may have confused and exhausted the reader to the point where the essential meaning and purport of this unfamiliar price-concept have been lost. It may be helpful, therefore, to offer a short and non-rigorous recapitulation at this point.

It seems best to start with the key concept of the eigencost-ratio ϕ, the eigenvalue of a defined matrix, from which the whole system takes its name.

Imagine a government forced to observe two principles in its revenue-raising (possibly imposed by some legally enthroned supranational watchdog or legislative commission):

1. It is debarred from enforcing unilateral transfers (i.e. direct taxes) out of incomes once they have accrued in return for factor services rendered, as this is regarded as spoliation. It can therefore get its (unearned) revenue only by 'indirect' (price-boosting) taxation.
2. Its taxes must not discriminate against any factor or branch of production.

The upshot of this would be a value added tax (VAT) levied at a uniform rate from all sectors of production. The eigenyield $\sigma_* (= 1/\phi_* - 1)$ is then the VAT rate the government would be able to impose if all factors earned their 'due' income (= marginal revenue productivity) without monopoly rents or other economically unjustified perks obtained by extortion or deceit, and if all products were sold at factor cost plus the VAT (= uniformly marked-up marginal cost). We believe we have shown that this VAT rate is computable and a unique function[1]

---

[1] But for problems relating to the existence and uniqueness of an economically meaningful dominant eigenroot of the relevant valuation matrices $\mathbf{F}$ and $\mathbf{P}$ (3.30).

of the coefficients and quotas of the 'Leontief technology'.[2] The corresponding factor-rentals and prices form the system of eigenprices—equally unique (up to a multiplicative constant) and specific to the economy under review.

We believe that these prices can be used for the computation of internal ratios of a structural or cost-benefit kind, and can enable unbiased comparisons of these to be made across time, space, and economic systems. The index-number problem is thereby avoided for *ratio* comparisons, though not for comparisons of *absolutes*; the latter must still await the formulation of internationally valid eigenprice systems which, though possibly definable on similar principles, are left outside the scope of this book as unfinished business.

For the computation of ϕ_* the direct taxes actually imposed ought to be obtained from factor-incomes before the calculation begins. If they cannot be (for lack of statistics), the ϕ-measure and corresponding eigenyield σ are vitiated. If they can be, these measures are clearly affected by arbitrary tax rates as well as technological imperatives, but are still meaningful if the tax rates are imposed by a democratically elected government and therefore represent what the factor-owners are collectively prepared to put up with. Even where tax rates are undemocratically enforced, however, they retain an economic meaning as measures of what the government is able to 'get out' of the factors, however unwilling they may be. Our σ is therefore best regarded not as a measure of efficiency *per* se, but as the combined effect of efficiency and self-abnegation (voluntary or enforced) which is perhaps best captured by the notion of 'cost effectiveness'. Inefficient military dictatorship might achieve lower ϕ_* (higher σ_*) than efficient consumer societies under the sway of free collective bargaining. Just as growth in productivity can fail to benefit living standards owing to faster population growth, so superiority in technology and the state of the arts might fail to yield greater cost effectiveness owing to parallel leads in real wages, profit-taking, and consumerism.

We conclude that the ϕ_*-measure must be treated with circumspection, but that it does capture a characteristic of the economy that is worth watching and comparing between different times, countries, and economic systems.

[2] Including also factor-input coefficients valued at the remuneration exacted or accepted by the factor-owners concerned.

8.2 Possible Uses

International and intertemporal comparison

This aspect of the matter has been fully explored in previous chapters and, indeed, provided the first impetus for the designing and construction of eigenprices. It is the comparison of ratios that is at issue, to be sure, and not a comparison of aggregates or absolute levels; but in this restricted sphere at least it may fairly be claimed that eigenprices are unbiased and relevant standards of comparison. They measure economic flows in terms of a yardstick reflecting each economy's own implicit view of the relative urgency of wants and scarcity of resources—the view that has motivated the economy to produce the observed network of physical flows in what was presumably a search for the greatest possible satisfaction of wants, whether individual or collective, in the face of existing constraints.

In Part III we shall test the general plausibility of the results obtainable from using eigenprices in this way.

Diagnostic use

Standardized eigenprices below unity reflect an overvaluation of the relevant sectoral products in terms of the operative price system, and therefore pinpoint the existence of monopoly elements or other conditions enhancing the capacity of the sectoral producers to exact higher rewards from their buyers than their rationally measured contributions to the economy justify. The same is true of factor-owners whose eigenrentals are below unity. Unless distributional considerations outweigh purely economic criteria, therefore, these deviations present a prima-facie case for scrutinizing institutional arrangements, customs, or tax-subsidy regimes with a view to reducing such excessive rewards in the interests of allocative efficiency. The signal that this was on the way to being achieved would be the gradual reduction of the offending prices towards the level of the corresponding eigenprices. To the extent that this would not automatically bring about the raising in the price of *under*valued commodities or factors (those with eigenprices *above* unity), opposite measures would need to be undertaken to counteract the non-economic disabilities under which these sectors (or factors) were operating.

In countries where rentals and prices are centrally controlled, of course, the adjustment in the direction of eigenprices could be undertaken by altering operative prices directly by fiat. However, if this were not accompanied by institutional measures to remove the concentrations of extra-economic power or disadvantage, it would result in putatively undesired changes in the final physical flows produced. In either case, therefore, the response to deviations from eigenprices would need to contain a strong element of institutional, legal, or fiscal readjustment. The mere change of operative prices to bring them into line with eigenprices would not be enough, unless such a movement was the result of deeper changes in the necessary direction.

It can therefore be said that eigenprices provide the means for a diagnosis of dysfunctions in the economy, but cannot by themselves be regarded as a remedy.

Functional use

A government that wished to replace a command economy subject to physical planning and control by a market orientated one yielding the same final physical flows or some other pre-defined set of final flows (y) for which it had a preference could, in the absence of friction, rely on a centrally decreed price structure for products and factors corresponding to the desired system's eigenprices. It would need to compute these from the desired bill of final goods y by first ascertaining the gross output flows needed from the sectors, i.e. $z = \overline{A}y$ (3.7), then computing the quota-matrix $D = \hat{z}A\hat{z}^{-1}$ (3.16). This, in conjunction with the 'factor technology' and factor-quotas B and R, would enable it to find the cost-and norm-matrices, $C = B\overline{A}$ (3.11) and $N = \hat{s}\overline{D}'E'$ and hence their product, $F = CN$ (3.28). The dominant eigenvalue of the latter ϕ_*, would furnish the uniform rate of VAT ($\sigma_* = (1/\phi_*) - 1$) to be levied on each sector to generate the eigenprices of commodities (p') from the eigenprices of the factors (r') that emerge as the left-hand eigenvector of F corresponding to ϕ. Thus, a knowledge of the assumed technologies A, B, and $\hat{S}$ and the total factor utilization w, in conjunction with the desired bill of final goods y, would furnish the factor- and product-price system to be enforced in substitution for physical targets. As long as institutional arrangements could ensure the competitive character of all markets, prevent the emergence of monopoly or other extra-economic friction, and maintain profit-maximizing behaviour, the price-planning could by this means achieve the result that may have eluded quantitative planners.

No doubt further analysis could reveal how price-planning of this sort could be combined with a residue of quantity-planning in certain crucial sectors, although to the extent that the latter would produce dysfunctions, the price-planners might be faced with awkward problems of the second-best variety.

It should be evident from this that, short of certain coincidences between the technology and allocation scheme resulting from the final bill of goods and the consumption patterns of working households, eigenprices could have a clearer and more effective functional role than traditional cost-fetishist price systems like Marxian labour-values, production prices, or the 'two-channel' prices recently so much in vogue in some European people's democracies.

8.3 Caveats and Open Questions

Having now arrived at the end of the theoretical exposition of eigen-prices, it is essential to pass in review the qualifications, defects, and loose ends that must abound in a new concept of this kind, and have so far been mentioned only in passing, if at all. They ought to be summarized and displayed to better disadvantage as a challenge to critics and improvers—without, however, claiming that anything like an exhaustive list has been achieved.

1. Eigenprices optimize nothing. They assume that the usual optimization problems have already been solved, possibly on the basis of some social welfare function that is left out of sight, with the result of yielding the technical coefficients, demand structure, and factor allocation that we observe to be at work in the economy under review. By equating product-prices to marginal costs (in terms of factor-rentals and each other) and factor-rentals to marginal revenue productivities (in terms of product-prices), they reveal a price structure that would have induced the economy to select the quantitative flows actually observed in search of an achievable optimum, and thereby give expression to the implicit view on the desirability of products and the scarcity of factors taken by the economy itself. They are thus a way of describing or explaining what is happening, not what ought to happen or what would happen if certain desiderata were met.

2. Eigenprices can at best measure efficiency at given levels of resource utilization. They contribute nothing to an appraisal of the economic system as a mobilizer or steward of the resources *available* to it. A system could be excellent in making the best possible use of all the resources it utilizes, but abysmal in drawing the stock of available resources into production—by keeping it idle or depleting it with reckless unconcern for the future. Indeed, the most glaring deficiencies of present or past systems may lie precisely in their inability to secure the full or rationally full employment of resources. One may conjecture that performance in this respect will depend on the general equilibrium characteristics thrown up by various systems, their reactions to rationing situations, multiplier effects, and the propagation of disequilibria between sectors, as treated in models of 'dual-decision' hypotheses, with Drèze- and Malinvaud-type equilibria. Our own model and its eigenprice structure is completely silent on all-important performance criteria of this type.

3. Eigenprices are heavily dependent on the measurement of physical flows, particularly where such flows are inferred rather than directly observable. This applies with particular force in the case of resources or factors of production whose physical flows cannot, without overstraining our conceptual apparatus, be measured independently of revenues or output values. The difficulties of measuring physical capital stock are well known and unresolved; so are the conundrums posed by the physical measurement of entrepreneurship, skill, or talent. Yet our concept of eigenprices blithely assumes that we can identify and unambiguously measure such flows as they are absorbed in various branches of production, and establish utilization-coefficients and quotas on this basis. The scope that this opens up for arbitrary choice and procedures justified by mere convention may well be greater than unbiased comparisons can bear.

4. Eigencost-ratios and eigenprices depend not only on the range and nature of physical factor flows that our statistical ingenuity may have brought to light, but also on the definition of the rewards in terms of which they are measured. Where this is only done unpurged of direct taxes, the eigencost-ratios will be overestimates of the true final-use flows mortgaged to the factors, and the eigenyield correspondingly understated, possibly even to the extent of reversing its sign from positive to negative. It is doubtful, however, if any statistical basis for estimating net-of-tax factor-rewards will in practice be available for any real economy in time or space. Our comparisons

will therefore inject a substantial bias against economies relying more on direct taxation for government revenue and in favour of those relying on indirect taxes. The mechanical reduction of all pre-tax factor-flows in the ratio that direct taxes bear to GNP would mitigate this, but would fail to differentiate between factor-owners, who are typically subject to widely different rates of direct taxation.

5. Calculated eigenprices are vulnerable to the frequent derogations from the uniform pricing rule between different consumers of the same product on which the raw input–output data are assumed to be based. The systematic price discrimination practised by some countries (in particular by centrally planned economies where collective farm markets sell agricultural products at 'free' or 'semi-free' prices greatly inflated in comparison with similar sales through the State retail network) is probably the most conspicuous case in point.

On a strict interpretation of the eigenprice concept such divergent selling ought to be split off and treated as proceeding from a separate sector before the input–output table is processed, a sector to be credited with the revenues obtained from the differentially priced sales and debited with the costs of the original sector inputs in proportions derived from the relative importance of the discriminated market. The same procedure ought to be applied to all supplier industries separately where particular consumers (e.g. agriculture) are disadvantaged or favoured by discriminatory prices for their inputs. The statistical effort and scope for error of such procedures are probably too large to justify this search for the extra precision obtainable, and the inexactitudes incurred by assuming non-discriminatory pricing (as has been done in the empirical parts of this book) may be judged a fair price to pay for the practical feasibility of the enterprise.

A good deal of research remains to be done on the likely size and directions of errors from the neglect of discriminatory pricing, but this must be left to future commentators.

6. Eigenprices are intended to reproduce the substratum of perfectly competitive prices hidden in the tangled networks of real economies beset by imperfections or wilful distortions. To the extent they are successful in this they naturally share all the inadequacies of which prices as they might emerge from universally competitive behaviour are traditionally and rightly accused. They fail to take account of inevitable derogations from perfect competition in those sectors which produce public goods, thereby ruling out universal optimization and enforcing second-best solutions on the rest of the economy.

They neglect externalities, scale economies, and distributional aspects of pricing. Above all, they are blind to social policy and social purpose. Add to this their essentially static nature and vulnerability to errors of compilation and aggregation in input–output tables, and our elaborate edifice may well dissolve into thin air, as so many of the best-laid schemes of mice and men.

Should we, then, consign the concept of eigenprices without further ceremony to the dustbin of speculative theory? This must be left to the critical reader to decide. But we can at least claim that the concept is no further from operational usefulness than a host of other price concepts that have profoundly influenced economic thought, and even policy, throughout historical time. It may, in particular, commend itself as a feasible method of overcoming the limits of a 'one-factor' world and various cost-based value-constructs which neglect the obvious role of utility or usefulness as a co-operant element in the formation of value. It is this, in our submission, that entitles it to serious consideration and further thought.

PART III

Eigenprices: A Foray into the Real World

9

Cross-Section Pilot Survey

9.1 Introduction to the Pilot Survey

NO theoretical construct as esoteric and unfamiliar as eigenprices should be offered to the public without some attempt, however cursory, to test its performance as a tool of analysis for the real world, whether as a pointer to the curing of ills or as a diagnosis for imperfections. With this in mind we venture to exhibit the results of two very different and qualitatively unequal experiments undertaken on the witch's brew of statistical data which the world has at present on offer.

The first of these is in the nature of a pilot survey designed to bring together a number of countries following divers policies, traditions, and ideologies, in an attempt to compare their eigenprices and related statistics at identical—or at least similar—points in time. This had to be undertaken under pressure of time and with inadequate means upon 'untreated' data, although devoted and expert help with computing facilities was generously offered and ruthlessly exploited.[1]

The dubiousness of the results will become evident as the makeshift methodology unfolds, and will be re-emphasized in fairness to the reader at as many points as concern over tedium will allow.

[1] For work carried forward from the first edition relating to the early 1970s I would like to record my gratitude to Mr Colin Carpenter of the Mathematical Department of Bradford University, who fought his way through the maze of that University's uniquely rich data-base on input–output statistics and put them to work in fulfilment of my intentions, and to Mr Guiseppe Mazzarino of the Oxford University Institute of Economics and Statistics, who acceded to my ever-changing demands with tolerance, courtesy, and consummate skill.

These contributions, however important and valuable, are greatly exceeded by the collaborative efforts of Dr Erik Dietzenbacher of the University of Groningen in The Netherlands. Not only did he accomplish the daunting task of assembling the 'harmonized' 1980 data on EEC countries and putting them through the massive and elaborate computations required, but also applied his considerable mathematical skills to a penetrating analysis of various facets of the eigenprice concept, and furnished a number of insights of great value and encouragement to the author. I am happy to record my particular gratitude to him as well as my admiration for his devoted and accomplished work.

Substantially fewer reservations need to be entered about the second experiment, reported in the Special Annex by Professor A. E. Steenge, which supplements the author's *ad hoc* cross-section tests by a more intensive exploration of two particularly well-documented countries, The Netherlands and Hungary, in which a number of consecutive years could be studied, with all the additional and corrective insights that only time-series analysis can furnish. Professor Steenge's residence in the first country and extended visits to the second have made it possible to penetrate further into the exact nature of the data offered, to question their validity in some instances, and to adapt them more closely to the purpose in hand. I am therefore inclined to place greater reliance on his results than on my own, even though there is little scope for direct comparison or contradiction between the two.

However that may be, it would be misguided to regard the results of either experiment as a litmus test of the relevance or validity of eigenprices, whether in a positive or negative sense. It would indeed be disappointing, and possibly destructive of further interest attaching to the methodology, if they did no more than confirm our preconceptions in regard to the countries under review. Some surprises, perplexities, and even counter-intuitive findings must clearly be expected, and all that can legitimately be hoped for is that the results, however much they may disturb us, should not be devoid of meaning, or so offensive to common sense as to invite instant dismissal. If that is so, we can at least claim that the first hurdle has been passed and the way is clear to the more thorough and stringent tests that must surely follow before the methodology can hope to gain acceptance.

It must be left to the reader to judge how well this hurdle has been negotiated, but let him be fully aware that it is an exercise only to *illustrate* what could be achieved, and not to reveal where the achievement will lead us. The horse is merely showing his paces, and not completing—let alone winning—the race.

9.2 The Data

At the time work proceeded on the first edition of this book in the early 1980s the input–output tables made available by the major countries, though fully articulated in terms of the matrices $\mathbf{X}$, $\mathbf{Y}$, and $\mathbf{W}$, were based on a bewildering variety of national accounting concepts, price systems, input definitions, etc. Their standardization and adaptation to the requirements of eigenprice computations as proposed in this book could have provided a rich vineyard in which many could have laboured for years, using resources and skills far beyond the reach, let alone the grasp, of this author. The tentative results of his pilot survey as offered here are therefore no more than a crude attempt to 'test the air', to ascertain whether an off-the-cuff experiment with ill-adapted data, taken wherever and in whatever form they happen to be available, will yield *meaningful* results, however uncertain or distorted they may later turn out to be. Our choice of countries and benchmark years at the beginning of the 1970s and earlier was determined by nothing more than easy availability, and had to accept the data in their crude form without any attempt to adjust or even interpret them where unclarity remained. When the precise meaning of data was doubtful, as in the case of capital services, imports (complementary, competitive, or both), or exports (gross or net), we simply assumed that it conformed to our requirements and set to work without further ado. Our results, displayed in the tables below, must be regarded in this light and not invested with an authoritativeness or finality to which they do not pretend.

The pitfalls opened up by this procedure, to mention but a few, are due to some countries quoting imports inclusive of import duties while others record them ex-tax, to different pricing conventions underlying official tables varying between factor-costs, producer prices, consumer prices, or a mixture of the last two, with intermediate and final outputs sometimes differently treated, or variations in the units of observation serving as the origins or destinations of the published flows. These may disaggregate the economy into industries, commodities, or establishments, thus affecting the intra-sector turnovers in the main diagonal of the table to an unknown extent. Add to all this that some statistical bureaux, lacking funds, time, or skilled manpower, substitute rules of thumb for painstaking and costly surveys, sometimes not even disclosing such practices, and it will be clear that the input–output statistics available must lure the experimenter with eigenprices into a minefield through which only impossibly fine tooth-combing or extraordinary luck can secure a passage unscathed.

We may derive some comfort from the fact that at least for the 1980-economies quoted here (1979 in the case of the UK) the tables are purportedly couched in producer prices throughout and generally harmonized according to SNA conventions,[2] so that distortions might be expected to affect all countries in similar ways without affecting their relative standing. It was this hope, as well as the desirability of updating earlier findings, which emboldened the author to offer the empirical extensions of the second edition. Even here, however, it is far from clear that harmonization has proceeded far enough and that the figures, for all the increased expertise and effort which has gone into their collection, can be accepted at face value in all instances.

We must conclude therefore that short of a large-scale, sustained research effort with sufficient resources and authority to enlist the co-operation of national bureaux of statistics, eigenprice calculations are bound to remain the hazardous undertakings exemplified in this book. A strict regard for truth and rigour would have compelled us to forgo the pilot survey altogether and to present the reader with nothing but the dry bones of theory. We have chosen the more perilous, not to say heroic course, but let the reader beware!

9.3 The Problem of Aggregation

It must have occurred to the reader by now that the ideal intersectoral flow table demanded by our methodology would be one in which the disaggregation of the economy went far enough to isolate production units or groupings producing no more than one homogeneous service or commodity. This might necessitate a table with anything from 200 to at least 500 sectors, depending on the size and complexity of the economy. As will be seen from the first column of Table 9.1, however, the input–output tables available are consolidations of such 'basic sectors' into some thirty to sixty sector groupings whose homogeneity in the above sense takes more than the eye of faith to see. A condensation-ratio in the region 7 : 1, such as must be assumed in most of these cases, is bound to give rise to aggregation errors whose direction and size is notoriously difficult, if not impossible, to gauge. The only way in which we may hope to obtain an indication of the robustness or sensitivity of our results in the face of such condensation would appear to be the parallel computation of our ratios and prices with data subjected to a similar degree of condensation in comparison with those presented by the original input–output tables.

[2] The United Nations' System of National Accounts, see e.g. *Eurostat—National Accounts ESA, Input–Output Tables 1980*, Theme 2, Series C, EEC, Brussels, 1986.

As may be seen from Table 9.1, such a condensation has the effect of reducing the eigencost-ratio, but not by as much as would alter it out of all recognition. The most substantial aggregation errors occur in the case of the UK in 1972 (– 13.2 per cent) and Sweden in 1969 (– 15.3 per cent). For the rest, they vary between 0.77 and 6.2 per cent. In any case the order of the economies listed remains virtually unaffected by the consolidation. We may conclude with due caution, therefore, that in this respect at least the distorting effects of aggregation, though noticeable, are unlikely to be so damaging as to make eigenprice calculations totally useless.

This is confirmed by the out-turn of eigenprices themselves (Table 9.3) which are in general only marginally affected by pre-consolidation, although there are some notable exceptions: Chemicals (D) are overpriced in Spain ($P_* < 1$) on micro-sector calculations, but emerge slightly *under*priced from the pre-consolidation exercise. The same is true in Belgium and W. Germany, while the opposite holds for Denmark, though the discrepancies in these cases are only marginal.

Structural eigenratios (Table 9.4) are also largely unaffected by our condensation as far as production sectors are concerned, but show discrepancies in the case of primary inputs, especially in W. Germany, where the consolidation results in a substantial shift in GNP-components from eigenyield to the wage categories. For the rest, the results emerging from pre- and post-consolidations are remarkably similar and, indeed, virtually coincident when allowance for rounding errors is made.

All in all, one may be tempted to conclude that the methodology is under only relatively weak threat from aggregation errors. We must, however, enter two caveats. Even a slight reduction in the eigencost ratio is bound to have the effect of raising the eigenyield $\sigma^* (= 1/\phi_* - 1)$ quite sharply, resulting, in some cases, in distortions by a factor of 2–5. It may be better therefore to give preference to ϕ over σ when quoting a characteristic parameter for various economies, even though the latter may have greater intuitive appeal. In the second place, the disturbing effects of aggregation may not be determined by the condensation-ratio independently of the *level* of aggregation to which that ratio is applied. Reducing articulation in the ratio 7 : 1 from sixty to nine sectors may well have different effects from those resulting from reducing it in the same ratio from 500 to sixty sectors, quite apart from the fact that the effects must depend on the exact structure of the original network and the similarity or discrepancies between its several row- or column-structures. To that extent our supplementary exercise cannot be regarded as conclusive, and the robustness of eigenprice calculations under aggregation has not been firmly established. But neither has that of a large variety of input–output-based calculations which have by now gained widespread acceptance.

9.4 Price Deviance and Eigenyield

Since eigenprices are defined as approximations to the perfectly competitive prices that would have generated the given configurations of economic flows, one might well expect operative price systems to differ from them more radically (i.e. expect the price deviances to be larger) in non-market than in market economies. With some notable exceptions this is roughly borne out by the second column of Table 9.1, where the two types of economy tend to appear near the top and the bottom of the table respectively. It must however be borne in mind that the fifteen economies listed differ both in the timing and articulation underlying our exercise, as well as in the reliability of their statistical reporting. Nor should it be forgotten that market economies may also suffer serious price distortions due to monopoly elements, oligopolistic practices, tariff- and non-tariff protection, and differential commodity taxation. Nevertheless the large price deviance of W. Germany (43 per cent in 1980 as against 12.3 per cent ten years earlier)[3] and the growing deviance of the United Kingdom (7.9 per cent in 1979 compared with 3.8 per cent in 1963)[4] come as a surprise. The increase in the UK's distortion in the ten years preceding 1979 may be due in part to the gain in importance of sector B (including oil-extraction) which may be expected to operate in less competitive conditions than the rest of the economy. The much larger increase in Germany's price distortion may also be associated with a shift from more to less competitive branches, particularly metals and engineering which gained in importance at the expense of agriculture, the food industry, and 'other manufacturing'. This, however, can hardly account for more than a fraction of the change, the major part of which must probably be ascribed to progressive derogations from competi-

---

[3] As calculated on a slightly different basis in the first edition of this book (*Cost, Use, and Value*, p. 116).

[4] Ibid.

tion in individual branches due to monopolization and mergers. Even this can hardly account for so spectacular a change, and we must once again remind ourselves that our calculations, being illustrative only, are too imperfect to give reliable results. In any case, the price deviances uncovered do not fly in the face of economic intuition with sufficient force to be summarily dismissed.

Table 9.1. *Fifteen economies in descending order of price deviance*

Economy	Articulation[a]	$\delta(\%)$[b]	$\phi(\%)$[c]
W. Germany 1980	44	43.0	91.3 (85.7)
Poland 1971	32	29.7	46.5 (45.2)
USSR 1972	56	28.6	95.4 (89.5)
Italy 1974	44	22.1	66.5 (66.0)
Czechoslovakia 1973	44	21.5	66.5 (66.0)
Belgium 1980	59	17.0	94.5 (93.1)
Yugoslavia 1972	29	14.5	90.0 (89.3)
Sweden 1969	35	13.4	86.5 (73.3)
Japan 1970	60	12.3	91.0 (90.3)
Denmark 1980	59	11.2	95.6 (94.0)
UK 1980	59	10.7	83.6 (82.5)
Spain 1980	44	8.7	96.8 (96.2)
Portugal 1980	45	8.4	94.7 (93.8)
Netherlands 1980	59	8.1	91.9 (91.3)
UK 1972	60	7.9	96.3 (83.6)

[a] Number of sectors distinguished in original input–output table used (n).

[b] For all 1980 economies computed as the root-mean square of all sectoral deviances weighted by their importance in GNP, i.e.

$$\delta^2 = \Sigma q_i (p_* - 1)^2/q_0, \text{ where } q_i = p_i y_i \text{ and } q_0 = y_* = \Sigma p_i y_i.$$

In the case of earlier economies the weights are *current*-value GNP contributions (q_i/q_0) and the variables inverse-eigenprice deviations from unity, i.e.

$$\delta^2 = \Sigma y_i (p_0 - 1)^2/y_0, \text{ where } p_0 = 1/p_* \text{ and } y_0 = \Sigma p_i y_i = y_*.$$

[c] ϕ is the dominant eigenvalue of the cost-norm matrix $\mathbf{F}(= \mathbf{CN})$,—see Sect. 3.5 and (3.30). Figures in brackets show the result of the same computation performed on the tables when first consolidated (preconsolidated) into the nine sectors of Table 9.3 below.

Sources: For all 1980 economies the input–output tables used are harmonized full tables at producers' prices, see *Eurostat, National Accounts ESA, Input–Output Tables 1980*, Theme 2, Series C, EEC, Brussels, 1986. For earlier economies input–output tables were supplied on tape by courtesy of the University of Bradford data-bank, compiled from published official sources.

Table 9.2. *Fifteen economies in descending order of eigenyield* (σ)

Economy	Articulation[a]	Eigenyield $\sigma(\%)$[b]
UK 1979	59	19.7
Austria 1964	54	16.9[d]
USA 1967[c]	76	16.0[d]
Sweden 1969	35	15.7[d]
Yugoslavia 1972	29	11.0
W. Germany 1970	44	9.9
Japan 1970	60	9.6
W. Germany 1980	44	9.5
Netherlands 1980	59	8.8
Belgium 1980	59	5.9
Portugal 1980	45	5.6
USSR 1980	56	4.8
Denmark 1980	59	4.6
UK 1972	60	3.9[d]
Spain 1980	44	3.3

[a] Number of sectors distinguished in original input–output table (n).

[b] Uniform surplus for all sectors in terms of eigenprices (see Sect. 3.6), related to the eigencost-ratio ϕ by $\sigma = 1/\phi - 1$.

[c] Result of earlier pilot survey; validity particularly doubtful.

[d] Based on final outputs gross of competitive imports and thereby an interpretation of z as total supply becoming available rather than total domestic output only. This is assumed to reduce input-coefficients and -quotas just sufficiently to eliminate the import-inflation of the $\mathbf{X}$-matrix, and allowing competitive imports to be added to complementary imports to form a cost element on a par with other primary inputs.

[*] *Sources*: See note to Table 9.1 above.

Our confidence may be slightly more shaken by the behaviour of our measure of cost effectiveness (low ϕ and high σ) as evidenced in the last columns of Tables 9.1 and 9.2. The seemingly brilliant performance of the United Kingdom in 1979 compared with W. Germany and Japan is of course highly counter-intuitive, in particular when we note that the UK was near the bottom of the league table in 1972. There has, however, been a substantial 'shaking out' of the disguised unemployed due to redundancies in the intervening years, which saw a rise in the number of unemployed (excluding school-leavers) from some 800,000 to over 1.3 million, a process which undoubtedly contributed to the rise in output per person employed. Add to this the progressive squeeze on non-wage incomes and the nearly fourfold increase in taxes on expenditure and it will be evident that the proportion of the surplus above the rewards of the statistically documented factors of production must have risen substantially. It will cause less surprise to find Spain in 1980 and the USSR in 1972 relegated to fairly low levels of performance, and Sweden and United States to somewhere near the top, though the position of Austria, Yugoslavia, Japan, and W. Germany is not quite what one would expect.

In view of Sect. 7.5 above the lack of correlation between price deviance and eigencost-ratio should not cause undue surprise, particularly when we remind ourselves that a high σ is not necessarily a measure of efficiency in the technological or allocational sense, but may be achieved by depressed factor-rewards arising from political coercion, self-abnegation, or supineness on the part of factor-owners (e.g. labour unions). This need not be accompanied by the underpricing of factors, but could be achieved by an imposed pattern of final demand which assigns to labour and/or other factors relatively low 'proper' rewards (eigenrentals **r**). A shift in government policy from direct to indirect taxation may also help in the deflation of (pre-tax) factor rewards, thus inflating the measured (pre-tax) surplus.

We conclude our comments on Tables 9.1 and 9.2 with the plea that, given the reservations we have repeatedly made, their findings do not invalidate the methodology by producing self-contradictory, nonsensical, or irrelevant results; and feel encouraged, with due diffidence, to advance the claim that the method appears to justify further and more detailed exploration beyond the scope of this book.

9.5 Measured Eigenprices and Current Pricing Behaviour

Before venturing to comment on Table 9.3, the author must once again sound his oft-repeated warning note, lest readers accuse him of representing as gospel truth a set of experimental findings which are at best illustrations of the application of his methodology to defective and ill-adapted data.

If for the moment we suspend scepticism and look down the p_*-columns of Table 9.3 we find that in our economies agricultural commodities appear to be generally underpriced with a margin of up to 6.8 per cent (Spain), except in Benelux where they are correctly priced and in W. Germany where they seem to be overpriced by nearly 9 per cent. Processed foods, drinks, and tobacco, on the other hand, tend to be overpriced, particularly in W. Germany and the UK, where the margin is around 12 per cent. Chemicals, plastics, and rubber are

Table 9.3. *Eigenprices* $(p*)$[a] *and current pricing* (p_0)[b] *in 1980*

Prod'n. sector[c]	Belgium $p*$	Belgium p_0	Denmark $p*$	Denmark p_0	Netherlands $p*$	Netherlands p_0	Spain $p*$	Spain p_0	Portugal $p*$	Portugal p_0	United Kingdom (1979) $p*$	United Kingdom (1979) p_0	W. Germany $p*$	W. Germany p_0
A	0.987 (.99)	0.957	1.045 (1.03)	0.957	1.000 (0.99)	1.000	1.073 (1.09)	0.932	1.062 (1.06)	0.942	1.043 (1.018)	0.959	0.918 (0.96)	1.089
B	0.990 (1.00)	1.01	0.910 (0.938)	1.10	0.990 (1.0)	1.010	0.922 (0.971)	1.08	1.048 (1.05)	0.954	0.928 (0.942)	1.078	0.953 (0.99)	1.049
C	0.930 (.93)	1.075	0.966 (0.960)	1.03	0.996 (0.99)	1.004	0.969 (0.976)	1.11	0.969 (0.98)	1.032	0.899 (0.878)	1.112	0.886 (0.91)	1.129
D	0.995 (1.01)	1.00	1.022 (1.02)	0.978	0.992 (1.00)	1.01	0.987 (1.01)	1.01	1.043 (1.04)	0.959	1.013 (1.022)	0.987	0.999 (1.02)	1.00
E	1.029 (1.03)	0.972	0.987 (0.99)	1.01	1.035 (1.03)	0.966	0.972 (0.97)	1.03	0.983 (0.988)	1.017	1.077 (1.063)	0.928	1.05 (1.04)	0.951
F	1.023 (1.03)	0.978	1.029 (1.03)	0.972	1.050 (1.05)	0.952	1.000 (1.00)	1.00	1.031 (1.03)	0.970	1.069 (1.058)	0.935	1.06 (1.08)	0.948
G	1.033 (1.03)	0.968	1.035 (1.04)	0.966	1.036 (1.03)	0.952	0.979 (0.994)	1.02	1.026 (1.03)	0.975	1.088 (1.071)	0.919	1.03 (1.05)	0.971
H	1.013 (1.01)	0.987	1.029 (1.02)	0.972	1.027 (1.02)	0.974	0.979 (0.970)	1.02	1.018 (1.026)	0.982	1.086 (1.079)	0.921	1.05 (1.05)	0.952
I	0.997 (0.99)	10.003	1.007 (1.01)	0.993	0.985 (0.985)	1.02	1.021 (1.02)	0.98	0.986 (0.980)	1.01	0.980 (0.989)	1.020	0.986 (0.974)	1.01
Primary inputs	$r*$	r_0	$r*$	r_0	$r*$	r_0	$r*$	r_0	$r*$	r_0	$r*$	r_0	$r*$	r_0
Wages[d]	1.034 (1.0)	0.967	1.009 (1.00)	0.991	1.012 (1.0)	0.893	1.022 (1.00)	0.98	1.014 (0.998)	0.986	1.028 (1.003)	0.973	1.13 (1.0)	0.884
Profit[e]	0.987 (0.99)	1.01	1.052 (1.00)	0.951	0.971 (0.99)	1.03	1.003 (1.00)	1.00	1.003 (0.998)	0.997	0.942 (0.998)	1.062	0.943 (0.99)	1.06
Imports[f]	1.01 (1.01)	0.99	1.004 (0.994)	0.996	1.017 (1.01)	0.98	0.973 (0.99)	1.03	1.03 (1.01)	0.984	1.027 (1.004)	0.974	1.023 (1.01)	0.98

[a] Eigenprice per unit-worth of local currency. Computed by consolidating eigenprices obtained from original (disaggregated) input-output tables for 59 production sectors (Belgium, UK, and Netherlands) or 44 production sectors (W. Germany, Spain, and Portugal) as left-hand eigenvectors of the derived matrix **P** and of the derived matrix **F** (in the case of factors). Bracketed figures show the results when tables are first consolidated into 9 sectors (preconsolidated). All eigenprices are 'scaled' to equate GNP values in the two price systems.

[b] Current price per unit-worth of eigenprice, i.e. reciprocal of $p*$.

[c] A = Agriculture, fishing, and forestry   F = Textiles, leather, clothing
B = Mining, quarrying, and fuel extraction   G = Other manufacturing
C = Food, drink, tobacco   H = Construction
D = Chemicals, plastic, rubber   I = Utilities, transport, trade, and services.
E = Metals and engineering

[d] Including wage-related insurance charges.

[e] Mainly incomes classified as 'operational surplus', assumed to be gross of depreciation charges, but excluding prescribed contributions to public budgets in the nature of production taxes.

[f] Both 'complementary' and 'competitive' where these cannot be distinguished.

often correctly priced, though slightly underpriced in Denmark, Portugal, and the UK. Engineering and metal products are underpriced by as much as 7 per cent in the UK, and by somewhat lesser margins in other countries except Denmark, Spain, and Portugal. Construction is generally underpriced, particularly in the UK (by about 8 per cent), while services tend to be slightly overpriced, except in Denmark.

Among the primary inputs labour appears to be underpaid everywhere except in Spain, while capital (profits) tends to get its just reward, except in Denmark where it is underpaid by about 5 per cent, and in the UK, where it appears to be overpaid by about 2 per cent. Our cavalier treatment of imports whereby competitive and complementary flows are hopelessly mixed up, renders the last row of the table all but meaningless and would disqualify any comment on it as spurious.

Table 9.4. *Cases of substantial overpricing* ($p > 1.25$) [a] *in 1980*

	Belgium	Denmark	Netherlands	Portugal	Spain	UK[b]	W. Germany[c]
Coking		1.2761					
Oil ref'g						1.277[d]	
Water			1.281			1.504	
Nuclear fuel						1.878	
Non-met. minerals							1.281[e]
Beverages	1.338		1.410			1.536	
Tobacco[f]	2.339	4.882	1.805			2.954	
Pulp and paper				1.535			
Bldg and civil eng'g							1.702
Recovery and repairs					1.270		
Credit and insurance		1.624					

[a] Current-price over 25% above eigenprice.

[b] Data for 1979. Earlier overpricing in vegetable and animal fats, and air and sea transport in 1970 (*CUV*, p. 123) no longer in evidence.

[c] W. Germany. Earlier overpricing in crude oil and gas and tobacco in 1970 (*CUV*, p. 123) no longer in evidence.

[d] More substantial overpricing (by a factor of 3.28) was found in 1963 and 1972, see *CUV*, p. 123.

[e] No overpricing found in earlier years investigated, see *CUV*, p. 123.

[f] Overpricing (by factors between 2.6 and 5.2) was found in earlier years also in Czechoslovakia, Italy, Japan, and W. Germany.

In most cases the deviation of current prices from eigenprices is so small as to be almost insignificant, and doubts have been expressed whether, in these circumstances, the whole elaborate exercise is worth undertaking at all.[5] While we have considerable sympathy with readers who may resent being taken through so many hoops only to find themselves where they started, we would like to plead the following in our defence. Even if eigenprices turned out to be identical with current prices in all sectors ($p_* = 1$ in every case), the resulting legitimation of current prices would not be an idle undertaking; for their 'correctness' could not have been known and proved without this exercise. The disenchantment with such an outcome could be likened to the annoyance of a book-keeper who checks a long addition of figures and regrets having done so because the addition turns out to have been correct in the first place. It should also be noted that the observed closeness between current prices and eigenprices emerging from this survey is evident only when eigenprices are consolidated into the nine macro-sectors we have defined—a process in which major discrepancies in different directions are 'averaged out'. When the comparison is between the original micro-price structures, even the average discrepancy varies between 8 and 43 per cent (see the δ-column in Table 9.1), while the eigenprices of individual micro-sectors may deviate from current prices by as much as a factor of 4.9 (see Table 9.4). Indeed, a few micro-sectors might show a pronounced tendency to overpricing in more than one country, and some of the usefulness of our method (if applied to well-adapted data) may lie precisely in pinpointing these in order to provide restrictive practices courts in market economies and price reform commissions in centrally planned ones with prima-facie evidence on the direction that further investigation could usefully take.

9.6 Structural Eigenratios

Owing to the closeness of macro-eigenprices to current price structures, already noted in previous sections, the structural ratios of various economies in the breakdown shown in Table 9.5 are only marginally different from the familiar ones in terms of current prices.

[5] G. Szakolczai in the Discussants' Comments on the author's paper presented at the IEA conference in Athens, Oct. 1981, published in the Conference Proceedings, edited by D. Hague. See also Szakolczai's comments on the translated paper (in Hungarian) in Csikós-Nagy, B. and S. György (eds.), *Alkalmazkodás az új árviszonyokhoz*, Budapest, 1983.

Table 9.5. *Structural eigenratios in various economies in 1980 (% of GNP)*[a]

Sectoral share[b]	Belgium	Denmark	Netherlands	Portugal	Spain	UK 1979	W. Germany
A	1.9 (1.9)	2.2 (2.3)	2.6 (2.6)	4.4 (4.4)	3.8 (3.7)	1.1 (1.1)	1.0 (1.0)
B	11.1 (10.9)	4.0 (3.8)	10.6 (10.5)	3.5 (3.5)	4.7 (4.5)	6.7 (6.6)	5.9 (5.6)
C	7.6 (7.1)	11.9 (12.0)	9.3 (9.3)	11.0 (11.0)	9.8 (9.7)	7.0 (7.2)	6.8 (6.7)
D	6.5 (6.4)	2.8 (2.8)	5.6 (5.6)	3.1 (3.1)	2.4 (2.3)	3.0 (3.0)	4.3 (4.2)
E	14.7 (15.1)	11.4 (11.4)	12.5 (12.6)	11.8 (11.8)	10.9 (11.0)	16.2 (16.4)	20.5 (20.6)
F	4.5 (4.6)	3.0 (2.9)	3.3 (3.3)	9.0 (9.0)	4.0 (4.0)	3.2 (3.2)	4.3 (4.2)
G	5.2 (5.4)	3.2 (3.2)	3.4 (3.4)	4.9 (4.9)	2.9 (2.8)	2.7 (2.8)	3.7 (3.6)
H	8.7 (8.8)	8.3 (8.3)	7.6 (7.6)	12.0 (11.9)	10.5 (10.6)	8.5 (8.5)	10.3 (10.3)
I	39.8 (39.7)	53.3 (53.1)	45.0 (45.0)	40.3 (40.5)	51.0 (51.3)	51.6 (51.2)	43.1 (43.7)
Primary inputs							
Wages etc.[c]	38.2 (39.6)	46.3 (46.5)	39.9 (40.5)	36.3 (36.9)	43.6 (44.5)	50.6 (51.8)	47.8 (53.9)
Profits etc.[d]	14.3 (14.2)	22.4 (23.5)	15.0 (14.6)	28.3 (28.5)	37.8 (37.8)	11.3 (10.6)	17.1 (16.2)
Imports[e]	40.6 (40.8)	25.4 (25.6)	36.4 (36.8)	29.1 (29.3)	14.8 (14.5)	20.6 (21.1)	20.9 (21.2)
Eigenyield[f]	6.9 (5.5)	6.0 (4.4)	8.7 (8.1)	6.2 (5.3)	3.8 (3.2)	17.5 (16.4)	14.2 (8.7)

[a] Figures in brackets show the result of parallel computations on the same data in pre-consolidated form.

[b] A = Agriculture, fishing, and forestry
　　B = Mining, quarrying, and fuel extraction
　　C = Food, drink, and tobacco
　　D = Chemicals, plastic, and rubber
　　E = Metals and engineering
　　F = Textiles, leather, footwear
　　G = Other manufacturing
　　H = Construction
　　I = Utilities, transport, trade, and services

[c] Including wage-related compulsory insurance charges.

[d] Mainly incomes classified as 'operational surplus', assumed to be gross of depreciation.

[e] Both 'complementary' and 'competitive' where these cannot be distinguished.

[f] Share of eigenyield in GNP, i.e. $\sigma_*/(1 + \sigma_*)$.

Sources: See note to Table 9.1 above.

More radical discrepancies would of course be pointed up if we disaggregated the economies down to the original micro-sectors, but their number is in most cases too large to be conveniently accommodated in the format of this book. Suffice it to say that the range of discrepancies between current and eigenprices (p_0) reaches from factors of 0.91 to 2.9 in the British economy and from factors of 0.75 to 3.7 in the case of W. Germany. This must imply a fairly radical revision of structural ratios in the wake of a revaluation of flows in eigenprices.

With factor-eigenrentals of 0.88 for wages in W. Germany and of 1.06 for capital in W. Germany and the UK in 1979/80, the share of these factors in GNP must also be affected more radically than the macro-sectoral shares in the first nine rows of the table.

9.7 Further Experiments with Eigenprices

Characteristics of eigenprice distributions

Table 9.6 shows that the range of sectoral price deviance (p_0) within countries tends to be wider than that of their averages (δ) between countries and that, moreover, their distribution is extremely skew. There are in fact typically one to three sectors, usually accounting for less than 5 per cent of GNP, whose overpricing ratio (p_0) exceeds the average by a factor of 1.5 to almost 5, while the remaining sectors are 'bunched up' within a range of 0.7 to 1.4. Only much deeper probing would reveal whether the overpricing sectors owe their position to monopoly power or simply to the fact that they serve as milch cows in the country's system of taxation at producer price level (excluding VAT). In the same way the exceptionally underpriced sectors ($p_0 < 0.5$), usually comprising less than 1 per cent of GNP, may be suffering from cutthroat competition in a buyers' market, or may be beneficiaries of substantial production subsidies which enable them to sell their products below cost or provide a portion of them free of charge as a public service.[6]

Distribution patterns similar to those of Table 9.6 also apply to what might be called 'sectoral trade terms' (t_0), defined as the ratio between

---

[6] Railway transportation services in W. Germany and the Netherlands, and manufactured gas in Belgium may come under this head.

output-pricing (p_0) and the analogous pricing of inputs (say q_0), which measure the net or total exploitation by a sector of the rest of the economy (both downstream and upstream) by overpricing its sales and, possibly gaining unfairly from the underpricing of its purchases. This variable, which is the analogue of effective protection rates in international trade, might well repay further study, but will not be investigated here.

A good deal of interest also attaches to the precise sectoral patterns of overpricing in various economies and the characteristics of sectors that tend to deviant pricing behaviour, whether by significant over-pricing or underpricing of their products. Cursory forays in this direction on data for the early 1970s in the first edition of this book have led the author along several false trails, of which only two will be mentioned here by way of illustration. It was found, for instance, that overpricing was positively correlated with labour-intensity in all market economies except the UK, but negatively correlated with this factor in the East European economies under review, although none of these correlations was significant even at the 10 per cent level. There was, in addition, some positive correlation between overpricing and consumer orientation (as measured by the proportion of sectoral output going to household consumption) in all countries investigated, but only the correlation coefficients for Italy and Czechoslovakia turned out to be significant (at the 5 per cent level). Again, the correlation between sectoral trade terms (t_0) and consumer-orientation turned out to be (insignificantly) positive in all countries except Italy, where it was negative; but a positive correlation between overpricing and material intensity (proportion of non-factor to total input costs) can be reported for all economies except Sweden, with significant results (at the 10 per cent level) in Czechoslovakia, Italy, Japan, and the USSR. These results are too weak to allow firm conclusions of any kind; they do, however, indicate the direction in which further research might go.

Some findings concerning comparative advantage

The comparative cost of any sector product can be measured as the ratio of that sector's eigenprice to the weighted average eigenprice of all other sectors in the economy under review, in accordance with the paradigm of the classical two-sector model. Tables (9.7 and 9.8)

Table 9.6. *The grouped distribution of sectors by price-deviance* (p_0)

Price deviance by group	Belgium	Denmark	Netherlands	Portugal	Spain	UK	W. Germany
0.2	—	—	1[a] (—)	—	—	—	1[b] (0.65)
0.3	1[c] (0.36)	—	—	—	—	—	—
0.4	—	1 (0.44)	—	—	—	—	—
0.5	—	—	—	—	—	—	—
0.6	—	—	1 (0.58)	—	1 (0.69)	1 (0.33)	1 (0.60)
0.7	2 (0.20)	1 (1.9)	1 (1.9)	—	1 (—)	3 (3.6)	1 (0.13)
0.8	32 (64.8)	32 (73.5)	26 (57.8)	4 (8.8)	3 (8.7)	26 (67.8)	2 (13.6)
0.9	13 (28.5)	9 (11.8)	10 (27.5)	25 (60.0)	16 (41.0)	8 (10.4)	19 (50.4)
1.0	2 (1.57)	4 (6.9)	2 (2.0)	6 (14.4)	17 (31.6)	3 (1.8)	9 (13.1)
1.1	1 (3.76)	1 (—)	2 (4.1)	2 (14.1)	2 (3.8)	2 (2.9)	5 (8.8)
1.2	1 (0.59)	—	—	1 (0.87)	2 (3.6)	—	1 (0.87)
1.3	—	—	—	—	—	—	1 (0.92)
1.4	—	—	1 (0.85)	—	—	1 (1.4)	—
1.5	—	—	—	1[d] (0.97)	—	—	1 (6.0)
1.6	—	1 (0.62)	—	—	1 (0.65)	—	—
1.7	—	1 (1.4)	—	—	—	—	1 (4.1)
1.8	—	—	1 (0.81)	—	—	1 (1.9)	1 (0.1)
1.9	—	—	—	—	—	—	—
2.0	—	—	—	—	—	—	—
2.1	—	—	—	—	—	—	—
2.2	—	—	—	—	—	—	—
2.3	1[e] (0.67)	—	—	—	—	—	—

Table 9.6. (*cont.*)

Price deviance by group	Belgium	Denmark	Netherlands	Portugal	Spain	UK	W. Germany
2.4	—	—	—	—	—	—	—
2.5	—	1[f] (1.23)	—	1[g] (0.9)	—	1[h] (1.2)	1[i] (0.69)

Note: The figures give the number of sectors within each group. Bracketed figures show the percentage of GNP covered by the sectors enumerated.

[a] Manufactured gases.
[b] Railway transport services.
[c] Railway transport services.
[d] Pulp and paper.
[e] Tobacco products.
[f] Tobacco products (over 4.8).
[g] Chemical products (over 4.0).
[h] Tobacco products (over 2.9).
[i] Chemical products (over 3.6).

present the results of such computations for the sample of economies investigated in the early and late 1970s respectively.

Table 9.7.   *The comparative costs (γ) of various sectors in the early 1970s*[a]

Sectors[b]	Czechoslovakia 1973	Japan 1970	UK 1972	USSR 1972	W. Germany 1970
A	1.133	1.096	0.966	1.144	1.087
B	1.182	1.016	1.013	1.045	0.905
C	0.854	0.960	0.861	0.992	0.913
D	0.933	0.931	0.758	0.906	0.993
E	1.061	1.016	0.930	1.043	1.011
F	0.907	1.013	0.866	0.760	0.982
G	1.020	0.994	0.874	0.950	0.971
H	1.083	1.001	1.046	1.096	0.961
I	1.089	1.057	1.129	1.100	0.971

[a] With π_r denoting the weighted average eigenprice of all sectors *other than* r, defined by:

$$(y_0 - y_r)\pi_r = \Sigma_{i \neq r} p_i y_i = y_* - p_r y_r = y_0 - p_r y_r$$

i.e. $\pi_r = (y_0 - y_r^*)/(y_0 - y_r)$, the comparative cost-ratio $\gamma_r (= p_r/\pi_r)$ can be computed as $[p_r(y_0 - y_r)]/(y_0 - p_r y_r)$ or:

$$\gamma_r = (p_r - a_r)/(1 - a_r), \text{ where } a_r \equiv p_r y_r / y_0 \equiv q_{r*}/q_*.$$

[b]   A = Agriculture, fishing, and forestry   E = Metal and engineering
      B = Mining, quarrying, and fuel   F = Textiles, leather, and clothing
      C = Food, drink, and tobacco   G = Other manufacturing
      D = Chemicals, plastics, and rubber   H = Construction
                    I = Utilities, transport, trade, and services

In spite of the dubious value of the data, compounded by the formation of ratios between variables which are themselves subject to considerable error, some of the findings appear to be consistent with universal impressions. The fact that in the sample of the early 1970s (Table 9.7) British agriculture showed the most favourable comparative cost-ratio and the USSR the least favourable supports widely held views about the outstanding degree of mechanization in British agriculture and the well-known and avowed facts of Soviet inefficiency and weak incentives in that branch. The relative advantage enjoyed by the UK in chemicals, engineering, and other manufacturing also accords with traditional views. More problematic is the low relative cost of textiles, leather, and clothing in the USSR and the high relative cost of these products in W. Germany compared with the rest of the sample. It should be borne in mind, however, that the inter-country discrepancies in the ratios of the table are not large, and probably well within the margin of error. The purpose of the tables is merely to display the *sort* of exploration that eigenprices might lend themselves to rather than to produce results allowing firm conclusions.

Table 9.8 *The comparative costs* (γ) *of various sectors among seven EEC countries in 1980*[a]

Sectors[b]	Belgium	Denmark	Netherlands	Portugal	Spain	UK[c]	W. Germany
A	0.987	1.917	1.000	1.076	1.076	1.043	0.917
B	0.989	0.906	0.989	1.050	0.981	0.923	0.950
C	0.925	0.961	0.966	0.965	0.966	0.891	0.878
D	0.995	1.023	0.992	1.044	0.987	1.013	0.999
E	1.034	0.985	0.040	0.981	0.969	1.092	1.066
F	0.024	1.030	1.052	1.034	1.000	1.071	1.057
G	1.035	1.036	1.037	1.027	0.978	1.090	1.031
H	1.014	1.036	1.029	1.020	0.976	1.094	1.056
I	0.995	1.015	1.973	0.976	1.043	0.959	0.975

[a] With π_r denoting the weighted average eigenprice of all sectors *other than r*, defined by: $(y_0 - y_r)\pi_r = \sum_{i \neq r} p_i y_i = y_* - p_r y_r = y_0 - p_r y_r$

i.e. $\pi_r = (y_0 - y_r^*)/(y_0 - y_r)$, +

the comparative-cost-ratio $\gamma_r (\equiv p_r/\pi_r)$ can be computed as $[p_r(y_0 - y_r)]/(y_0 - p_r y_r)$

or: $\gamma_r = (p_r - a_r)/(1 - a_r)$, where $a_r \equiv p_r y_r/y_0 = y_r^*/y^*$.

[b] A = Agriculture, fishing, and forestry E = Metal and engineering
B = Mining, quarrying, and fuel F = Textiles, leather, and clothing
C = Food, drink, and tobacco G = Other manufacturing
D = Chemicals, plastics, and rubber H = Construction
I = Utilities, transport, trade, and services

[c] 1979

Table 9.8 for 1980 holds a number of mild surprises: The UK appears to have lost its position of relatively lowest-cost agricultural producer in the sample of countries—a position which is now held by W. Germany, though the change of the comparative cost-ratio between 1972 and 1979 is only marginal in both countries. Likewise the UK has become the relatively highest-cost producer of metals, engineering products, textiles etc., other manufacturing, and construction, while Spain has overtaken the rest of the sample in the comparative advantage enjoyed by the same industries in the wake of the much-vaunted Spanish economic miracle of the 1970s. It must be noted, however, that the composition of the sample between the two tables has changed and it is therefore not to be wondered at that particular countries show changed positions within it. Nevertheless the loss of comparative advantage by the UK in engineering, textiles, leather, clothing, and other manufacturing is striking, whatever the composition of the sample of which it forms part.

The relative cost advantage of Denmark in mining and fuel extraction and of the W. Germany in food, drink, and tobacco would need to be explained if any reliance were placed on the results. Again, however, the data available and our cavalier way of dealing with them rule out the firm conclusions which only a much more thoroughgoing research project could yield. It is the hope that such a project may some day be launched and the author's belief that it could conform to the pattern outlined here that encouraged the author to offer the defective findings of this chapter.

10

Time-Series Analysis for
The Netherlands and Hungary

(*Special Annex contributed by Professor A. E. Steenge,*
University of Groningen)

10.1 Introduction

IT is well known that prices in centrally planned or socialist economies have different functions to fulfil than in market economies.
Here the debate on 'functional' (policy-geared) prices versus 'diagnostic' prices (aiming to reflect social relations, whether actual or
idealized) is of great relevance.[1] It might be considered, for instance,
that prices should stimulate the production of qualitatively superior
goods and discourage that of outdated products, or that they should
stimulate the introduction and use of new technologies. Thus, on the
one hand, they must be high enough to cover production costs and
secure appropriate profit rates, but not so high as to discourage the
use of alternative technologies which might become available shortly
thereafter.[2]

To highlight price differences in planned and market economies a
number of economic models have come into use, of which linear
models are probably the most popular, because of their rich history
in intersystem comparisons. One of the most serious defects of existing models, however, is their total neglect of demand factors, which
deprives them of the capacity to reflect real-world scarcities. More-

---

[1] F. Seton, 'The Question of Ideological Obstacles to Rational Price Setting in Communist Countries', in A. Abouchar (ed.), *The Socialist Price Mechanism*, Duke University Press, Durham, NC, 1977.

[2] For such and other observations see e.g. G. Fink, 'Price Distortions in the Austrian
and in the Hungarian Economy', *Zeitschrift für Nationalökonomie*, 41 (1981), and
*Preisverzerrungen und Unterschiede in der Produktionsstruktur zwischen Östtereich
und Ungarn*, Studien über Wirtschaft-und Systemvergleiche, Springer-Verlag, Vienna,
1981.

over, these models fail to provide suitable criteria for the efficiency with which inputs are used. If, for example, the factor capital is used inefficiently in a particular sector, the model being used may simply adjust prices in order to enable that sector to obtain the same rate of profit on capital as others without signalling the defect. Further difficulties arise from the lack of comparability of basic statistics, e.g. the conformity of Western input–output tables with the System of National Accounts (SNA), in contrast to East European tables, which mostly follow the MPS (Material Product System).[3]

The system presented here is designed to fill an important gap in synthesizing 'cost-fetishism', which imputes total value to one or more primary factors, with 'use-fetishism', which derives factor-rentals from the value of final products. The synthesis is achieved by the use of left-hand eigenvectors corresponding to the dominant eigenvalues of certain matrices appearing in linear transformations (see Part I above). If the relevant matrices have no eigenvalue equal to unity, this signalizes the existence of an 'eigenyield' or 'eigensurplus', positive or negative, extracted from the factors by (or acquired by them from) an—as yet—unspecified agency (foreign countries, monopolists, future generations, the state, or simply 'others').

Seton proposed his system primarily as a tool for international comparison of structural characteristics and performance criteria and took the first tentative steps towards empirical testing, which are supplemented in greater detail in the following chapters. Some of the results are easy enough to interpret, while others need further attention. The general picture, however, promises well for the potential interest of the method.

The relevance of eigenprices for international comparison would no doubt be documented most clearly if it could be shown that different economic systems tended to exhibit different eigenprice structures, so that the revealed structure could be used as a basis for systemic classification at any point in time. A necessary condition for this would be that the annual fluctuations in the eigenprice profile of a particular country should not be so large as to obscure systemic differences from other countries. To test for this condition, we must

---

[3] After 1968, national income accounting in Hungary was extended to include the value of services as well. However, minor discrepancies between the Hungarian system of national accounts and the United Nations system remain. See *Hungary: An Economic Survey*, Occasional Paper 15, International Monetary Fund, Washington, DC, 1982.

of course trace the development of eigenprices in a number of different years in contrasting economies, in order to highlight how different economies coped with emerging disequilibria, thereby revealing systemic peculiarities which might remain hidden in a simple cross-section analysis at a given point in time.

In what follows we present two empirical studies, one for a Westerntype country, The Netherlands, and one for a socialist centrally planned economy, Hungary. We calculated eigenprices and eigensurpluses for the Dutch post-war economy 1948–78, using data compiled by the Central Bureau of Statistics (Centraal Bureau voor de Statistiek) (CBS). During this period the organizational framework of the economy remained substantially unchanged, although the share of government increased from roughly one-third to about two-thirds of the national income without, however, resulting in a substantial increase in government intervention in the private sector. The importance of the foreign sector also remained roughly constant. We may expect, therefore, that a study of eigenprices implying the over- and under-pricing of specific flows in terms of current prices will provide information on the time-profile typical of a medium-sized open economy based on free enterprise with some elements of state control.

In the case of Hungary, we analysed the period 1970–9, using tables prepared by the Central Statistical Office of that country (Központi Statisztikai Hivatal). This period is of considerable interest, as it is the period of the 'second wave of reforms'.[4] The New Economic Mechanism (NEM) of 1968 resulted in systemic changes of considerable scope by East European standards. After the 1968 reform, the system of planning directives was abolished altogether and enterprises were given a relatively free hand in determining their output and cost structure. The planning agencies still drew up the national plan as usual, but this plan was no longer broken down to enterprise level. Central policy was imposed on lower echelons through economic regulators instead of administrative command. The NEM did not quite fulfil the aspirations of 1968. After a temporary recourse to centralization during the years 1973–7, the period 1979–80 again saw considerable changes, particularly the adoption of 'competitive market prices'.[5] At the same time, the Hungarian system had to cope with

[4] The terminology is borrowed from W. Brus, 'The Eastern European Economic Reforms: What Happened to Them?', *Soviet Studies*, 31 (1979).

[5] J. Kornai, 'Comments on the Present State and Prospects of the Hungarian Economic Reform', *Journal of Comparative Economics*, 7 (1983).

the world price shocks in the field of energy and other resources, and to grapple with worsening balance-of-payments problems. A comparison of the two systems is therefore of special interest. Both countries are medium-sized; both experienced an agricultural phase followed by a period of rapid industrialization. Holland is a member of the EEC and OECD, while Hungary is a member of the CMEA, and since 1982 also of the IMF. We start with a brief discussion of the economic background of both countries, followed by the presentation of the data, and conclude with a number of observations on the method in the light of this.

The author of this annex is particularly indebted to Francis Seton for discussions and comments on an earlier draft. Special thanks are also due to Andrew Bródy of the Institute of Economics of the Hungarian Academy of Sciences for providing the opportunity for a stay of several months at the Institute. He also wishes to thank Ferenc Bánhidi of the Hungarian Central Planning office, György Szakolczai of the Econometric Laboratory of the Institute of Economics, and György Molnar, also of the Institute of Economics of the Hungarian Academy of Sciences, for providing additional information on the Hungarian economy. For the processing of the Dutch data, thanks are due to Erik Dietzenbacher of the Econometric Institute of the University of Groningen, and to Jaap Stellingwerff for help at an earlier stage. Financial support from the Netherlands Organization for the Advancement of Pure Research (ZWO) is gratefully acknowledged.

10.2 Brief Characterization of the Post-War Dutch Economy

As in most other West European countries, several stages can be quite easily distinguished in the post-war economic development of the Netherlands. A fairly common division is the following one into four periods.[6]

Reconstruction and recovery, 1945–50

Economic damage, both national and personal, wrought by the war was enormous. Material damage alone was estimated at 25 billion

---

[6] Here we follow broadly the classification of W. S. P. Fortuyn, *Kernciifers 1945–1983 van de sociaal-economische ontwikkeling in Nederland*, Kluwer, Deventer, 1983. Another source is J. P. Windmuller and C. de Galan, *Arbeidsverhoudingen in Nederland*, 3rd edn., pt.2, Het Spectrum, Utrecht, 1979.

guilders at current prices.[7] However, recovery was fast owing to a number of favourable circumstances. In the earliest post-war years, employers and employees were prepared to accept strong government intervention in the form of strict wage, credit, and foreign currency controls; social harmony was a decisive factor here. Another factor was the substantial American support given in the form of Marshall aid in 1948. Each year large portions of the growth in national income could be invested in industry. This guaranteed rapid industrialization, which could absorb the growing working population and help to compensate for the loss of the colonial empire in South-East Asia. The policy of strict wage controls ensured the country's favourable position in foreign markets. Commodity exports almost doubled in the period 1948–50 (from 2.8 to 5.5 billion guilders), while national income increased by 28 per cent (from 13.4 to 17.1 billion guilders in 1950). The balance of payments still remained weak, however, owing to the persistence of grave shortages of all kinds. The whole period was characterized by a rapid transformation from a traditional type of society based on agriculture, trade, and services to a modern industrial economy. Particularly fast expansion was registered in the production of metals, chemicals, and food, while trade and services remained important.

Recovery and expansion, 1950–63

This rapid industrialization policy continued throughout the period. In the early 1950s, most economic controls were lifted. According to the Dutch Central Bank, the recovery period was completed by about 1953 in the monetary sphere. However, a strict wages policy remained a cornerstone of national policy and was a major factor in keeping inflation down to 2–3 per cent per annum. Equally important was the fact that Dutch firms had become highly competitive in foreign markets. Exports were concentrated on Western Europe, with W. Germany emerging as the largest trading partner. The balance of payments showed surpluses year after year, a process mitigated only by the appreciation of the guilder by 5 per cent in 1961. But two

[7] This compares with a national income (net, market prices) of 13.4 bn. guilders in 1948, the first year for which detailed national accounts are available, when the government budget was 4.0bn. guilders (in 1975 prices). See Fortuyn, *Kerncijfers 1945– 1983*: 14–15, and *Tachtig jaren statistiek in tijdreeksen 1899–1979*, Centraal Bureau voor de Statistiek, 's-Gravenhage, Staatsuitgeverij, 1979: 144.

consequences of the national policy orientation became obvious only gradually. In the first place, because of the relatively low level of wages, industrialization was extensive rather than intensive in comparison with neighbouring countries. Textiles became less competitive than before, followed somewhat later by metals. In the second place, owing to the strong concentration on exports, domestic consumption was squeezed, creating a large overhang of postponed demand. This, combined with general excess demand for labour, gave rise to various 'grey' and 'black' markets to overcome disequilibria, and to an influx of foreign workers from southern Europe. However, overall growth continued and national income almost trebled. Social security legislation greatly expanded, leading among other things to a significant raising of old-age pensions in 1957 (the 'AOW' law).

Growth and reorganization, 1963–74

In 1963 tensions in the labour market became so serious that the policy of wage controls had to be abandoned. The breakdown of the system resulted in explosive wage increases. Nominal wages rose by 17 per cent in 1964, increasing real wages by 10 per cent. Profits then rapidly fell in a number of already weakened sectors such as textiles, metals, and other labour-intensive branches. A period of reorganization and restructuring ensued, characterized by shut-downs, takeovers, and mergers, which changed Dutch industry fundamentally. For a time, newer developments in expanding sectors such as electronics, information-processing, transport, trade, and government services were able to take over the role of traditional industries in providing employment for the still growing population. Towards the 1970s, however, it became clear that the newer branches would not be able to absorb all those seeking employment, and 'industrial innovation' became the keynote of the current debate. Growth in industrial investment came to a stop fairly abruptly in 1971, and in the following year trade unions called attention to the necessity of maintaining employment for the first time.

During the period 1963–74 as a whole, the rate of inflation doubled from 4 to 8 per cent per annum, showing an average rate of 5.6 per cent, while national income, investment, and labour productivity still continued on their fast upward trend. The balance of payments, however, became weak, mainly because of overconsumption. Thus unemployment became an issue only at the beginning of the 1970s.

Government expenditure rose faster than national income, with its share rising from 40.8 per cent in 1964 to 53.7 per cent in 1974.

Reorganization and stagnation, 1974

The first oil crisis was a turning point for The Netherlands, as it was everywhere else. The government reacted with restrictions on expenditure on fuels of every kind combined with wage and price controls. In 1974 and 1975 the growth in national income slowed down, while unemployment rose apace. (The number of unemployed, already 100,000 in 1972, passed the 200,000 mark in 1975.) Anti-cyclical measures failed to bring unemployment down, but the rate of inflation remained high and reached 10.2 per cent in 1975, while budget deficits increased. After 1975, the Keynesian approach gave way to policies of a more monetary kind, and public expenditure was cut significantly in the hope of reducing the still rising deficit. This brought about a slow-down in inflation but increased the number of unemployed, thus increasing the pressure on the social security system. In the wake of the second oil crisis and other causes, the economy stagnated in the late 1970s, and growth rates turned negative in the 1980s: by the end of 1981, about 400,000 people were unemployed. Public expenditure had to be cut once again, causing further changes in wages policy (with specially severe effects in the public services) and in the social security system. Thanks to the export of large quantities of natural gas, however, the balance of payments went into persistent surplus. This, of course, had the effect of strengthening the guilder and adversely affecting the less competitive sectors of the economy.

10.3 Eigenprices for The Netherlands, 1948–78

Our calculations are based on yearly input–output tables published by the Dutch Central Bureau of Statistics (CBS).[8] The original tables were based on a breakdown into thirty-odd sectors following standard international classification. Substantial changes in the CBS classification occurred in 1969 in regard to the oil and gas sector; until 1969

---

[8] Centraal Bureau voor de Statistiek, *De produktie-struktuur van de Nederlandse volkshuishouding*, various years, 's-Gravenhage, Staatsuitgeverij, and *Nationale rekeningen*, various years, 's-Gravenhage, Staatsuitgeverij.

oil and gas exploration and exploitation activities were recorded under 'Chemicals', while in subsequent years these activities were recorded under a separate heading. At about the same time, because of the shut-down of the Dutch mines in the province of Limburg, coalmining virtually disappeared as an economic activity. The CBS sought to overcome a discontinuity in the time series of input–output tables by publishing two figures for the year 1969, labelled 1969(1) and 1969(2) in Tables 10.1–10.4, where the latter stands for the new classification.

A further break in the series occurred in 1969, when the tables were adapted to the introduction of the value added tax (BTW), which replaced earlier turnover taxes. The main difference with previous usage was that indirect taxes paid on final deliveries were now recorded in the corresponding columns of the fourth quadrant. (This was the case for both the series 1969(1) and 1969(2) mentioned above.) No set of figures was published for 1971.

To facilitate comparison with the pilot survey in this book and to avoid the excessive detail of the CBS classification, we have aggregated the tables into nine 'macro-sectors' (henceforth to be called 'sectors' *tout court*):

A   Agriculture, forestry, and fishing
B   Mining, oil, and gas
C   Food, drink, and tobacco
D   Chemicals
E   Metals and engineering
F   Textiles, leather, and clothing
G   Other manufacturing
H   Construction
I   Utilities, transport, and services.

Primary input categories were aggregated into three:

1   Wages and salaries (including employers' contributions to social security)
2   Other incomes (profits, dividends, etc.)
3   Imports of commodities and services (c.i.f.)

This classification leaves the 'τ-row' to record the sum of all indirect taxes and price-decreasing subsidies. The above-mentioned CBS shift in the classification of the oil and gas activities corresponds to a shift from sector D to B in the aggregation. Above we also mentioned the break in the CBS publications regarding the taxes on final purchases, starting from 1969. We have adhered to this in the aggregation scheme, because of the impracticality of recalculating figures according to the pre-1969 schedule. For the numerical consequences of this, refer to the tables and Sect. 10.4.

Table 10.1 *Sectoral eigenprices for The Netherlands, 1948–78*

Year[a]	Sector[b]								
	A	B	C	D	E	F	G	H	I
1948	1.145	0.953	1.029	0.974	1.019	1.011	1.010	1.003	0.953
1949	1.138	0.983	0.966	0.990	1.034	1.029	1.022	1.019	0.970
1950	1.051	0.980	1.002	0.987	1.038	1.036	1.021	1.020	0.964
1951	1.048	1.009	1.000	0.980	1.039	1.027	1.019	1.017	0.964
1952	1.047	1.041	0.962	0.981	1.041	1.022	1.024	1.023	0.990
1953	1.040	1.032	0.968	0.996	1.039	1.023	1.021	1.027	0.984
1954	1.045	1.035	0.979	1.005	1.037	1.025	1.019	1.023	0.976
1955	1.050	1.019	0.976	0.996	1.024	1.025	1.013	1.016	0.985
1956	1.052	1.019	0.978	0.997	1.017	1.046	1.007	1.012	0.984
1957	1.083	1.006	0.986	0.983	1.017	1.050	1.009	1.010	0.980
1958	1.119	1.007	0.979	0.972	1.016	1.047	1.007	1.008	0.984
1959	1.077	1.009	0.970	0.972	1.022	1.047	1.015	1.013	0.989
1960	1.085	1.007	0.971	0.976	1.025	1.048	1.015	1.013	0.983
1961	1.096	1.012	0.968	0.979	1.029	1.053	1.019	1.018	0.978
1962	1.078	1.018	0.961	0.975	1.033	1.053	1.021	1.019	0.982
1963	1.077	1.016	0.965	0.973	1.035	1.056	1.022	1.020	0.981
1964	1.080	1.012	0.972	0.958	1.036	1.056	1.023	1.022	0.978
1965	1.065	1.015	0.961	0.975	1.038	1.061	1.025	1.027	0.978
1966	1.045	1.020	0.964	0.961	1.041	1.062	1.028	1.031	0.979
1967	1.046	1.028	0.976	0.984	1.041	1.049	1.027	1.029	0.974
1968	1.038	1.053	0.981	0.966	1.041	1.051	1.026	1.030	0.976
1969 (1)	1.003	1.022	0.979	0.948	1.042	1.030	1.027	1.025	0.989
1969 (2)	1.002	0.835	0.978	1.036	1.042	1.032	1.024	1.024	0.987
1970	1.004	0.857	0.993	1.029	1.034	1.028	1.020	1.023	0.986
1971	n.a.	n.a.	n.a.	n.a.	n.a.	n.a.	n.a.	n.a.	n.a.
1972	1.003	0.853	0.987	1.022	1.031	1.028	1.020	1.024	0.993
1973	1.006	0.874	1.009	1.014	1.026	1.023	1.015	1.019	0.991
1974	1.010	0.928	1.003	1.010	1.023	1.020	1.013	1.016	0.994
1975	1.000	0.939	0.992	1.010	1.024	1.025	1.015	1.018	0.996
1976	1.004	0.957	1.001	1.007	1.021	1.021	1.012	1.015	0.993
1977	1.007	0.947	1.014	1.010	1.025	1.026	1.017	1.020	0.989
1978	1.006	0.937	1.018	1.010	1.026	1.025	1.017	1.021	0.989

[a] 1969 (1) = Old classification, 1969 (2) = new classification (see text); data for 1971 are not available.

[b] A = Agriculture, forestry, and fishing; B = Mining and oil; C = Food, drink, and tobacco; D = Chemicals; E = Metals and engineering; F = Textiles, leather, and clothing; G = Other manufacturing; H = Construction; I = Utilities, transport, and services.

Table 10.2 *Eigenrentals and eigenyield for The Netherlands, 1948–78*

Year	Factors[a]			Eigenyield[b] (σ in %)
	1	2	3	
1948	0.96	1.007	1.005	8.03
1949	1.001	1.004	1.001	9.71
1950	1.000	0.997	1.007	9.77
1951	1.000	0.997	1.006	9.87
1952	1.004	0.998	1.001	9.90
1953	1.003	0.997	1.003	9.72
1954	1.002	0.997	1.004	9.52
1955	1.001	0.999	1.002	8.68
1956	1.001	0.999	1.002	8.06
1957	1.000	1.000	1.002	7.08
1958	1.001	1.003	0.999	6.79
1959	1.002	1.001	0.999	7.41
1960	1.001	1.001	1.001	7.37
1961	1.002	0.999	1.003	7.78
1962	1.003	0.998	1.003	7.94
1963	1.002	0.997	1.004	8.03
1964	1.002	0.998	1.004	8.05
1965	1.003	0.996	1.005	8.42
1966	1.003	0.995	1.005	8.81
1967	1.002	0.995	1.006	9.18
1968	1.002	0.996	1.006	9.71
1969 (1)	1.004	0.996	1.002	3.55
1969 (2)	1.006	0.997	1.001	3.40
1970	1.005	0.997	1.001	3.34
1971	n.a.	n.a.	n.a.	n.a.
1972	1.006	0.997	0.999	3.70
1973	1.004	0.996	1.001	3.11
1974	1.004	0.998	0.998	2.67
1975	1.005	0.995	0.999	2.73
1976	1.003	0.996	1.000	2.31
1977	1.003	0.995	1.003	2.79
1978	1.003	0.995	1.003	2.81

[a] 1 = Wage factors; 2 = Other factors; 3 = Imports.
[b] $\sigma = 100(1/\phi - 1)$, where ϕ = eigencost-ratio.

Table 10.3 *The GNP by origin in eigenprices, The Netherlands, 1948–78*[a]

Year	Sector[b]								
	A	B	C	D	E	F	G	H	I
1948	8.52	0.15	17.59	3.85	10.45	9.79	3.23	9.77	36.66
1949	7.44	0.12	18.93	4.15	10.90	10.55	2.85	9.14	35.65
1950	5.84	0.12	20.18	5.54	11.27	11.22	2.96	8.39	34.48
1951	5.40	0.14	20.02	6.49	12.93	10.04	3.47	8.35	33.17
1952	5.90	0.14	19.61	6.69	13.62	8.08	2.84	8.77	34.37
1953	5.03	0.10	19.42	6.72	13.72	8.44	2.68	10.20	33.70
1954	5.40	0.12	19.12	6.86	14.35	8.11	2.84	9.19	34.02
1955	5.09	0.12	17.85	7.00	15.12	7.91	2.91	9.40	34.61
1956	4.94	0.14	16.98	7.40	15.00	7.78	2.72	9.95	35.09
1957	4.94	0.12	16.69	8.31	14.71	7.49	2.66	10.35	34.73
1958	5.24	0.12	17.42	8.29	14.09	6.72	2.67	10.13	35.34
1959	4.76	0.12	17.00	8.21	14.95	6.74	2.83	10.28	35.12
1960	5.16	0.11	16.19	8.68	16.05	6.74	3.04	9.86	34.19
1961	4.86	0.11	15.63	8.52	16.18	6.90	3.05	10.41	34.35
1962	4.76	0.11	15.07	8.41	16.47	6.57	2.98	10.32	35.33
1963	4.23	0.11	15.46	8.05	16.19	6.89	3.08	10.32	35.68
1964	4.36	0.11	15.12	7.66	16.31	6.62	3.08	11.75	35.00
1965	4.39	0.10	14.56	8.08	16.21	6.16	3.14	11.94	35.43
1966	3.89	0.13	14.53	7.98	15.82	6.17	3.16	12.68	35.66
1967	3.76	0.17	14.84	8.12	15.14	5.23	3.10	13.46	36.18
1968	3.50	0.32	14.42	8.46	15.16	5.17	3.12	13.72	36.13
1969 (1)	3.63	0.40	13.74	9.02	16.48	4.99	3.30	11.97	36.47
1969 (2)	3.17	2.91	14.42	6.50	15.58	5.29	3.36	12.21	36.56
1970	2.94	3.47	13.99	6.26	16.36	4.50	3.32	12.10	37.07
1971	n.a.	n.a.	n.a.	n.a.	n.a.	n.a.	n.a.	n.a.	n.a.
1972	2.99	3.63	13.58	6.19	15.57	4.07	3.29	12.38	38.30
1973	3.21	4.23	13.60	6.54	15.66	3.72	3.38	11.54	38.13
1974	2.59	6.87	12.61	8.20	16.07	3.32	3.42	9.98	36.95
1975	2.56	6.85	13.01	6.34	15.05	2.89	3.06	10.28	36.97
1976	2.91	7.72	12.44	6.74	14.84	2.70	3.11	9.94	39.60
1977	2.75	7.13	11.65	5.66	13.91	2.45	3.06	10.30	43.09
1978	2.65	6.35	11.50	5.49	13.47	2.33	3.06	19.77	44.38

[a] Sectoral shares in value added, neglecting factor-services rendered directly to final users (fourth quadrant of input–output table).
[b] For the definition of the sectors, see Table 10.1

Table 10.4 *The GNP in eigenprices by factor share and final use, The Netherlands, 1948–78*[a]

Year	Factor[b]			Final use[c]				
	1	2	3	Pc	Gc	Gi	Ex	Oth.
1948	32.31	35.29	24.96	56.01	2.45	13.92	23.72	3.89
1949	30.78	36.39	23.99	54.66	2.08	13.89	27.74	1.63
1950	28.76	34.34	28.00	49.86	2.04	12.80	32.13	3.17
1951	27.23	33.21	30.58	45.68	2.69	11.99	36.12	3.52
1952	27.94	34.52	28.54	45.61	3.30	12.05	39.01	0.04
1953	28.19	34.95	28.00	44.83	3.56	13.78	37.64	0.19
1954	28.51	34.46	28.33	44.08	3.42	13.45	36.73	2.32
1955	28.78	35.37	27.86	43.36	3.51	14.40	37.23	1.51
1956	29.12	34.29	29.13	43.13	3.77	15.32	36.59	1.20
1957	30.06	33.99	29.35	41.90	3.42	15.76	37.30	1.62
1958	31.61	34.21	27.82	43.81	3.02	14.60	38.13	0.45
1959	30.88	34.38	27.84	42.97	2.49	15.44	38.91	0.20
1960	30.87	34.57	27.71	41.21	2.55	15.13	39.50	1.61
1961	32.46	33.13	27.19	42.13	2.53	15.45	38.08	1.81
1962	33.22	32.55	26.87	42.65	2.75	15.53	38.02	1.06
1963	34.20	31.35	27.01	43.30	2.96	12.42	38.07	0.25
1964	34.57	31.05	26.93	41.54	2.79	16.77	37.20	1.70
1965	35.64	30.94	25.65	42.30	2.46	16.95	37.30	1.00
1966	36.94	29.46	25.50	42.47	2.57	17.84	36.44	0.68
1967	37.12	30.04	24.43	42.89	2.70	18.45	35.92	0.05
1968	37.06	29.73	24.37	42.12	2.50	18.93	36.16	0.28
1969 (1)	39.54	30.76	26.27	41.06	2.46	15.90	38.89	1.68
1969 (2)	40.17	30.11	26.43	40.52	2.42	16.19	39.24	1.64
1970	40.78	28.56	27.43	39.49	2.48	16.38	40.43	1.22
1971	n.a.	n.a.	n.a.	n.a.	n.a.	n.a.	n.a.	n.a.
1972	41.98	28.96	25.49	39.45	2.60	16.10	41.77	0.08
1973	42.15	28.71	26.12	38.57	2.46	15.34	43.09	0.54
1974	40.53	26.35	30.52	36.17	2.47	13.47	46.69	1.20
1975	43.23	26.02	28.09	39.31	2.89	13.35	44.83	− 0.37
1976	41.52	27.76	28.46	38.65	2.80	12.32	45.83	0.39
1977	41.62	29.03	26.64	41.30	2.59	14.31	41.51	0.30
1978	42.50	29.30	25.47	42.29	2.67	14.82	39.99	0.23

[a] As in Table 10.3 the GNP neglects factor-services rendered directly to final users (the fourth quadrant of the input–output table).

[b] 1 = Wage factors; 2 = Other factors; 3 = Imports; $1 + 2 + 3 + 100(1 - \phi) = 100$, where $\phi = 100/(100 + \sigma)$. (For σ see Table 10.2.)

[c] Pc = Personal consumption; Gc = Government consumption; Gi = Gross investment; Ex = Exports; Oth. = Other. Pc + Gc + Gi + Ex + Oth. = 100.

10.4 Discussion of the Results for The Netherlands

Tables 10.1–10.4 summarize the results for The Netherlands for 1948–78. Recalling that an eigenprice below unity implies overpricing of the commodity or factor in terms of current prices, and an eigenprice above unity a corresponding underpricing, we may call attention to a few especially interesting features.

Tables 10.1 suggests that agricultural production was underpriced throughout the post-war period, although the degree of underpricing appears to have diminished steadily, possibly reflecting the improved organization of agricultural interests in the late 1960s and 1970s. The relatively large underpricing in 1948 and 1949 may reflect the government's efforts to keep down the prices of primary products in the immediate post-war years. The jump in eigenprices in 1969 can be attributed to the aforementioned shift in the recording of the value added tax on final deliveries. The economy's eigenyield having fallen under the post-1969 tax registration schedule to somewhat more than 3 per cent, agriculture has approximately the 'right' proportion of indirect taxes under the new scheme. (The same is valid, *mutatis mutandis*, for other sectoral eigenprices for 1969 and following years.) The data of the table also suggest an inverse correlation between the eigenprices of sector A and the food-handling and processing activities represented largely in sector C. For the latter sector, the picture is complicated by the qualitative differences between its constituent commodities. A more detailed breakdown may easily give substantially different results.

Sectors B and D could also be viewed in conjunction, as they might be even more complementary than A and C. It appears that up to 1969 the basic primary products of sector B were underpriced, while the processing activities of sector D were overpriced. The substantial change evident in 1969 may be traced to the shift in classification affecting the oil and gas industry which is known to favour monopolistic elements; from then on we note that the over- and underpricing of the two sectors is reversed. The effects of re-classifying the oil and gas sector are also interesting from a purely statistical point of view. Sector B's eigenprice falls from 1.022 to 0.835, while that of sector D rises from 0.948 to 1.036, a considerably smaller change. This is due largely to the fact that the total output of sector B in 1969 was 1.4 billion guilders under the old classification while that of sector D was 15.9 billion. Under the new classification, however, the same figures were 7.0 and 10.0 billion guilders respectively. Thus, 'over-valued' oil and gas account for some four-fifths of sector B's output under the new classification. In the year designated 1969(1), the effect of these overvalued commodities on the eigenprice of sector D was exerted by only about one-third of its output-mix.

Another interesting feature is the behaviour of these eigenprices for 1974 and the years immediately following. Contrary to what one might expect, we observe a *rise* in the eigenprice for sector B, from 0.874 to 0.928 in 1974. That is, there is *less* measured overvaluation in the period of the severe oil price shocks. The reason for this may be found in the fact that sector B's imports (mainly oil) more than doubled (from 5.9 billion guilders in 1973 to 14.4 billions in 1974), while indirect taxes increased only moderately (from 2.1 to 2.2 bil-lion). The other relevant entries in the third quadrant also increase, but much less than (the value of) imports. Thus, the entry in the τ-row decreased in proportion to the totality of the primary factors, which entails an increase in eigenprice.

As for the typical manufacturing sectors E–H, the table suggests a tendency to underpricing, which may be the result of greater compet-itiveness in these sectors and a lack of concerted action by the inter-ests concerned. The systematic overpricing of sector I (eigenprices below unity), on the other hand, may be indicative of a substantial degree of government participation in the revenues of this sector through taxation; it is also in line with the lack of competitiveness of public utilities in The Netherlands.

Table 10.2 appears to indicate fewer and less radical changes through the years, but nevertheless presents interesting features. There is a slight, but systematic, underpricing of the wage-factor; but it is interesting to note that the wage restraint shown by labour in the recovery period (late 1940s and early 1950s) is not reflected in the data. This may reflect the fact that consumption goods were broadly 'correctly' priced in relation to the amount of labour 'embodied' in them. We also note that the wage increases of 1963 and subsequent years do not entail any significant fall in the eigenprice for labour. Perhaps the tentative conclusions drawn for the earlier period of wage restraint may apply here also, *mutatis mutandis*.

The eigenyield concept seems to provide a good indicator for cyc-lical phenomena. For example, the recession of 1957–8 is reflected in a fall in eigenyield, signalling a decline in indirect tax revenues. The same is possibly true for 1974 and following years, although here

the situation is complicated by the changed treatment of final purchases. Furthermore, we may observe that, during the recession of
1958–9, both labour and 'other incomes' become underpriced when
compared with 1957. This is consistent with a degree of oversupply
of production factors, such as is typical of a recession. Imports, on
the other hand, became overpriced in 1958, reflecting a stable and
relatively high level of demand for foreign goods and services. However, this switch from over- to under-pricing in the non-labour factor
of production is not in evidence in the recession following the oil-
price increase of 1973. This may be due to the considerable change
in general conditions that had taken place. While the recession trig-
gered off by the cost-push of 1973 brought immediately increased
revenues to the oil-processing companies, no such phenomenon had
occurred in 1958–9. This is documented by the overpricing during the
years following 1973. Later years, however, again saw a gradual
erosion here.

Tables 10.3 and 10.4 were included to show the effects of eigenprice calculations on the structure of the gross national product, in
line with the results of the pilot survey presented in Sects. 6.6–7.2.
Table 10.3 shows the structural shifts in the Dutch economy during
the period under review. The fact that the eigenprices of the traditional sectors (textiles, metals, etc.) stabilized from the late 1960s
onward may point to the disappearance of the less efficient enterprises
in these sectors, while the surviving firms were operating under 'normal' competitive conditions. Table 10.4 shows the breakdown of GNP
according to factor-shares and final use structure.

The pronounced discontinuity in the time-series for sectors B and
D points up the sensitivity of the results to sectoral aggregation of the
crude data. The same is valid for changes in tax schedules, as is
illustrated by the contrast in eigenyields for the pre-1969 years and
the later years. It should be noted in conclusion that eigenrentals of
factors of production are in general very close to unity—a finding that
evidently needs to be put on the agenda for future research.

10.5 A Brief Characterization of Post-War Hungary

The Hungarian People's Republic, when launched in 1949, introduced
a centrally planned economic system. This meant that five-year plans
spelled out interim targets for important economic aggregates in the

necessary breakdown, while annual and quarterly plans provided a detailed disaggregation down to enterprise level. Firms were given specific directives on output, investment, wages, prices, and employment, and all inputs were centrally allocated. In this system, prices had in the main no more than an accounting function, and generally did nothing to reflect demand or supply conditions in the markets for goods or factors. Producer and consumer prices were fixed at a level determined by a large variety of turnover taxes and subsidies. International price movements had little influence on domestic price developments, as the discrepancy between foreign and domestic prices was covered largely by financing out of special funds.[9]

From the very beginning, major efforts were made to establish a firm industrial base for the country's development. The centrally planned system met with a measure of success, particularly in the 1950s when resources were being extensively reallocated. Very high rates of investment were realized, and as a consequence output, employment, and industrial capacity grew rapidly, signalling the onset of a period of extensive growth in these early years. With the exhaustion of labour supplies, however, further economic growth became dependent on the increasing productivity of an almost static labour force.[10] Economic pressures arising from this dictated a change from extensive to more intensive growth policies. However, the formulation of plans that were both flexible and sufficiently detailed became an increasingly complex task, largely dependent on up-to-the-minute statistical reporting of high quality; and their implementation was hampered by the general lack of incentives for workers and management alike.

To alleviate the administrative burden of central agencies, a full-scale consolidation of enterprises into larger units was initiated in the early 1960s. In a series of mergers, the number of state industrial enterprises was reduced from over 1,300 in 1961 to some 850 in the mid-1960s. But this heavy concentration of industry had adverse effects on the production of consumer goods, semi-finished products,

---

[9] For an extended discussion of the institutional characteristics, we refer to J. Kornai, *Economics of Shortage*, vols. A and B, North-Holland, Amsterdam, 1980. For a recent economic survey see the earlier-mentioned study, *Hungary: An Economic Survey*. Other references include P. Hare, H. Radice, and N. Swain (eds.), *Hungary: A Decade of Economic Reform*, Allen & Unwin, London, 1981; E. A. Hewett (ed.), 'Hungary: The Third Wave of Reforms', *Journal of Comparative Economics*, 7 (1983); and P. Mihályi, 'Das Ungarische Modell', *Osteuropa Wirtschaft*, 28 (1983).

[10] Hare *et al.*, *Hungary: A Decade of Economic Reform*, 5.

and spare parts, which was dependent mainly on small- and medium-size enterprises.[11] Moreover, Hungary's limited domestic market and its relative lack of natural resources encouraged an increasing orientation towards Western markets. With some 50 per cent of the national product going to exports and one-third of this dependent on hard-currency areas, industry had to be organized so as to be geared to the demands of foreign trade and export promotion. The flexibility that this required was difficult to achieve within a tightly organized central planning system. It was generally accepted by the mid-1960s, therefore, that only a fairly thorough reform of the system would guarantee the country's future economic performance.

The second wave of reforms that followed took about two years to prepare; the 'New Economic Mechanism' (NEM) came into force on 1 January 1968, with an overall package of measures. The scope of centralized price determination was reduced, domestic prices of exports and import-substitutes were linked to world market prices, and a major part of investment decisions was decentralized. Annual plans ceased to be enforced by direct instructions to enterprises, and were implemented indirectly by means of 'regulators'. To facilitate this, producer prices were recalculated to reflect domestic and foreign costs more accurately than before. The degree of plan-fulfilment became less decisive as a factor in determining workers' premia, yielding place to the profits of the firms that employed them. Moreover, the division of enterprise profits remaining after tax into a 'sharing' fund and a 'development' fund brought about a certain degree of decentralization in wage determination and investment decisions.

When the NEM was introduced, a number of 'brakes' were built in to mitigate the shock of the transition from the previous system. In essence, there were three price categories operative in the system: a

[11] Here it may be interesting to quote W. Brus, 'The Eastern European Economic Reforms: What Happened to Them?': 'One of the elements which should secure the required degree of control under conditions of various degrees of devolution of economic authority was thought to be a higher level of organizational concentration. If we take the schematic three-tier organization of industry (ministry; intermediate—most frequently branch—organization; enterprise), it was the status of the intermediate organization which, sooner or later, was enhanced. In the course of this development the intermediate organizations underwent in some cases substantial transformation: in Hungary, where amalgamation of existing enterprises preceded the reform, the amalgamated units took over the name of enterprises, underlining the fact that the function of enterprises, with all their enhanced autonomy, became vested in these units.'

fixed-price category (prices set directly by the government); a flex-ible-price category (prices fluctuating between officially set upper and lower limits); and a free-price category (prices determined largely by market forces). Controls were removed mainly on producer prices, although consumer prices were affected as well. However, even the 'free' prices were subject to a certain amount of control through general rules linking them to costing and profit margins, through the continued regulation of wages and raw material prices, and through limitations deriving from the government's wish to avoid excessive price adjustments.[12] Operative prices were regularly examined by the price control authorities.

The main form of government intervention in producer prices was the wide range of taxes and subsidies that continued to be negotiated between the government and individual enterprises. After the reform of 1968, consumer prices overtook producer prices in the case of industrial goods, but remained below them in the case of foodstuffs, transport, communication, and a number of services which continued to be subsidized via the state budget.

The intention was gradually to eliminate restrictions. But during the early 1970s the system was partially modified in the reverse direction, i.e. away from the market. The main reason for this was the intention to prevent large income inequalities, excessive labour turn-over, and over-investment at enterprise level. Initially, these changes were introduced in response to a number of shortcomings that had emerged during the implementation of the new system. However, the policy responses to the external shocks were frustrated by the infla-tionary boom of 1972–3 and the world recession of the mid-1970s. The deterioration of the Hungarian terms of trade after 1973 led to reduced reliance on the market mechanism, and to a certain return of central direction and government intervention. By 1974, for instance, over two-thirds of the increase in world market prices was compen-sated for by subsidies on imports. The price disparity was particularly large for crude oil, whose domestic price remained well below the world market price for several years. However, since intra-CMEA trade prices are normally fixed annually at the level of a five-year moving average of world market prices, the price of oil imports from the USSR—Hungary's main supplier of oil—rose steadily towards the international level.

[12]   *Hungary: An Economic Survey*, 9.

10.6 Empirical Results for Hungary, 1970–9

Our eigenprice calculations for Hungary are based on twenty-six sector input–output tables published by the Central Statistical Office (Központi Statisztikai Hivatal).[13] It is evident that these tables were compiled with an eye to the interests of the immediate users operating within the Hungarian economic system. Ideally, we should have processed tables conforming to the definitions of economic activities current in international practice, where the various subdivisions of light industry are aggregated into a single sector and building activities are similarly condensed. While this is the proper breakdown for most decentralized production systems, it does not correspond to the needs of the Hungarian set-up. Hungarian enterprises operate under the jurisdiction of larger economic organizations which play a dominant role in preparing production plans, dealing with parallel echelons in other industries, 'bargaining' with central authorities, etc. Many of these organizations comprise both horizontally and vertically related production stages. Accordingly, Hungarian input–output tables embody a compromise between the 'branch-type' and the 'administration-type' systems of classifying enterprises, designed to facilitate subsequent aggregations into either of these two classification schemes, as the need may dictate. In the case of building, for example, the table specifies not only 'building proper', but contains separate entries for building in agriculture, railway construction, water works, and construction activities carried out in various organizations directly financed by the state. Thus, to obtain an overview of the entire building industry, these entries can be summed up to give a reasonably accurate picture, while alternative aggregations will allow the activities of administrative divisions to be supervised. The latter subdivision can focus on the centres of integrated supply-planning, smoothing out seasonal fluctuations in revenue, centred on self-supporting entities arising from cross-subsidization, etc.

For our purpose aggregation according to the administrative principle is to be preferred. In the first place, many of the data are available exclusively in this breakdown. (This refers particularly to primary inputs, for which the 'branch-type' breakdown is usually

[13] Központi Statisztikai Hivatal, *Ágazati kapcsolatok mérlege 1970–1979*, Budapest, 1981. Another source of information was the *Statisztikai Évkönyv 1980* (Statistical Yearbook 1980) from the same publisher.

missing.) In the second place, the computations for planning purposes usually follow the organizational classification, with the Ministry of Finance and the Planning Office distributing available funds in conformity with it. Given the dominant role of the administrative principle, it seems appropriate to analyse price patterns in accordance with the classification that flows from it.[14]

In our classification scheme, we distinguish the following administrative sectors:[15]

1   Mining
2   Electricity
3   Metals
4   Machinery
5   Building materials
6   Chemicals
7   Light industry
8   Food
9   Construction
10   Agriculture
11   Forestry
12   Transport and telecommunications
13   Domestic trade
14   Foreign trade
15   Water supplies
16   Personal and economic services
17   Health, social, and cultural services
18   Communal and administrative services

[14] For example, sector 10 (Agriculture) is the result of merging the following headings in the original tables: 'Agriculture', 'Food processing activities in agriculture', 'Other industrial activities in agriculture', 'Building activities in agriculture', and 'Commercial activities in agriculture'. Sectoral nomenclature will mostly speak for itself; however, a few remarks seem in order. 'Mining' includes the exploitation and processing of Hungarian oil and gas, bauxite, etc.; refining of domestic and imported oil is registered under 'Chemicals'. The construction of highways and railways is entered under 'Transport and telecommunications'. 'Domestic trade' includes hotels and restaurants, catering services, travel agencies, and the like. By 'Foreign trade' is meant the organization of import–export-related activities. 'Personal and economic services' include housing facilities, insurances, banks, repairs, etc.

[15] The sectoral numbering follows established Hungarian practice. We have followed this practice to avoid confusion with the nine-sector classification we used for The Netherlands, and to facilitate the exposition of the various aggregation schemes we have employed.

The input–output tables are in current producer prices, i.e. the entries record the receipts of producers rather than the (usually different) payments made by the purchasers, while final demand is also recorded in producer prices.

The quantitative estimate of eigenprices and eigenyield is critically dependent on the availability and quality of the data supposedly representing the current remuneration of each primary factor. Given that Hungary followed a strict wages policy, the identification of the rewards of the factor 'labour' causes no special difficulty, and the same should apply to the primary factor 'imports', *mutatis mutandis*. When it comes to the factor 'capital', however, a strict application of the rules of Part I is a delicate matter, mainly because of the important role played by 'bargaining' in determining the financial position of the enterprise, when 'bailing out' in the face of adverse results is an everpresent possibility.

In trying to overcome the problems involved, we resorted to alternative aggregation schemes. In the first instance, we identified the variable w_1 with the remuneration of labour including social security payments paid by employers, the variable w_2 with the totals of pretax profits and amortization, and the variable w_3 with the sum of rouble and non-rouble imports. This relegates to the residual τ-row a number of headings, such as price discounts or price premia on the use of home-produced goods and various subsidies and taxes on imports and exports, as well as additional corrections connected with the difference between producer and consumer prices (Table 10.5).

The great flexibility of the theoretical framework of Part I enables us also to incorporate certain degrees of 'hardness' into our calculations. In the second exercise, therefore, we dispensed with the pre-tax profits in row w_2 except for amortization, thereby relegating the flow of 'net profits' to the τ-row. This must result in the Frobenius eigenvalue of the ensuing system measuring not the eigenyield as strictly defined in Part I, but the surplus yielded to the reduced factor-complement 'labour, imports, and amortization'. We have thereby eliminated a source of error arising from the 'bargaining skill' of enterprise management in dealing with the central authorities rather than from truly economic effort or performance, even though this has been achieved by narrowing the scope of true primary factor-inputs to a subset of those that the economy may be presumed to require. The results of this exercise are recorded in Table 10.6, which follows the same sector classification as the previous table.

Table 10.5 *Hungarian eigenprices for eighteen macro-sectors (on standard factor-base), 1970–9*

Sectors[a]	1970	1971	1972	1973	1974	1975	1976	1977	1978	1979
1	0.917	1.095	1.113	1.135	1.169	1.009	0.865	0.855	0.883	0.899
2	0.901	0.950	0.955	0.946	0.915	0.936	0.871	0.885	0.839	0.872
3	0.858	0.866	0.878	0.894	0.864	0.925	0.909	0.898	0.861	0.854
4	0.900	0.909	0.925	0.929	0.903	0.924	0.897	0.889	0.888	0.889
5	0.887	0.941	0.909	0.897	0.892	0.940	0.918	0.899	0.925	0.938
6	0.870	0.880	0.884	0.898	0.985	0.894	0.811	0.820	0.837	0.846
7	0.941	0.949	0.967	0.958	0.984	0.939	0.940	0.931	0.932	0.944
8	1.080	1.026	1.015	0.971	1.035	1.039	1.060	1.113	1.081	1.086
9	0.940	0.948	0.946	0.953	0.938	0.955	0.944	0.930	0.952	0.960
10	1.131	1.132	1.106	1.117	1.134	1.110	1.103	1.113	1.121	1.120
11	1.004	1.012	1.005	0.987	0.965	0.988	1.031	1.018	1.044	1.034
12	0.926	0.925	0.927	0.931	0.929	0.919	0.954	0.950	0.958	0.977
13	0.877	0.852	0.852	0.864	0.844	0.925	0.906	0.904	0.939	0.938
14	1.187	0.951	0.900	0.956	0.837	0.778	0.799	0.741	0.725	0.781
15	0.986	1.014	1.017	1.022	0.994	1.013	1.044	1.018	1.038	1.039
16	1.327	1.385	1.430	1.501	1.411	1.494	1.598	1.554	1.479	1.436
17	1.058	1.074	1.078	1.097	1.092	1.081	1.127	1.120	1.137	1.117
18	1.012	1.011	1.012	1.012	0.982	0.982	1.030	1.005	1.011	1.006
Primary factors[b]										
1	1.020	1.020	1.017	1.018	1.018	1.019	1.024	1.024	1.026	1.025
2	1.015	1.018	1.022	1.026	1.019	1.023	1.043	1.041	1.029	1.028
3	0.700	0.680	0.706	0.715	0.722	0.721	0.704	0.692	0.671	0.723

Table 10.5 *(cont.)*

Sectors[a]	1970	1971	1972	1973	1974	1975	1976	1977	1978	1979
Eigenyied (σ in %)	11.53	14.38	14.24	12.65	10.29	10.53	16.33	12.58	15.23	13.56
Price deviance (%)	10.88	10.83	10.69	11.03	11.32	10.72	13.28	13.90	12.85	12.20

[a] 1 = Mining; 2 = Electricity; 3 = Metals; 4 = Machinery; 5 = Building materials; 6 = Chemicals; 7 = Light industry and other; 8 = Food; 9 = Construction; 10 = Agriculture; 11 = Forestry; 12 = Transport and telecommunications; 13 = Domestic trade; 14 = Foreign trade; 15 = Water supplies; 16 = Personal and economic services; 17 = Health, social, and cultural services; 18 = Communal and administrative services.
[b] 1 = Wage factors; 2 = Other factors; 3 = Imports.

Table 10.6 *Hungarian eigenprices for eighteen macro-sectors (on reduced factor-base), 1970–9*[a]

Sectors[b]	1970	1971	1972	1973	1974	1975	1976	1977	1978	1979
1	1.017	1.105	1.154	1.198	1.215	0.984	0.930	0.897	0.914	0.931
2	0.827	0.860	0.858	0.881	0.876	0.932	0.901	0.914	0.851	0.896
3	0.854	0.883	0.904	0.896	0.830	0.924	0.941	0.958	0.896	0.894
4	0.806	0.810	0.815	0.821	0.783	0.799	0.804	0.780	0.787	0.800
5	0.865	0.890	0.852	0.871	0.865	0.888	0.876	0.881	0.891	0.908
6	0.826	0.845	0.844	0.875	0.986	0.882	0.816	0.836	0.850	0.867
7	0.913	0.912	0.921	0.943	0.976	0.907	0.911	0.925	0.920	0.926
8	1.118	1.067	1.062	1.009	1.102	1.121	1.119	1.170	1.151	1.154
9	0.901	0.899	0.890	0.898	0.871	0.889	0.900	0.884	0.888	0.893
10	1.251	1.244	1.247	1.224	1.257	1.248	1.238	1.230	1.238	1.241
11	0.992	1.024	1.041	1.020	0.962	1.001	0.999	1.007	1.018	1.004
12	0.950	0.965	0.989	0.986	0.980	0.986	0.979	0.981	0.979	0.992
13	0.657	0.674	0.669	0.687	0.663	0.714	0.730	0.735	0.737	0.739
14	0.638	0.664	0.603	0.616	0.543	0.504	0.623	0.546	0.545	0.654
15	1.012	1.046	1.068	1.075	1.085	1.113	1.139	1.113	1.108	1.119
16	1.114	1.098	1.092	1.113	1.053	1.112	1.102	1.066	1.077	1.063
17	1.231	1.257	1.270	1.308	1.293	1.281	1.319	1.326	1.340	1.307
18	1.209	1.237	1.271	1.301	1.264	1.280	1.299	1.298	1.269	1.262
Primary factors										
1	1.052	1.051	1.052	1.050	1.054	1.054	1.060	1.060	1.060	1.057
2	1.028	1.028	1.030	1.031	1.037	1.040	1.041	1.041	1.041	1.039
3	0.700	0.683	0.711	0.722	0.735	0.733	0.713	0.702	0.681	0.732
Eigenyield (σ in %)	57.54	61.06	62.12	64.35	58.47	58.69	65.16	63.79	64.91	59.63
Price deviance (%)	19.31	18.69	19.11	18.61	20.95	19.91	19.03	20.24	20.05	18.83

[a] Net profits being imputed to the τ-row (see the text). Primary factors now are: 1 = Wage factors; 2 = Amortization; 3 = Imports.
[b] We have followed the sectoral classification of Table 10.5.

Table 10.7 *Hungarian eigenprices for nine macro-sectors, 1970–9*[16]

Sectors[a]	1970	1971	1972	1973	1974	1975	1976	1977	1978	1979
A	1.134	1.136	1.114	1.122	1.140	1.114	1.111	1.120	1.129	1.126
B	0.918	1.040	1.033	1.037	1.046	0.988	0.900	0.885	0.915	0.928
C	1.088	1.036	1.027	0.980	1.045	1.049	1.074	1.127	1.096	1.098
D	0.873	0.882	0.888	0.900	0.990	0.903	0.828	0.837	0.856	0.862
E	0.896	0.908	0.925	0.928	0.902	0.932	0.912	0.903	0.897	0.894
F	0.909	0.925	0.951	0.943	0.977	0.937	0.944	0.940	0.943	0.956
G	1.014	1.019	1.031	1.011	1.031	0.977	0.979	0.967	0.962	0.966
H	0.956	0.968	0.970	0.977	0.960	0.970	0.959	0.945	0.965	0.973
I	1.008	1.002	1.007	1.020	0.989	1.012	1.043	1.029	1.031	1.036
Primary factors										
1	1.017	1.016	1.013	1.013	1.012	1.013	1.016	1.017	1.017	1.018
2	1.000	1.000	1.000	1.001	0.998	0.999	1.004	1.006	1.004	1.005
3	0.701	0.682	0.710	0.717	0.725	0.725	0.709	0.696	0.676	0.728
Eigenyield (σ in %)	12.17	15.25	15.34	13.87	11.32	11.65	18.12	14.20	16.54	14.63
Price deviance (%)	8.27	7.29	6.02	6.18	6.96	6.09	8.06	9.09	8.46	8.45

[a] A = Agriculture, fishing, and forestry; B = Mining and oil; C = Food, drink, and tobacco; D = Chemicals; E = Metals and engineering; F = Textiles, leather, and clothing; G = Other manufacturing; H = Construction; I = Utilities, transport, and services. Primary factors are as in Table 10.5.

[16] In terms of the classification of Table 10.5, we have: A = sectors 10 and 11; B = sectors 1 and 5; C = sector 8; D = sector 6; E = sectors 3 and 4; F = part of sector 7; G = remaining part of sector 7; H = sector 9; I = sectors 2 and 12–18.

Table 10.8 *Hungarian eigenprices for five macro-sectors, 1970–9*[17]

Sectors[a]	1970	1971	1972	1973	1974	1975	1976	1977	1978	1979
A	0.943	0.946	0.954	0.941	0.963	0.952	0.931	0.941	0.932	0.935
B	0.955	0.954	0.953	0.955	0.945	0.957	0.948	0.937	0.956	0.963
C	1.123	1.125	1.105	1.114	1.123	1.105	1.105	1.116	1.118	1.113
D	0.933	0.897	0.896	0.902	0.878	0.904	0.919	0.908	0.928	0.943
E	1.121	1.138	1.157	1.182	1.145	1.166	1.237	1.222	1.197	1.175
Primary factors										
1	1.019	1.020	1.019	1.022	1.018	1.020	1.025	1.023	1.024	1.021
2	1.000	1.000	1.001	1.004	1.001	1.001	1.012	1.011	1.008	1.006
3	0.699	0.685	0.713	0.720	0.724	0.726	0.709	0.694	0.675	0.728
Eigenyield (σ in %)	12.17	14.92	14.83	13.21	10.98	11.18	17.31	13.77	16.10	14.40
Price deviance (%)	8.09	8.88	8.75	9.59	8.84	8.67	10.85	10.41	9.97	9.15

[a] A = Industrial sectors; B = Construction; C = Agriculture; D = Productive services; E = Other services. Primary factors are as in Table 10.5.

[17] In terms of the classification of Table 10.5, we have: A = sectors 1–8; B = sector 9; C = sectors 10 and 11; D = sectors 12–15; E = sectors 16–18.

As a further step, we aggregated the 18 sectors of the first tables into nine macro-sectors, following, as far as possible, the sector classification used for The Netherlands in Chapters 34–6 and the analysis of the pilot survey. Table 10.7, which shows the results, defines these sectors by letter in a footnote to the table. Finally, to test the effects of further aggregations, we added yet one more exercise in which the system is condensed into five major sectors (see Table 10.8).

10.7 Discussion of the Results for Hungary

Although in the Hungarian case aggregation took place along administrative and organizational lines, conclusions regarding the associated products or product groups emerge quite naturally. A first impression is that our results reveal substantial differences between the eigenprices calculated for The Netherlands and for Hungary. In contrast to Holland, the Hungarian eigenprices appear to show greater variations between commodities and commodity groups, generally with fairly revealing time-profiles.

This is certainly the case for the first sector quoted in Tables 10.5 and 10.6. In the first half of the 1970s energy became increasingly underpriced in relation to the pricing of other activities within the economy. This may be traced to the fact that more than two-thirds of the increase in world market prices was neutralized through subsidies on imported goods, where the price divergence was particularly large for crude oil. Keeping the domestic price of oil low was helped, naturally, by the slow adaptation of official CMEA prices for energy to developments in other markets (more than 80 per cent of Hungarian oil is imported, mostly from the USSR). This is possibly also a factor in explaining the declining trend in eigenprices for electrical energy (sector 2) until 1975. The sudden impact of the increase in world market prices is probably reflected by the relatively high eigenprice for Chemicals (sector 6) in 1974, about half of its imports stemming from Western countries; though still indicative of overpricing, it is markedly higher than in previous—and later—years. (The same is true, though to a lesser extent, for sector 7, Light industry.)

A number of price adjustments occurred in the years 1975–6, following general world trends. Producer prices were raised by about 10 per cent in 1975 and by another 4 per cent in 1976, the largest revisions affecting the prices for energy and raw materials. To a certain extent this is reflected in the data for these years. In Table 10.5 we observe a *fall* in eigenprices for basic sectors such as mining and chemicals, and a *rise* for their users such as metals, machinery, and building materials. In the subsequent years the pattern that developed was more or less maintained. The shift in energy prices in 1975 and 1976 is also reflected in the eigenprice of the second sector quoted, reflecting as it does the significant increase in electricity prices in a fall from 0.936 in 1975, to 0.871 in 1976 and 0.839 in 1978. (Producer prices for electricity were substantially increased both in 1976 and 1978.)

Eigenprices for food and agriculture reflect underpricing throughout the period, which is consistent with observations from many other sources. Moreover, a number of services still financed from the state budget are typically underpriced. The exception here is foreign trade, which is grossly overpriced. However, this need not surprise us, since the eigenprices of these services reflect substantial margins in the import–export trade. The outcome for sector 12 (transport and telecommunications) is something of a surprise, showing an eigenprice that seems too low in view of the fact that this sector (like communal and administrative services) is supposed to operate on a non-profit basis.

Overall consumer prices rose by 5 per cent in 1976, almost double the average increase per annum during the previous five years. Given that wages were lagging behind prices, the rise in the eigenrental for the wage factor need not surprise us. The calculated values of 'Other factors' (in essence, the factor capital) are comparable with those of labour; with wages linked to enterprise profits through various devices, the simultaneous increase in the eigenprice for 'Other factors' in 1976 is not surprising either. The fact that our tables reflect pre-tax situations need not detract from their interest, as a supplementary 'post-tax' exercise with tax rates assumed to vary between 40 and 60 per cent, revealed no significant changes in either commodity or factor-eigenprices. Accordingly, its results are not quoted here.

Imports are largely overpriced in comparison with the other primary factors, a result that may reflect the various devices used in import–export trade. (Because of the presence of multiple price arrangements between the CMEA countries, an analysis in terms of rouble and non-rouble imports might have been interesting. This, however, would have required more extensive material.) The relatively high eigenyield figure for 1976 seems consistent with the picture drawn above. We would also point out that the observed eigenyields are of the same order of magnitude as those emerging from the pilot survey in the case of Austria, Sweden, and Yugoslavia. The two aggregation exercises distinguishing nine and five macro-sectors respectively, confirm our results in broad outline, again *mutatis mutandis*.

Price deviances (for definition see Table 9.1) are seen to be quite sensitive to aggregation or to the changing factors (inclusion or exclusion of net profits from the factor base). The fact that in our tables aggregation decreases deviances is not surprising, as the sectoral differences will have a tendency to average out. The exclusion of profits will affect especially the sectors that use some of the primary factors in relatively small amounts, such as certain services where amortization and imports are of relatively minor importance. Here a shift of profits to the τ-row will decrease the proportion of the remaining primary factors in the value-added components to a greater than average extent. The consequences for the eigenprice of those sectors may be expected to be larger than for other sectors, thus causing an increase in overall price deviance.

10.8 Concluding Remarks

The concept of eigenprices is intended to furnish a tool to gauge whether a product or primary factor is over- or under-priced in relation to the market prices of an economy's final deliveries. As such, eigenprices may be looked on as 'true' prices, i.e. prices that would exist in a situation producing the same final flows without imperfections in the markets for commodities or factors. We have seen in this study that the methodology may be useful (1) in studying the historical development of a specific country, and (2) in making international or inter-system comparisons.

When comparing The Netherlands (Tables 10.1 and 10.2) with Hungary, we note that the two sets of eigenprices present radically different patterns. In the case of the Netherlands, deviations from unity are quite small in the domain of commodity prices, while in Hungary these deviations tend to be considerable. This may reflect the fact that Dutch prices are to a large extent determined 'freely' by the forces of demand and supply. Similarly small deviations from unity may well be found for comparable market economies. This is partly confirmed by the pilot study; but it is an area in which further research could usefully be undertaken. In Hungary, where the government still plays a dominant role in the process of price determination independently of market-clearing considerations, eigenprices are clearly seen to deviate from unity quite substantially.

J. Kornai stated that it was the declared intention of the 'third wave of reforms' (1978–82) to 'harden' the financial constraints on state-owned enterprises by imposing a tax subsidy system not easily modifiable by a bargaining process. The 1980 price revision was designed to replace the common 'cost-plus' pricing principle by a price system that would adjust Hungarian domestic prices more readily to prices realized in foreign trade with inconvertible currencies. In official Hungarian terminology, this system is referred to as 'the competitive price system'.[18] We must evidently wait for further research on other East European countries to deepen our understanding of the patterns observed in this exercise.

Two final remarks seem to be called for. First, it should be recalled that the absolute level of eigenprices depends on the method chosen for their 'standardization'. We have here followed the procedure recommended in Part I and the pilot survey, which leaves the total of final demand (i.e. the conventional GNP) invariant. Different types of standardization will lead to a different level of eigenprices, although the relative proportions will remain unaffected. Second, eigenyield and eigenprices are crucially dependent on the interpretations given to such terms as 'labour', 'capital', 'tax', etc., and will also vary with the treatment of social security payments, depreciation, and the like. The allocation of these items to various types of primary inputs must impart a measure of arbitrariness to the calculation, thus tending to vitiate international comparisons. Clearly, whenever two countries fail to record their primary inputs according to a unified definition or breakdown, the comparison between them by the present methods is fraught with considerable danger, and should be undertaken with the utmost care.

---

[18] J. Kornai, 'Comments on the Present State and Prospects of the Hungarian Economic Reform'.

Appendix A

(contributed by Professor A. E. Steenge)

Data for the USA: An Experiment with Alternative Methods of Dealing with Multiple Production

A.1 Introduction

A basic feature of Leontief's input–output model is that each industry produces only one product, and that each product is produced by only one industry. Because of this built-in one-to-one relation between an industry and a commodity, Leontief's table of intermediate deliveries is square and 'homogeneous'. That is, the table can be interpreted as being of dimension of either commodity × commodity (c × c) or industry × industry (i × i). From the table the all-important multipliers linking changes in final demand to changes in total output can be obtained straightforwardly as the elements of the so-called 'Leontief inverse'.

A major advantage of the Leontief model framework is that its analytical power is based on a type of mathematics that has been available since the beginning of the twentieth century. Non-negative matrix theory dates back to the German mathematicians Perron and Frobenius. On the basis of their theoretical work, for example, it became known that the Leontief inverse is positive if the matrix of input-coefficients is indecomposable.

As already mentioned by Seton in Sect. 7.1, multiproduct production occurs quite often in reality. In such cases it is customary to distinguish between several types of product. First of all, to 'label' the activities, a choice should be made as to which product is to count as the industry's main or primary product. Assuming that this does not pose any serious problem, this product then serves to characterize the industry. If a specific industry produces commodities that are primary to another industry, these commodities are termed 'secondary'. If the products are technically related they are called 'by-products'. And finally, if a certain jointly produced commodity cannot be identified with a particular industry as its main product, this commodity is called a joint product. As we shall see later on, these distinctions are relevant for the interpretation of results obtained using the tables in money values that we usually work with.[1]

---

[1] In order to indicate the general case—and to avoid too much detail—we shall usually employ the term 'multiple production'. The last case (i.e. 'joint production' in the 'strict' sense) has been presented for the sake of completeness; it is generally

After World War II industrial production rapidly diversified, and multiple production became the rule rather than the exception. These diversification effects, however, cannot be handled by the Leontief framework. This implies that to obtain the sought-after production multipliers, complicating reallocations or redefinitions of the basic raw material are required in order to obtain *homogeneous* tables. Forcing real world data into the Leontief mould via a sequence of reallocations of cost and benefits clearly entails the risk of introducing irrealistic and artificial constructs. The need to construct tables based on mono-product industries increasingly meant that artificial and arbitrary elements were introduced, thus potentially leading to a reduction of the value of the end-product, the 'homogenized' tables. (From a purely descriptive statistical point of view, a further complicating tendency was the marked shift from the traditional agricultural and manufacturing industrial sectors to services, electronics, and other new types of industry. Statistical handling of the various input and output categories of these relatively new industries has become increasingly more complex.)[2]

Table A.1

	Commodities	Industries	Final outputs	Totals
Commodities		**U**	**e**	**q**
Industries	**V**			**g**
Primary inputs		**y′**		
Totals	**q′**	**g′**		

In its System of National Accounts (SNA) the United Nations proposed a departure from the established Leontief approach.[3] The new system did away with the explicit one–one relation between product and industry. The possibility of multiple production was now explicitly accounted for and, vice versa, a specific good could be the product of more than one industry. The SNA-system distinguished a 'use-matrix', of dimensions commodity × industry (c × i), and 'make-matrix' of dimensions industry × commodity (i × c). Although squareness of the tables is not explicitly required, we shall assume, following many empirical studies, that squareness is present. Table A.1 sets this out in tableau-form, and in a by-now-familiar notation. Here **U** represents the commodity by industry-use or absorption matrix, **V** the industry by commodity make-matrix, **e** the vector of final demands, and **y′** the (row) vector of primary inputs (the prime denotes transposition). The use-matrix

not relevant to us. For a full survey of these issues, see R. E. Miller and P. D. Blair, *Input–Output Analysis: Foundations and Extensions*, ch. 5, Prentice-Hall, Englewood Cliffs, NJ, 1985.

[2] See A. Carter, 'Input–Output Recipes in an Information Economy', *Economic Systems Research*, 1 (1989).

[3] See United Nations, *A System of National Accounts. Studies in Methods*, Series F, No. 2, New York, 1968.

can be viewed as an extension of the traditional input-coefficients-matrix; the make-matrix as an extension of the output-coefficients matrix, i.e. the unit-matrix.[4]

A.2 The UN's Technology Assumptions

Although the new framework solved many problems of a purely descriptive nature, from an analytical point of view many questions remained. For example, how should multipliers be calculated? Or rather, how should they be defined in the new context? Clearly, in the SNA-framework they cannot be straightforwardly obtained because the basic make and use tables, being of $i \times c$ or $c \times i$ format, are *not* homogeneous. This meant that the whole Perron–Frobenius mathematical foundation was no longer available, while new mathematics to fill this gap were not yet available.

The UN proposes several approaches. A well-known suggestion is to assume a *commodity technology*. That is, we assume commodity-specific input proportions independent of the industry in which the commodity is produced. A second suggestion is to assume an *industry technology*, which requires, among other things, fixed output shares. Both are based on the following assumptions regarding the existence of constant-coefficient matrices:

$$U = B\hat{g}, \qquad (A.1)$$

where B is a matrix of constant use or absorption coefficients, and

$$V' = C\hat{g} \qquad (A.2)$$

with C a matrix of fixed-output coefficients.

The commodity–technology model immediately leads to an input–output matrix, either in commodity $\times$ commodity ($c \times c$) or industry $\times$ industry format ($i \times i$).[5] Denoting the $c \times c$ input–output matrix by M^c, we have

$$M^c \equiv BC^{-1} = U(V')^{-1}. \qquad (A.3)$$

(From $BC^{-1} = U(\hat{g})^{-1}(V'(\hat{g})^{-1})^{-1} = U(\hat{g})^{-1}(g)(V')^{-1} = U(V')^{-1}$). Denoting the $i \times i$ variant by M^i we have

$$M^i \equiv C^{-1}B = (\hat{g})(V')^{-1}U(\hat{g})^{-1}. \qquad (A.4)$$

Mathematically, both approaches thus simply postulate the existence of a non-negative matrix connecting the make and use matrices. The columns of this matrix are to be interpreted as the columns of commodity- or industry-specific input requirements. The sought-after production multipliers now

---

[4] Because the UN's notation has been adopted here, the symbols differ from the ones used in Sect. 7.1.

[5] For additional argumentation and derivations of both forms, see United Nations *System of National Accounts*, or R. Stone, 'Accounting Matrices in Economics and Demography', ch. 2 in F. van der Ploeg (ed.), *Mathematical Models in Economics*, Wiley, Chichester, 1984.

could be obtained by using matrices $\mathbf{M}^c$ or $\mathbf{M}^i$, provided of course these matrices were non-negative.

If we do not adopt a strategy like that used by the UN, we are stuck with matrices such as $(\mathbf{C} - \mathbf{B})^{-1}$, as an analogon of the Leontief inverse. Interpretations of the result given by this approach may be difficult to accept. For example, in that case we may have to decide how to interpret the fact that an *increase* in final demand may, according to the model, lead to a *decrease* of total outputs.[6] Calculating eigenprices on this basis seems to be rather risky.

A.3 Empirical Investigations

The UN's methods clearly were a step forward. However, there is absolutely no guarantee that matrices $\mathbf{M}^c$ or $\mathbf{M}^i$ are indeed non-negative. For want of a theoretical basis, empirical testing may provide indications whether the ideas are potentially fruitful. (Note that also in Sect. 7.1 above, the exposition proceeds with matrix $\mathbf{A} = \mathbf{X}\mathbf{Z}^{-1}$ (notation Seton), without any guarantee regarding its non-negativity.)

Empirical testing of the relevance of the commodity–technology model gave disappointing results, however. The problem was that negative elements invariably kept appearing in the calculated matrices. Because these negatives have no interpretation in an input–output framework, this implied that the commodity–technology model did not produce meaningful results.

Several attempts have been made to provide a statistical explanation of the occurrence of the negatives. Statistical methods usually postulate a known distribution for the entries in the tables. However, the problem here is how to establish the appropriate distribution and its parameters for each entry. Based on several assumptions, the intervals thought to be relevant could be calculated.[7] Unexpectedly, these approaches invariably resulted in the rejection of the commodity–technology model as an appropriate description of economic reality.

The verdict of the empirical tests resulted in a lack of generally acceptable techniques to tackle the problem of the negatives. As a consequence, many countries have turned to the industry–technology approach (although this method is theoretically inferior to the commodity–technology approach) or have adopted one of many alternative mixed forms, thereby sacrificing transparency. Those mixed forms, however, do have the advantage that they

---

[6] See G. Abraham-Frois and E. Berrebi, 'La demande, face câchée de la production jointe', *Revue Economique*, 32 (1981), or A. E. Steenge, 'On the Wage-Profit Relation in a Sraffa System with Joint Production', *Revue Economique*, 37 (1987).

[7] For such an approach, see e.g. R. van der Ploeg and Th. ten Raa, 'A Statistical Approach to the Problem of the Negatives in Input–Output Analysis', *Economic Modelling*, 6 (1989).

provide the desired homogeneity *and non-negativity*.[8] They lack, however, a sufficient theoretical basis, and therefore are not really satisfactory.

There is no reason for despair, however. A question that has not yet been addressed in the discussion is under which conditions a non-negative matrix connecting the make and use matrix actually does exist. It can be shown that if the economy satisfies a certain elementary condition, such a matrix does in fact exist. From this matrix multiplier matrices *and* eigenprices can then be calculated. Below we shall first briefly discuss this approach, after which we go into the exact interpretation of the result.[9]

A.4 The Commodity–Technology Model Revisited

The existence of a non-negative matrix connecting matrices **B** and **C** as defined above, can be provided with a theoretical basis if the economy is such that a positive output vector requires a positive vector of inputs. (Recall that we are working with square matrices here.) To see why this should be the case, let us consider a traditional single product input–output model with non-singular input-coefficients matrix, to be denoted by the symbol **M**. Further let **x** represent an arbitrary positive output vector, i.e.

$$\mathbf{x} > 0. \tag{A.5}$$

Then obviously

$$\mathbf{Mx} > 0. \tag{A.6}$$

That is, the traditional input–output model is such that normally

$$\mathbf{x} > 0 \Rightarrow \mathbf{Mx} > 0. \tag{A.7}$$

The vice-versa relation is not generally valid: **x** may have negative elements (thereby allowing an interpretation as a vector of increments, for example). Non-negative outputs thus are guaranteed only if non-negative inputs are available. Analogously, for the price side of the model, we find that a non-negative price vector implies non-negative input costs

$$\mathbf{p} > 0 \Rightarrow \mathbf{pM} > 0. \tag{A.8}$$

---

[8] See Interindustry Economics Division, 'The Input–Output Structure of the US Economy, 1977', *Survey of Current Business* (1984), 42–84, but also U.N. Statistical Office, 'Input–Output Standards in the SNA Framework', in A. Franz and R. Rainer (eds.), *Problems of Compilation of Input–Output Tables*, Orac, Vienna, 1986, or N. Rainer, 'Descriptive versus Analytical Make-Use Systems: Some Austrian Experience'. Paper presented at the Eighth International Conference on Input–Output Techniques, Sapporo, Japan, 28 July–2 Aug. 1986.

[9] A. E. Steenge, 'Second Thoughts on the Commodity Technology and the Industry Technology Approaches', in A. Franz and N. Rainer (eds.), *Compilation of Input–Output Data*, Vienna, 1989, and Steenge, 'The Commodity Technology Revisited', *Economic Modelling*, 7 (1990).

Extensions to the case of multiple production are self-evident. Here we should realize that **x** in (A.6) stands for both the vector of sectoral output levels and the total output vector. In joint production models these two functions should be considered separately, and we should distinguish between a vector of commodity outputs, a vector of industrial outputs, and a vector of production levels. Now let us consider a joint production variant like

$$\mathbf{Cx} > 0 \Rightarrow \mathbf{Bx} > 0. \tag{A.9}$$

(Note that **x** need not be non-negative here; for example, it may stand for a vector of—positive or negative—production increments. Mangasarian provided a basic result here.[10] He discussed a number of implications of the above type. Suppose, for example, that **B** and **C** are rectangular real m x n and k × n matrices, then we have

$$(\mathbf{Cx} \geqslant 0 \Rightarrow \mathbf{Bx} \geqslant 0) \Leftrightarrow \text{(There exists an } \mathbf{M^c} \geqslant 6\ 0\text{: } \mathbf{B} = \mathbf{M^c C}),$$
with $\mathbf{M^c}$ a real $m \times k$ matrix).

It is clear that Mangasarian's theorem may provide a theoretical basis for the commodity–technology model. The proof of the theorem is quite complicated. However, in case matrices **B** and **C** are *square* and if **C** is non-singular, a much simpler proof can be given.[11] We should also note that if our matrices **B** and **C** are square and if **C** has full rank, $\mathbf{M^c}$ is easily seen to exist. For the price implication a similar equivalence is straightforwardly derived.

Mangasarian's results have importance for the interpretation of the UN's commodity–technology model. The above tells us that if **B** and **C** have the property that for any **x** we have $\mathbf{Cx} \geqslant 6\ 0 \Rightarrow \mathbf{Bx} \geqslant 6\ 0$, a column of a non-negative matrix $\mathbf{M^c}$ can be associated with each commodity. Its columns can be interpreted as columns of commodity-specific bundles of imputed input proportions. However, by no means has it yet been shown that they represent *technologically interpretable* commodity-specific limitational production functions of the standard Leontief type. Clearly, if the set of commodities contains only primary and secondary products, we may expect that in certain cases they will allow an interpretation in terms of technologically interpretable Leontief production functions.

In the case of pure by- or joint-production, the interpretation of the columns of $\mathbf{M^c}$ is already much more complicated. Interpreting them as engineering input–output functions makes no sense here because these processes are by definition lacking. Nevertheless, the columns of $\mathbf{M^c}$ do represent imputed commodity-specific input proportions, consistent with the overall make-use framework. If, as in our case below, matrix $\mathbf{M^c}$ is calculated from

---

[10] O. L. Mangasarian, 'Perron–Frobenius Properties of $Ax = \lambda Bx'$, *Journal of Mathematical Analysis and Applications*, 36 (1971), 86–102.

[11] Steenge, 'Commodity Technology Revisited'.

tables in money values, its columns represent input shares imputed to each commodity being produced by the economy. The relation between these imputed shares, in money value, and possible interpretations in terms of sectoral technological characteristics needs a lot of further study. Here only some preliminary steps have been taken.

A.5 The Location of Inaccuracies

Underlying the statistical approaches to the problem of finding an acceptable basis for the commodity–technology model, of course, is the fact that a substantial degree of arbitrariness is present in the balancing process of the commodity-flow system. Here we may mention certain redistribution techniques, such as the RAS or Lagrange methods, problems in distinguishing stock or flow characteristics, the use of inter- or extra-polation techniques, errors in sampling and sampling methods, incorrect homogeneity assumptions, and aggregation problems.[12]

If we are unable to achieve meaningful results by imposing certain distributions to account for the fact that inaccuracies are present in the make and use tables, how else could we proceed? One approach that has not yet been explored is to try to profit from the fact that negatives can often be linked straightforwardly to specific elements in the make or use matrices. That is, experience up to now has indicated that the negativity of a certain element can be explained in terms of the magnitude of only a very limited number of other entries, i.e. if those entries would have (possibly only slightly) different values, the negatives might disappear. Now suppose we have identified certain such elements. If sector specialists would be able to tell us about the 'quality' of the published figures on these entries, we might have located a potential element 'explaining' one or more negatives. If indeed the statistician who built the table is able to give us further indications regarding the reliability of the published figures, the basic use or make tables should be corrected in the indicated way, and a new matrix $\mathbf{M^c}$ be calculated.[13] A systematic way to proceed is to calculate the matrices

$$\mathbf{X_{ij}} = \frac{\delta \mathbf{M^c_{ij}}}{\delta \mathbf{C}} = \frac{\delta (\mathbf{BC^{-1}})_{ij}}{\delta \mathbf{C}} = -(\mathbf{C^{-1}})'\mathbf{B}'\mathbf{E_{ij}}(\mathbf{C^{-1}})', \tag{A.10}$$

$$\mathbf{Y_{ij}} = \frac{\delta \mathbf{M^c}}{\delta \mathbf{C_{ij}}} = \frac{\delta \mathbf{BC^{-1}}}{\delta \mathbf{C_{ij}}} = -\mathbf{BC^{-1}}\mathbf{E_{ij}}\mathbf{C^{-1}}, \tag{A.11}$$

and

---

[12] For comments on the many fundamental issues of classification that are involved here, see R. Eisner, 'Extended Accounts for National Income and Product', *Journal of Economic Literature*, 24 (1988), 1611–84.

[13] Concerning the—not discussed—industry × industry variant, a similar argumentation can be employed.

$$\mathbf{Z_{ij}} = \frac{\delta \mathbf{M_{ij}^c}}{\delta \mathbf{B}} = \mathbf{E_{ij}}(\mathbf{C}^{-1})', \qquad (A.12)$$

where $\mathbf{E_{ij}}$ is an elementary matrix which has unity in its (i,j)th position while all other elements are zero.[14] If certain elements of, say, $\mathbf{X_{ij}}$ are large, this means that small errors in the corresponding elements of $\mathbf{C}$ will have a large effect on $\mathbf{M_{ij}^c}$. Therefore, it may be worth while to investigate the accuracies of *these* elements in particular. Generally, this will imply a thorough reconsideration of the way these elements have been compiled.

In Steenge, 'Commodity Technology Revisited', we discuss a number of exercises with the small American BEA table published in Young, 'US Input–Output Experience',[15] (1986). It appeared that by changing only seven entries (only two of which were relatively large) a non-negative matrix $\mathbf{M^c}$ could be generated. In view of the way in which the basic data for the American make and use tables are assembled, this outcome does not seem particularly surprising.[16]

The example we have presented (based on the small BEA tables for the US for 1977) illustrates that only very few corrections may be required to obtain (corrected) make and use matrices such that the implied third matrix does not contain any negatives. However, further research on much larger tables is required here before a definite verdict can be reached.

A.6 Eigenprices for the USA

We have seen in the previous section that by working with the functions $\mathbf{X_{ij}}$, $\mathbf{Y_{ij}}$, and $\mathbf{Z_{ij}}$, entries in the use and make tables can be discovered that may be the cause of the negatives in the calculated matrices $\mathbf{M^c}$ and $\mathbf{M^i}$. Our exercise involved only a small table. For large tables the number of possible 'candidates' rapidly becomes unmanageable and mechanistic devices are asked for. Nevertheless, for small aggregated tables our approach may work quite well, because as a result of the aggregation process the output matrix may have only a limited number of off-diagonal elements.

For our exercise, we worked with only twelve sectors. This was a consequence of the fact that the sectors 'Non-comparable Imports' and 'Scrap and Special Industries' did not use any inputs of the intermediate kind. Distinguished are the following twelve sectors: Agriculture, Mining, Construction, Manufacturing, Transportation and Communication, Electric, Gas, and Water Services, Wholesale and Retail Trade, Finance and Insurance, Real Estate,

---

[14] See Steenge, 'Commodity Technology Revisited' for proofs.

[15] P. C. Young, 'The US Input–Output Experience—Present Status and Future Prospects', in Franz and Rainer (eds.), *Problems of Compilation of Input–Output Tables*.

[16] The tables are compiled using data collected by the Census Bureau. Unfortunately, the Census procedures and classification schemes do not always coincide with input–output convention.

Eating and Drinking Places, Services, and Government Enterprises. On the factor side we distinguish Labour, Capital, and Imports. The residual taxes and surpluses then complete the tables.

The eigenprices for the twelve sectors and the three primary factors were calculated from matrix $\mathbf{M}^c$ and its corresponding matrix of primary input coefficients (Table A.2). The influence of the relatively large entry for the American imports is quite considerable. This is a consequence of the fact that imports consist for a large part of foreign oil and other energy carriers. At our level of aggregation this means that the outcomes of the American energy policy debates are passed on into the economy via the mining sector. Its large eigenprice implies that the sectors that are dependent on its deliveries also tend to large eigenprices. It may appear a bit surprising that the American eigenprices fluctuate much more than the eigenprices for The Netherlands. However, as we have an observation for only one year, we leave a detailed discussion of the individual values to the cases for Hungary and The Netherlands, where time-series are available.

Table A.2

Sectoral eigenprices for the USA, 1977	
Agriculture	1.060
Mining	1.106
Construction	1.014
Manufacturing	1.028
Transportation and communication	0.975
Electric, gas, and water services	1.049
Wholesale and retail trade	0.904
Finance and insurance	1.000
Real estate	0.961
Eating and drinking places	0.993
Services	1.039
Government enterprises	1.092
Corresponding primary factor eigenprices	
Labour	1.019
Capital	0.992
Imports	1.036
Eigenyield = $100(1/\phi - 1) = 1000(1/0.922 - 1) = 8.46\%$	

The above eigenprices were calculated using the approach based on the Mangasarian theorem. By way of experiment we have also calculated the American eigenprices via the approach advanced by Seton discussed in Sect. 7.1. We obtained a very close result (Table A.3).

It is likely that the fact that the eigenprice patterns are quite similar is due to the fact that only very small corrections were needed to obtain a non-negative matrix $\mathbf{M}^c$. The primary factor eigenprices show a much larger range, which may be due to the fact that one entry needed a substantial correction to obtain a non-negative factor coefficients matrix. Finding the general pattern here is another area for additional research.

Table A.3

Sectoral eigenprices for the USA, 1977 Seton method

Agriculture	1.027
Mining	1.112
Construction	1.031
Manufacturing	1.041
Transportation and communication	0.975
Electric, gas, and water services	1.027
Wholesale and retail trade	0.911
Finance and insurance	1.006
Real estate	0.894
Eating and drinking places	0.003
Services	1.038
Government enterprises	1.105

Corresponding primary factor prices

Labour	0.975
Capital	1.024
Imports	1.166

Appendix B

Eigenprices and Cost-Values

SINCE eigenprices are constructed with the special object of avoiding the twin defects of factor-monomania and cost-fetishism, which—in my submission—distort traditional model prices of a diagnostic nature, it is of particular importance to measure and analyse their deviations from such prices in the context of an empirical study. The computation by which eigenprices are obtained (Chapters 6–10) throws up a number of cost-fetishist and monomaniac values as intermediate steps in the procedure, which are therefore readily available for the purpose in hand.[1]

Table B.1 compares the Marxian labour-values λ with eigenprices p_* for our nine macro-sectors in five countries, and analyses the multiplicative correction-factor $\iota = p_*/\lambda$ ('inflator'), which provides the link, and factorizes into the part played by the admission of 'co-factors' other than labour (co-factor-inflator i_1) and the part played by influences from the demand-side (use-value inflator i_2). The first of these components defines the effect of eliminating 'monomania', while the second measures that of amending 'cost-fetishism' by admitting use-value alongside costs into value formation.

The table makes it clear that the effects of eliminating monomania (i_1) are nearly everywhere considerably stronger than those of correcting for cost-fetishism (i_2), with the latter being virtually of uniform size in all the sectors of a given country. This is indeed to be expected whenever the standardized eigenrentals r_*^1, r_*^2 differ only marginally from unity, thus making eigenprices:

$$\mathbf{P}_*' = 1/\pi \,.\, \mathbf{r}_*'\mathbf{C}$$

virtually equal to full total factor costs:

$$\lambda' + \mathbf{K}' = \mathbf{i}'\mathbf{C}.$$

As a result the ration i_2 becomes nearly identical with $1/\pi$ throughout the system.

---

[1] Similar computations for Austria and Hungary, though without direct comparisons with eigenprices, are presented in a particularly valuable monograph by G. Fink, *Preisverzerrungen und Unterschiede in der Produktionsstruktur zwischen Österreich und Ungarn* (Springer-Verlag, Vienna, 1981), which also explains derivation and rationale in a most illuminating way. For a shortened version see also Gerhard Fink, 'Price Distortions in the Austrian and in the Hungarian Economy', *Zeitschrift für Nationalökonomie*, 41 (1981), 111–32.

Table B.1. *Eigenprices and cost-values compared*

		A	B	C	D	E	F	G	H	I
Czechoslovakia 1973										
Labour value	λ	0.589	0.387	0.386	0.232	0.348	0.304	0.358	0.389	0.424
'Capital value'	κ	0.130	0.373	0.164	0.341	0.341	0.255	0.296	0.309	0.277
Cofactor inflator	t_1	1.221	1.964	1.425	2.470	1.980	1.839	1.827	1.794	1.653
Use-value inflator	t_2	1.527	1.531	1.531	1.532	1.533	1.531	1.532	1.530	1.531
Eigenprice	$p*$	1.098	1.164	0.842	0.878	1.056	0.856	1.002	1.068	1.073
Japan 1970										
Labour value	λ	0.195	0.438	0.273	0.322	0.427	0.465	0.416	0.447	0.429
'Capital value'	κ	0.781	0.497	0.573	0.500	0.481	0.453	0.480	0.465	0.487
Cofactor inflator	t_1	5.005	2.135	3.099	2.553	2.126	1.974	2.154	2.040	2.135
Use-value inflator	t_2	1.104	1.104	1.104	1.105	1.105	1.105	1.104	1.104	1.104
Eigenprice	$p*$	1.077	1.032	0.934	0.908	1.003	1.104	0.989	1.007	1.011
United Kingdom 1972										
Labour value	λ	0.407	0.682	0.451	0.429	0.619	0.558	0.523	0.560	0.595
'Capital value'	κ	0.492	0.215	0.296	0.218	0.164	0.164	0.216	0.304	0.285
Cofactor inflator	t_1	2.209	1.315	1.656	1.508	1.265	1.294	1.413	1.543	1.479
Use-value inflator	t_2	1.206	1.203	1.205	1.206	1.204	1.205	1.206	1.205	1.206
Eigenprice	$p*$	1.084	1.079	0.900	0.780	0.943	0.870	0.891	1.041	1.061
W. Germany 1970										
Labour value	λ	0.285	0.499	0.360	0.525	0.585	0.561	0.523	0.542	0.523
'Capital value'	κ	0.701	0.327	0.465	0.395	0.326	0.342	0.374	0.336	0.397
Cofactor inflator	t_1	3.460	1.655	2.292	1.752	1.557	1.610	1.715	1.620	1.759
Use-value inflator	t_2	1.106	1.110	1.108	1.108	1.110	1.109	1.108	1.108	1.109
Eigenprice	$p*$	1.109	0.917	0.914	1.019	1.011	1.002	0.994	0.973	1.020

USSR 1972		A	B	C	D	E	F	G	H	I
Labour value	λ	0.687	0.365	0.494	0.299	0.427	0.367	0.429	0.552	0.452
'Capital value'	κ	0.288	0.576	0.366	0.508	0.490	0.347	0.425	0.402	0.525
Cofactor inflator	ι_1	1.419	2.578	1.741	2.699	2.148	1.946	1.991	1.728	2.162
Use-value inflator	ι_2	1.125	1.122	1.124	1.123	1.123	1.124	1.123	1.125	1.123
Eigenprice	p_*	1.097	1.056	0.967	0.906	1.030	0.803	0.959	1.073	1.097

Notes: The nine sectors retain the meaning of Tables 9.3 and 9.4, i.e.
A = Agriculture, fishing, and forestry; B = Mining, quarrying, fuel extraction; C = Food, drink, and tobacco; D = Chemicals, plastics, rubber, etc.; E = Metals and engineering; F = Textiles, leather, and clothing; G = Other manufacturing; H = Construction; I = Utilities, transport, trade, and services.

All values are pure numbers (£ per £).

Labour- and 'capital'-values are defined in (3.10), (6.17), and Sect. 6.3 as $1' = 1'A$ and $\kappa' = k'A$, so that the first two rows above for each country reproduce the cost-matrix $C(= \mathbf{BA})$; see (3.11). The cofactor-inflator $\iota_1 =$ coefficient by which labour-value λ must be multiplied to give total factor-cost of each product, i.e. $\iota_1 + \kappa/\lambda$, such that $\kappa + \lambda = \lambda \iota_1$.

The use-value-inflator $\iota_2 =$ coefficient by which total factor-cost of each product must be multiplied to give standardized eigenprice, i.e. $\iota_2 = [(1 + \kappa_* \lambda_*)/(1 + \kappa/\lambda)] r_*$, such that $p_* = \lambda \iota_1 \iota_2$.

The product of the two inflator $\iota_1 \iota_2$ thus measures the 'labour-inflator' i by which labour-value must be multiplied to give the standardized eigenprice of each product, i.e. $p_* = \lambda i$.

It should be noted that the table is based solely on computations on 'preconsolidated' data, i.e. on input–output tables condensed into the same nine macro-sectors in each country.

Appendix C

The Current and Standardized Eigenstructure
of the United Kingdom in 1979

As an illustration of the computations undertaken on the original 59-sector data for the United Kingdom (and other fully disaggregated input–output tables whose articulation is shown in Table 9.1), we present here the data and results of the pre-consolidation exercise which condensed all country tables into the nine 'macro-sectors' defined in tables 9.3 and 9.4. The eigenprices emerging from this are of course the macro-prices quoted in brackets in Table 9.3, which differ from the proper micro-prices discussed in the other text tables, owing to inevitable aggregation errors. The use of the latter would have necessitated a transformation in which the flows from any given production sector were subjected to *differential* revaluation according to their sectors of destination, to take account of the different micro-mixes making up these flows. The use of macro-prices, however, though tainted by aggregation errors, allows the transformation procedures and results to be shown up in a more transparent way.

Table C.1 presents the current price structure in the upper tableau (above the middle line) and transforms this into the standard structure (i.e. the same structure in terms of standard eigenprices) in the lower tableau, as indicated by the asterisk subscripts on the left-hand margin. Only the first quadrant (A to I), the factor-inputs W, and the total output column z are directly taken from the data (in consolidated form). The final-demand column y is supplied by the author as the residual between total output z and total sectoral deliveries x, and the surplus-row τ' as the residual within value added (i.e. $z - \omega - \xi$). The last column of the upper tableau shows the standardized macro-eigenprices p_* and eigenrentals r_* by which the corresponding rows are multiplied (revalued) to give the lower tableau. The row-totals of the latter are then carried over into the penultimate row z_* and the residual eigensurplus τ_* is ascertained by subtraction ($z_* - \omega_* - \xi_*$).

The crucial effect aimed at by the transformation is clearly visible from a comparison of the last rows of each tableau, in which the surplus-margin $\sigma(= \tau/\omega)$ is shown: this is highly variable from one sector to another in terms of current prices, ranging from over -1 to 0.0632 nearly 16 per cent, but reduces to the single ratio σ_* (21.2 per cent) which is uniform (but for rounding errors) for all sectors. The 'standardized' scaling of eigenprices has moreover ensured that our proxy for the GNP (sum of y-column) remains invariant to the transformation at £271,764 million. Readers will recall that

Table C.1 *Preconsolidated flows in the United Kingdom (1979) in current- and eigenprices (fm.)*

	A	B	C	D	E	F	G	H	I	x	y	z	p*
A	2,131	16,421	8,705	84	2	290	68	7	429	11,718	2,919	14,637	1.0180
B	385		886	2,029	7,612	216	1,150	4,566	9,606	42,871	19,299	62,170	0.9419
C	2,218	39	4,476	282	38	235	47	24	7,787	15,147	21,736	36,883	0.8775
D	785	667	634	6,576	2,123	920	872	653	3,143	16,375	7,965	24,340	1.0216
E	178	1,497	939	747	13,763	208	524	2,125	10,070	30,052	41,380	71,432	1.0630
F	59	32	37	125	150	3,279	214	131	1,370	5,397	8,245	13,642	1.0577
G	115	363	966	571	993	185	4,992	1,526	6,097	15,759	6,923	22,682	1.0710
H	78	760	33	3	53	22	38	7,566	3,747	12,299	21,333	33,632	1.0793
I	1,747	5,286	3,767	3,395	7,951	1,292	8,250	2,273	41,159	70,122	141,964	212,086	0.9880
ξ	7,698	25,065	20,444	13,814	32,636	6,647	11,157	18,872	83,407	219,741	271,764	491,504	r*
W_1	1,757	7,454	3,880	4,234	19,055	2,968	5,255	8,379	84,101	137,083			1.0032
W_2	1,561	6,098	1,479	506	888	56	509	4,939	14,641	30,678			0.9983
W_3	2,797	14,673	4,724	4,306	15,268	3,218	4,776	565	5,416	55,742			1.0044
ω	6,115	28,225	10,083	9,046	35,211	6,242	10,540	13,883	104,158	223,503			
τ	824	8,880	6,356	1,480	3,585	753	985	877	24,521	48,261			
z	14,637	62,170	36,883	24,340	71,432	13,642	22,682	33,632	212,086	491,504			
σ($\equiv$ τ/ω)	0.1348	0.3146	0.6304	0.1636	0.1018	0.1206	0.9345	0.0632	0.2354				
A*	2,170	1	8,862	85	2	295	70	7	437	11,928	2,972	14,900	
B*	362	15,966	835	1,911	7,169	204	1,083	4,300	9,047	40,379	18,177	58,556	
C*	1,947	34	3,927	248	33	206	42	21	6,833	13,291	19,073	32,364	
D*	802	681	698	6,719	2,169	940	891	667	3,211	16,729	8,137	24,866	
E*	189	1,591	998	975	14,631	221	557	2,258	10,705	31,946	43,988	75,934	
F*	62	34	40	132	159	3,468	226	139	1,448	5,709	8,720	14,429	
G*	123	389	1,035	611	1,010	199	5,346	1,635	6,530	16,878	7,414	24,293	
H*	84	820	36	3	57	23	41	8,166	4,044	13,275	23,024	36,299	

I_*	1,726	5,223	3,722	3,355	7,856	1,276	3,211	2,246	40,664	69,279	140,257	209,536
ξ	7,467	24,239	20,101	13,860	33,087	6,832	11,468	19,441	82,919	219,414	271,764	491,178
W_1^*	1,763	7,478	3,893	4,248	19,117	2,978	5,272	8,406	84,373	137,526		
W_2^*	1,558	6,088	1,476	505	886	56	508	4,931	14,617	30,626		
W_3^*	2,809	14,738	4,745	4,325	15,336	3,232	4,797	568	5,440	55,989		
ω_*	6,130	28,304	10,114	9,078	35,339	6,266	10,577	13,904	104,429	224,141		
τ_*	1,302	6,014	2,149	1,929	7,508	1,331	2,247	2,954	22,188	47,622		
z_*	14,900	58,556	32,364	24,866	75,934	14,429	24,293	32,299	209,536	491,178		
$\sigma_* (\equiv \tau_*/\omega_*)$	0.2125	0.2125	0.2125	0.2125	0.2125	0.2124	0.2124	0.2125	0.2125			

this differs considerably from the GNP of the official national accounts by virtue of the exclusion of factor-services directly absorbed in final uses, the special treatment of imports, and other discrepancies between input–output and national accounts statistics.

Appendix D

Notation and Directory of Symbols

Notation

In this edition we use the established notation in which vectors and matrices are distinguished from scalars by bold-face lower-case and capital letters respectively. Row-vectors are distinguished from column-vectors by means of a prime ('), and diagonal matrices by a circumflex (^) over the vector of the main diagonal. In particular, I stands for the unit matrix, i and i' for its rth column and row, and i and i' for all-unit vectors (with 1 in all positions). Row- and column-sums are denoted by Roman and Greek letters corresponding to the vectors summed, without affixes, e.g.

$$Xi = x \qquad i'X = \xi'$$
$$Wi = w \qquad i'W = \omega'$$

Directory of the Most Frequently Occurring Symbols

(Numbers in brackets indicate the equation and/or surrounding text where definitions and explanations may be found.) Some of the symbols are also 'borrowed' to convey different meanings specific to particular chapters or sections.

$A = X\hat{z}^{-1}$	$n \times n$ matrix of sectoral (product-) input coefficients (3.6)
$\overline{A} = (I - A)^{-1}$	the $n \times n$ synthesizer—Leontief inverse of A ((3.7) and Sect. 3.1, n. 5)
$B = W\hat{z}^{-1}$	$n \times n$ matrix of primary (factor-) input coefficients (3.6)
$C = B\overline{A}$	$m \times n$ cost-matrix showing in row r the full (direct and indirect) costing of n products in terms of the single factor r (3.11)
$D = \hat{z}^{-1}X$	$m \times n$ matrix of sectoral delivery quotas (output allocations of m factors to n sectors) (3.16) and (3.24)
$\overline{D} = (I - D)^{-1}$	Leontief inverse of D
$E = \hat{w}^{-1}W$	matrix of earnings quotas (allocations of m factors to n sectors)
c_r'	row-vector of full absorption (cost) of factor r per unit output of n sectors (3.8)–(3.10); rth row of C
$c'(r) = r'C$	row-vector of composite factor-costs of n products per unit output when factors are valued at r' per unit each

$\mathbf{e}' = (\mathbf{p}', \mathbf{v}')$ complete vector of eigenprices (goods and factor) (p. 52)

$\mathbf{e}_*' = (\mathbf{p}_*', \mathbf{v}')$ complete vector of standardized eigenprices (p. 59)

$\mathbf{F} = \mathbf{CN}$ $m \times n$ cost-norm matrix (3.30 et seq.); see also Sect. 3.5, n. 11 and 12

ϕ_* eigencost-ratio = dominant eigenvalue of matrix $\mathbf{F}$, defined by $\mathbf{r}'(\phi \mathbf{I} - \mathbf{F}) = \mathbf{0}'$ or $|\phi_* \mathbf{I} - \mathbf{F}| = 0$ (3.30) and Sect. 3.5, n. 13 and 14

$\mathbf{G} = \mathbf{A} + \mathbf{H}$ $n \times n$ matrix of total prime-costs (product-inputs + workers' consumption) per unit output (p. 84)

g, g_* crude and standardized norm of notional factor earning the eigenyield or surplus (6.2)–(6.6) and surrounding text (pp. 57–8 ff.). In Sect. 7.2 'warranted employment structure'

$\mathbf{H}$ $n \times n$ consumption-coefficient matrix showing consumption of n products by workers of each of n sectors per unit output (p. 84)

$\mathbf{i}, \mathbf{i}'$ all-unit column- and row-vector, taken to be conformable for multiplication with its co-factor in any product and having the effect of simple summation, e.g. $\mathbf{z}'\mathbf{i} = \Sigma z$, $\mathbf{i}'\mathbf{y} = \overset{x}{\underset{i}{\Sigma}} y_r$, etc.

$\mathbf{i}_r, \mathbf{i}_r'$ rth column- and row-vector of the unit matrix $\mathbf{I}$, taken to be conformable for multiplication with its co-factor in any product, and having the effect of isolating the rth array or element of that co-factor, e.g. $\mathbf{z}'\mathbf{i}_r = \mathbf{i}'\mathbf{z} = z_r$; $\mathbf{A}\mathbf{i}_r = \mathbf{a}_r$

$\mathbf{k}'$ n-dimensional row-vector of direct absorption (cost) of capital-services (gross operational surplus) per unit of each product; short for $\mathbf{b}_2'$, second row of factor-input matrix $\mathbf{B}$

$\mathbf{K}' = \mathbf{k}'\mathbf{A}$ row-vector of full (direct and indirect) capital costs per unit of n products (see Sect. 3.2); short for $\mathbf{c}_2'$, second row of cost-matrix $\mathbf{C}$

$\mathbf{l}'$ labour-services (measured in wages) directly used per unit of each of n products; short for $\mathbf{b}_1'$, first row of factor-input coefficient matrix $\mathbf{B}$

$\boldsymbol{\lambda}' = \mathbf{l}'\mathbf{A}$ row-vector of full (direct and indirect) labour costs of n products; short for $\mathbf{c}_1'$, first row of cost-matrix $\mathbf{C}$ (see Sects. 3.2 and 6.3)

$\mathbf{M}$ $n \times n$ symmetric singular matrix $= \mathbf{C}'\hat{\mathbf{w}}^{-1}\mathbf{C}$, see (7.20)

m (scalar) number of primary inputs or factors specified in the model = number of rows in third quadrant of (3.1) exclusive of

$\mathbf{N} = \hat{\mathbf{s}}\,\overline{\mathbf{D}}'\mathbf{E}'$ $n \times m$ norm-matrix of (factor-) norms ((3.22), (3.26) and
$= \hat{\mathbf{y}}\mathbf{C}'\hat{\mathbf{W}}^{-1} = \mathbf{V}'\mathbf{E}'$ Sect. 3.4, n. 9)

n	(scalar) number of (micro-) sectors in the first quadrant of (3.1); dimension of square matrices $\mathbf{X}$, $\mathbf{A}$, $\mathbf{D}$, etc.
$\mathbf{P} = \mathbf{NC}$	$n \times n$ norm-cost matrix (3.30 ff.); see also Sect. 3.5, n. 12
$\mathbf{p}'$	eigenprices of n products = dominant left-hand eigenvector of $\mathbf{P}$, defined by $\mathbf{p}'(\phi_* \mathbf{I} - \mathbf{P}) = 0$ up to a multiplicative constant (3.29)–(3.30)
$\mathbf{p}_*' = \alpha \mathbf{p}'$	$\mathbf{p}'$ with α chosen to ensure that $\mathbf{p}_*'\mathbf{y} = y_0$; row-vector of standardized eigenprices of n products per \$-worth of output, see Sect. 3.7
$\mathbf{q} = \hat{\mathbf{p}}_* \mathbf{y}$	n-dimensional column-vector of eigenfinals = right-hand dominant eigenvector of $\mathbf{P}$ = warranted supply (7.12) and Sect. 7.2
$\mathbf{r}'$	eigenrentals of m factors (primary inputs) = dominant left-hand eigenvector of matrix $\mathbf{F}$, defined by $\mathbf{r}'(\phi_* \mathbf{I} - \mathbf{F}) = 0'$ up to a multiplicative constant (3.30)
$\mathbf{r}_*' = \beta \mathbf{r}'$	$\mathbf{r}'$ with β chosen to ensure that $\mathbf{r}_*'\mathbf{w} = w_0$; row-vector of standardized eigenrentals of m factors per \$-worth of factor-input; Sect. 3.7.
$\rho' = \tau' \mathbf{Z}^{-1}$	row-vector of n surplus/output ratios in current prices (Sect. 3.6, n. 16)
$\hat{\mathbf{s}} = \hat{\mathbf{y}} \hat{\mathbf{z}}^{-1}$	$n \times n$ diagonal matrix of final-use quotas (3.16 ff.).
$\sigma' = \tau' \hat{\omega}^{-1}$	row-vector of n surplus/value added ratios in current prices
$\sigma = \tau_*' \hat{\omega}^{-1} i$ $= 1/\phi_* - 1$	(scalar) eigenyield; uniform surplus/value-added ratio for all sectors in terms of eigenprices and rentals (3.31ff.). In Sect. 7.5 index of scarcity (σ) of commodity r
τ'	row-vector of residual cost-elements or surpluses of n sectors after accounting for the cost of all factors specified in the model, conventionally identified, but not necessarily identical with indirect taxes net of subsidies
U_n	in Sect. 6.4 border-price content of non-tradable good k
$\mathbf{V} = \overline{\mathbf{D}}\hat{\mathbf{s}}$	$n \times n$ matrix of sectoral use-norms ((3.19) and preceding text)
$\mathbf{v_k} = \mathbf{V} i_k$	column-vector of n sectoral 'use-norms' based on the final use of product k ((3.14)–(3.19) and surrounding text); in Sect. 6.4 border-price content of factor k.
$\mathbf{W}$	$m \times n$ matrix of primary input (factor-) flows; third quadrant of (3.1) excluding the τ'-row
$\mathbf{w} = \mathbf{W} i$	column-vector of m primary inputs (factors) employed; row-sums of third quadrant of (3.1) excluding the τ'-row
$= i' \mathbf{W}$	row-vector of total factor-use by n sectors; column-sums of third quadrant of (3.1) excluding the τ'-row

$\boldsymbol{\omega}' = \mathbf{i}'\mathbf{W}$	row-vector of total factor-use by n sectors; column-sums of third quadrant of (3.1) excluding the $\boldsymbol{\tau}'$-row
$\mathbf{X}$	$n \times n$ matrix of intersectoral flows in current prices; first quadrant of (3.1)
$\mathbf{x} = \mathbf{Xi}$	column-vector of n sector outputs for intermediate use; row-sum of first quadrant of (3.1)
$\boldsymbol{\xi} = \mathbf{i}'\mathbf{X}$	row-vector of n total sectoral ('non-factor') inputs; column-sums of first quadrant of (3.1)
$\mathbf{y} = \mathbf{z} - \mathbf{x}$	column-vector of final uses or 'finals' supplied by n production sectors in current prices; second quadrant of (3.1)
$y_0 = \mathbf{i}'\mathbf{y}$	GNP in current prices
$\mathbf{y}_* = \mathbf{i}'\mathbf{y}_* = \mathbf{p}_*'\mathbf{y}$	GNP in standardized eigenprices scaled to equal y_0 (Sect. 3.7)
$\mathbf{z} = \mathbf{x} + \mathbf{y}$	column-vector of n total sectoral outputs in current prices
$= \boldsymbol{\xi}' + \boldsymbol{\omega}'\boldsymbol{\tau}'$	= inputs + surplus; row-sums of first plus second quadrants of (3.1), equal to column-sums of first plus third quadrants of (3.1)

Index

Subject headings are in bold, proper names without emphasis unless qualifying as subjects (i.e. Marx, Pareto).

References are to pages and notes and distinguished as follows:

> ack   Acknowledgment
> bbg   Bibliographic reference
> qtd   Quotation

Entries in quotes (' ') refer to terms coined by the author, not in common use or commonly used in a non-specific sense.